D1179633

ASPECTS OF ORKNEY 2

THE BIRDS OF ORKNEY

This series has been developed in order to provide detailed and thorough texts on a range of aspects of the life, history and environment of the Orkney Islands. Each book is designed to make specialist knowledge available to the general reader.

Consultant Editor — William P. L. Thomson

*Publication 1985

Marwick Head (P. Reynolds)

ASPECTS OF ORKNEY 2

THE BIRDS OF ORKNEY

by

CHRIS BOOTH, MILDRED CUTHBERT and PETER REYNOLDS

With black and white photography by Arthur Gilpin
bird vignettes by John Holloway
seascape drawings by Ian MacInnes
and figures by Anne Leith Brundle

1984
THE ORKNEY PRESS

Published by The Orkney Press Ltd., 72 Victoria Street, Stromness, Orkney

ISBN 0 907618 07 3

Printed by The Kirkwall Press, "The Orcadian" Office, Victoria Street, Kirkwall, Orkney
Bound by James Gowans Ltd., Glasgow

The publishers acknowledge the financial assistance of Orkney Islands Council and the Highlands and Islands Development Board in the publication of this volume.

CONTENTS

ILLUSTRATIONS

Black and White Photographs by Arthur Gilpin

Colour Photographs

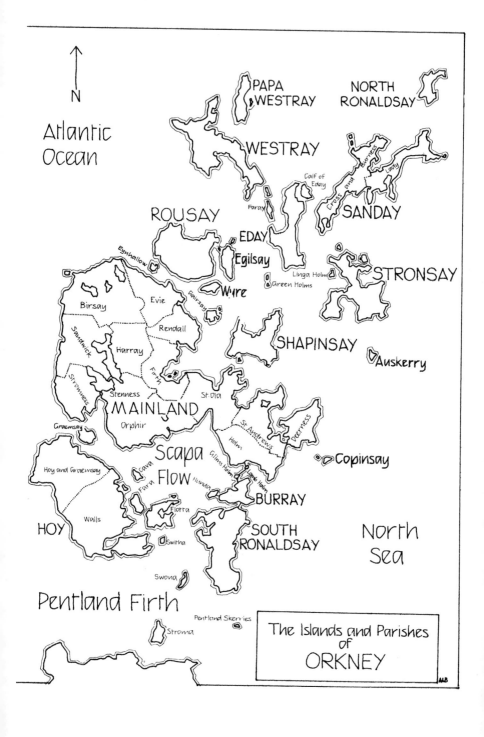

Atlantic Ocean

N

PAPA WESTRAY

NORTH RONALDSAY

WESTRAY

Calf of Eday

Cross and Burness

Lady

Faray

SANDAY

ROUSAY

EDAY

Egilsay

Eynhallow

Wyre

Linga Holm

Green Holms

STRONSAY

Birsay

Evie

Gairsay

Sandwick

Rendall

SHAPINSAY

Auskerry

Harray

Firth

Stromness

Stenness

St. Ola

MAINLAND

Orphir

Graemsay

St Andrews

Holm

Deerness

Copinsay

Scapa Flow

Glims Holm

Hoy and Graemsay

Cava

Farra

Hunday

Lamb Holm

BURRAY

HOY

Walls

Flotta

Switha

SOUTH RONALDSAY

North Sea

Swona

Pentland Firth

Pentland Skerries

Stroma

The Islands and Parishes of ORKNEY

ACKNOWLEDGEMENTS

The production of a book of this type is dependent on the support given to the authors by many people and we should like to acknowledge the help we have received.

We are greatly indebted to Arthur Gilpin for allowing us to use some of his black and white bird photographs, to John Holloway and Ian MacInnes for their vignettes and to Anne Leith Brundle for preparation of the maps and figures used in the text. Our thanks must be accorded to Beverley Smith for her chapter on birds in Orkney prehistory.

The personal scrap-book of the late Eddie Balfour and the diary of Mrs Marjorie Traill Clouston were very kindly lent by Eddie's widow, Mrs Robina Balfour, and Miss Alison Sutherland-Graeme respectively. We thank Alastair Pierse-Duncombe for his useful advice and assistance; W. G. Harper, Librarian at the Scottish Ornithologists' Club, Edinburgh for providing information; Robin Fenton for advice; the British Trust for Ornithology for information on ringing; the Fair Isle Observatory for the use of their library during our visit there and David Salmon of the Wildfowl Trust, Slimbridge, for providing details of Orkney Wildfowl Counts.

The staffs of *The Orcadian* newspaper and the Stromness Museum were unfailing in their help in allowing us access to their records and specimens. Our publishers, The Orkney Press, have provided valuable assistance and advice, especially Howie Firth, who also undertook the reading of the manuscript.

We must express our appreciation to all the people who have contributed records or articles to the *Orkney Bird Report* since 1974, for, without those, this book would not have been written.

Jean Booth has spent many hours deciphering our notes and typing the manuscript and, finally, we should like to thank our families for accepting, with such good grace, the disruption we caused in our homes!

Christopher J. Booth
Mildred F. Cuthbert
Peter Reynolds

June 1984

INTRODUCTION

The first attempt at producing a status of Orkney birds was by Low, in 1813, when his *Fauna Orcadensis* was published. This was followed in 1848 by Baikie and Heddle's *Historia Naturalis Orcadensis*. There was then a gap of over forty years, until Buckley and Harvie-Brown's important and much more detailed *Vertebrate Fauna of the Orkney Islands* was produced in 1891. From 1892 to 1911 the *Annals of Scottish Natural History* and, from 1912 to 1957, the *Scottish Naturalist* contain many records, including, in 1893 and 1894, those of Briggs from North Ronaldsay. The observations of Dr. W. Eagle Clarke, migration records from lighthouse keepers on Auskerry, Pentland Skerries and Sule Skerry and W. Serle's notes from Hoy in 1933 are also contained in these publications.

The status was reviewed by Omond in his *How to know the Orkney Birds* in 1925, but it was almost another twenty years before Lack's "List of Breeding Birds of Orkney" was published in the *Ibis* in 1942 and 1943. Lack relied greatly on G. T. Arthur's knowledge and it is unfortunate that the latter's bird notes are no longer available for reference, as there are few dated records for the period of 1920 to 1950. However, nature articles in *The Orcadian* and *The Orkney Herald*, especially "Nature Notes" written by J. G. Marwick and later by W. Groundwater, provided useful information.

Baxter and Rintoul's *The Birds of Scotland* (1953) summarises much of the data available up to 1950 and the production of *Scottish Birds* in 1958, with its "Current Notes", made possible the collection of more systematic records. K. G. Walker in *Island Saga* (Mary Scott, 1967) gives information, up to 31st December 1966, from North Ronaldsay and Mrs. M. Traill Clouston's diaries were also a source of valuable records. Balfour's "Breeding Birds of Orkney" (*Scottish Birds*, 1968) revised Lack's previous list and that same year saw the first *Scottish Bird Report*.

Orkney Birds: Status and Guide (Balfour, 1972) brought the status up to date and this was supplemented by Groundwater's *Birds and Mammals of Orkney* (1974). The annual collection of records, begun in 1974 by David Lea and resulting in the publication of the *Orkney Bird Report*, has given us a considerable amount of data on which to base this book.

Finally, Eddie Balfour's private scrap-book and notes, compiled over a long period, have yielded much interesting and useful material.

THE GEOGRAPHY OF ORKNEY

The county of Orkney consists of approximately seventy islands, about twenty of which are inhabited. It is separated from the north-east coast of Scotland by the Pentland Firth and lies at 59°N, only 80 km south of the latitude of the southernmost tip of Greenland. The island group measures 70 km from north to south and 60 km from east to west and the total land area is 976 sq.km, of which more than half is the Orkney Mainland.

Most of Orkney is composed of rocks of the Middle Old Red Sandstone series and only west Hoy consists of younger rocks, which are considerably harder than those of the Middle Series. There are no extensive areas of igneous or crystalline rocks, these types being confined to small intrusions found throughout the county.

The pattern of numerous small islands, separated by shallow water areas, is indicative of a submerged landscape; as a consequence of this submergence, the Orkney coastline is long, extending to approximately 800 km. Despite a relatively uniform underlying geology, the height and sharpness of the coastline is varied. Just under 20% is high cliffs (i.e. cliffs above 15 metres in height), 11% is in the form of sand or shingle beaches, and the remaining 70% consists of low rock or till cliffs, low rocky shores and man-made coastline in the form of sea walls and causeways. Inland there are gently rolling hills and shallow valleys, with fresh-water lochs. There is very little high ground, except in Hoy, where ten summits exceed 300 metres.

The climate can be considered to be cool and equable, reflecting Orkney's location and exposure to strong maritime influences, including the warm North Atlantic Drift. Daily and seasonal temperature ranges are reduced as a consequence of these maritime influences. For instance, summer temperatures tend to be subdued, with a mean temperature in July (the warmest month) of 12.8°C. This is the lowest in the British Isles, with the exception of Shetland. Average winter temperatures are correspondingly mild, with a mean winter temperature of 4°C, similar to Genoa or Venice. The annual range of mean monthly temperatures is around 9°C; this is the lowest range in the United Kingdom apart from Shetland, the Outer Hebrides and the west coast of Ireland.

XIII

The comparatively high winter temperatures result in snow lying for an average of only 16 days in the year on the lower lying parts of the county and frost is not common. On the other hand, high winds are frequently experienced, with October to March being the worst period; records show that gale-force winds occur on a mean of 30 days a year at Kirkwall. Rainfall is very variable over the islands, with an annual average ranging from 90-100 cm at Deerness to 150-200 cm on Hoy. May and June are the driest months.

In some places, soils are derived directly from the underlying bedrock, but most have their origin in glacial deposits. The depths and fertility vary considerably from one district to another, but in general, Orkney soils are deep and fertile. Where drainage has been impeded, extensive peat deposits in the form of blanket bog have developed.

THE ISLANDS

Auskerry

A seasonally inhabited island of moorland and rough pasture, it is grazed by sheep; there are colonies of seabirds, including Storm Petrels.

Burray

An island mainly under cultivation, with low rocky shores and beaches. There is an extensive dune system at The Bu, part of which is used for commercial sand extraction. Echna Loch is the only area of open water and faces Echnaloch Bay, a good locality for wintering sea duck, as is Water Sound to the South. The only remaining moorland is situated on the island of Hunda, which is linked to Burray by a causeway.

Calf of Eday

This uninhabited island consists of moorland and rough pasture, grazed by sheep. There are seabird colonies, particularly on the cliffs at the north end, and a large cliff-top Cormorant colony.

Cava

The highest point is approximately 30 metres. There are localised areas of reclaimed grassland, the rest is sheep-grazed moorland.

Copinsay

Apart from the lighthouse keepers, Copinsay is uninhabited. The rough pasture was formerly sheep-grazed. The island, which is an R.S.P.B. reserve, has spectacular south-east-facing cliffs which support a very large seabird colony.

Eday

On Eday, the reclaimed agricultural land occurs only in a peripheral zone in parts of the island. The moorland, which has hills up to 101 metres, has in the past been extensively cut for peats. The Loch of Doomy has now been drained, but several other lochs and wetland areas remain. At Fersness Bay, a narrow strip of sand dunes, grading into moorland, can be found. Cliffs in the north and north-east of the island have small seabird colonies. On the slope of Vinquoy Hill, at the north end of the island, is Orkney's oldest tree plantation, dating from the 1830's.

Egilsay
Egilsay consists of a mixture of reclaimed and semi-natural ground, with several small wetlands, particularly along the east side. The sea areas are good for wintering wildfowl.

Eynhallow
This island is the site of Aberdeen University's long-term Fulmar studies. It has sheep-grazed rough pasture and moorland, with some low cliffs.

Fara
Fara, in Scapa Flow, is now uninhabited. The island is mainly sheep-grazed moorland and bog, with some reclaimed grassland and rushes, and does not rise above 50 metres.

Flotta
The only area of moorland lies in the south-east of the island, the remainder consisting of cultivated land and the Flotta Oil Terminal.

Gairsay and Sweyn Holm
Gairsay is inhabited by one family. Part of the island is farmed and consists of grazed reclaimed pasture; the remainder is moorland and rough pasture.

Graemsay
There are several small farms and some localised areas of unreclaimed ground; the highest point is 62 metres. The surrounding sounds are very good for wintering wildfowl.

Hoy
Hoy is an island of high moorland, distinctly montane in character, with the Ward Hill rising spectacularly from the sea to a height of 479 metres. The hill tops, many of which are over 300 metres high, are stony and extremely exposed and examples of Arctic Alpine plants occur in certain areas. Having escaped burning

and grazing for over 25 years, the moorland plant communities of North Hoy are well developed although the recent fire has done some damage. Trees (largely Willows and Rowans) have spread along many of the sheltered gulleys and valleys and at Berriedale, the northernmost native woodland in the British Isles, can be found Rowan, Downy Birch, Aspen and Hazel. There are also several small conifer plantations. Hill lochans are numerous and there are stream systems at the Rackwick Burn, Summer of Hoy and Pegal Burn. The vertical cliffs of the west side of Hoy reach their highest point at St John's Head (335 metres) and support extensive seabird colonies. The cliffs on the east side, facing Scapa Flow, are lower and overlook areas of importance for wintering wildfowl. In Orkney, Hoy is unique for its combination of physical, botanical and ornithological features.

Linga Holm

This is an uninhabited island of moorland grazed by North Ronaldsay sheep and is administered by the Rare Breeds Trust. There is one loch.

Mainland

This, the largest of the Orkney Islands, is mainly under cultivation but has extensive moorland on the relatively low rolling hills, which reach a height of 268 metres. These moorlands hold important numbers of breeding Hen Harriers, Kestrels, Merlins, Red-throated Divers and Short-eared Owls. Botanically they are predominantly submontane in character.

Farming is primarily concerned with beef production and the cultivated land is sown largely with agricultural grasses; much of the grass is made into silage. Within the cultivated landscape are remnant wetland areas with variable amounts of open water. The most important of these areas are The Loons and the Dee of Durkadale, Birsay, the latter grading into the dome-shaped raised bog of Glims Moss. Smaller but nevertheless important wetlands are scattered throughout the Mainland and many contain patches of willow scrub. Shallow, nutrient-rich lochs are well represented and are especially important for wintering wildfowl, the Lochs of Harray, Stenness and Boardhouse all having nationally important concentrations.

The Orkney Mainland has a varied coastline extending for 234 kms. Approximately 21% of this coastline consists of cliffs over 15 metres in height. Many of these cliffs are characterised by well-developed ledges which have been fully exploited by cliff-nesting seabirds, with large colonies in both the East and the West Mainland. The low rocky shores and sandy inter-tidal areas, together with adjacent cultivated ground, provide food for many wading birds, some of them in nationally important numbers, particularly during the winter.

Garden habitats in Stromness and Kirkwall are frequented by a wide range of species, especially during migration. There are well established tree plantations at Binscarth (Firth), Woodwick (Evie) and Berstane (St Ola).

Binscarth Wood (Orkney Field Club Slide Library)

Aerial View over Finstown, looking towards Hoy (P. Reynolds)

Moorland lochan, Hoy (C. J. Booth)

The Loch of Hundland (M. F. Cuthbert)

Muckle and Little Green Holms

These are uninhabited sheep-grazed islands of rough pasture.

North Ronaldsay

This island has a mixture of reclaimed land and semi-natural habitat, its highest point being 20 metres. Rough grazing and machair dominate the part outside the stone dyke which surrounds the island and there is a small sand dune area behind South Bay. Wetland habitat is represented in the form of several small lochs, some of which support much emergent vegetation and peripheral marsh. The island is well placed for the observation of migratory birds and can be regarded as "Orkney's Fair Isle".

Papa Westray

Although much of the island is reclaimed agricultural land, several small wetland areas remain, together with the grazed moorland and the maritime heath habitat of the North Hill. Bounded by low cliffs, the North Hill is of considerable interest for its breeding seabirds and is an R.S.P.B. reserve. A small fixed dune area of machair has developed behind the Bay of Moclett and the Loch of St Tredwell is the only open fresh water on the island. The highest point is 45 metres.

Pentland Skerries

Muckle Skerry is a flat, low-lying island of sheep-grazed rough pasture with several small lochs and its only inhabitants are the lighthouse keepers. There are small colonies of seabirds, including Puffins. Little Skerry is a rock outcrop, virtually devoid of vegetation, where a small Cormorant colony has become established.

Rousay

High moorland hills reaching 250 metres dominate this island. The moorland, which is sheep-grazed in part, is relatively rich in bird life, with several small open water areas and the larger lochs of the Muckle Water and the Peerie Water. Trumland House has a wood which was planted in the 19th century and there is a smaller wood at Westness.

Rysa Little

This is an uninhabited island of sheep-grazed moorland.

Sanday

Sanday is a predominantly low-lying island consisting mainly of reclaimed agricultural land, but large parts are covered by dune and associated machair, which is grazed. There are several lochs, some of open water and others, such as the Bea Loch, with peripheral emergent vegetation. Extensive inter-tidal areas, sand and shingle spits and ayres all occur. The only moorland is confined to the Gump of Spurness, but this is undergoing gradual fragmentation due to reclamation for agricultural purposes.

Shapinsay

This island is almost entirely agricultural and the last vestige of moorland survives in a fragmented state in the south-east of the island. The cliffs on the east side support very small seabird colonies and Lairo Water and The Ouse attract wintering wildfowl. Balfour Castle has the largest area of woodland in Orkney, consisting mainly of deciduous trees which were planted in the 19th century.

South Ronaldsay

The undulating landscape is mainly agricultural, with very few semi-natural areas remaining. 38% of the coastline is high cliff with localised seabird colonies.

South Walls

South Walls is connected to Hoy by a shingle ayre, across which the road runs; the land is all below 60 metres and is predominantly cultivated.

Stronsay

Stronsay is another mainly agricultural island. Rothiesholm Head is the largest area of intact moorland and, with its lochs and cliffs, is ornithologically diverse; there are small seabird colonies. The cliffs between Burgh Head and Lamb Head, in the south-east of the island, also support small seabird colonies and the lochs of Stronsay are of importance for breeding wildfowl.

Sule Skerry

Sule Skerry lies 60 km west of Brough Head, Birsay and formerly had a manned lighthouse. This flat, low-lying island has Orkney's largest Puffin colony, and there are small seabird colonies on the cliffs.

Sule Stack

A rock of just over 42½ metres in height and lying 66 km west of Brough Head, this is the site of Orkney's only Gannet colony.

Switha

This is an uninhabited island of rough grassland, which is sheep-grazed. The cliffs support small seabird colonies.

Swona

This island, which is now uninhabited, is partly cattle-grazed; it has rough pasture with a marsh and a small loch. The low cliffs have small seabird colonies, including Puffins.

Westray

Reclaimed land dominates Westray and the moorland, together with maritime heath, is restricted to the western slopes of the main line of hills, which rise to 169 metres. On the west side, the high cliffs hold the largest and most extensive seabird colonies in Orkney. There are several lochs, most of them open water, but the Loch of Burness has much peripheral vegetation, including reeds. Small sand dune areas occur locally.

Wyre

With the exception of The Taing, the entire island consists of reclaimed land. The surrounding waters are good for wintering wildfowl.

FACTORS INFLUENCING THE BIRDS OF ORKNEY

The islands are situated at the crossroads of two major migration routes. The western route includes birds from Greenland, Iceland and the Faeroes, while the eastern route is used by birds from Scandinavia and Russia. Drift migrants are also recorded, those from America being much less frequent than ones from the east.

The location of the islands has, to some extent, determined the number of regular breeding species of which there are approximately 90—intermediate between Caithness and Sutherland with 127 species and Shetland with 66. Rich feeding, combined with the cliff structure, has resulted in the development of some of the most important seabird colonies in the North Atlantic. Extensive sheltered, shallow-water areas between the islands are ideal for wintering seaduck, such as Long-tailed Duck, and for inshore species including Eider and Black Guillemot. Wintering wildfowl from Iceland, Scandinavia and Russia are attracted by the numerous ice-scraped, shallow, nutrient-rich lochs. The generally mild winter temperatures and lack of frost are of considerable importance to both wildfowl and other birds wintering in the islands.

Ever since his arrival in the islands, approximately 5000 years ago, man has clearly had an important influence on the environment. Prior to his arrival, the pollen records suggest that Birch-Hazel scrub, associated with a rich ground flora of tall herbs and ferns, was extensive. This vegetation community subsequently declined and was replaced by large areas of scrub-free herbaceous vegetation and pasture, and by 1600 BC blanket peat formation had begun on the hills. The grazing of domestic animals, together with climatic factors, such as increased oceanicity, is thought to have been responsible for these changes (Keatinge, Dickson, 1979; Moar 1969).

The Orkney farmer has traditionally had a keen interest in the land and the wildlife about him. In recent years, however, economic pressures have made farms expand their cultivated land in order to remain viable. The result has been a decline in the amount of moorland and wetland to the point where, in some islands, there is little uncultivated land left.

Although arable land provides a good source of food for various birds, the loss of moors and wet places reduces the variety of habitat available, and hence some species have declined and could yet vanish completely. It may be that, with Europe moving into agricultural self-sufficiency, the system of farming grants will be phased out and the big reclamation and drainage schemes of the past thirty years come to an end.

The depth of feeling that can exist in Orkney for the land and its wildlife was expressed in a 1972 issue of the *Orkney Field Club Bulletin* by the distinguished Orcadian ornithologist, the late Eddie Balfour, writing in response to the drainage of a particular wetland site. "Everywhere, even in Orkney, bits of natural habitat are being despoiled . . . Now is the time to stop the eroding away of our natural heritage, our flora and fauna and their habitats, whether it be loch, marsh, moorland or seashore."

SYSTEMATIC LIST

The majority of the summarised information in the systematic list has been obtained from records supplied for the *Orkney Bird Reports* 1974-1982. Some additional records have been taken from the "Current Notes" in *Scottish Birds* 1959-1967 and the *Scottish Bird Reports* 1968-1973. No acknowledgement of these sources has been made in the text unless it was thought to be of special relevance.

There is an uneven distribution of records from the islands, with Shapinsay, Stronsay and Westray being less well covered for breeding and migrant birds than the other main islands. Although some of the breeding counts given in the species summaries involve only small numbers, it is thought that they are important as they are from discrete areas or small islands and could be repeated easily in future years. This would allow direct comparison and give an indication of population trends.

Only extreme rarities, seen prior to 1959, that are mentioned in the 1971 British Ornithologists' Union list and all rarities, since 1959, in the British Birds Rarities Committee Reports have been included.

A brief description of the status of each species, during the period 1974-1982, is given above the summary texts. To provide some indication of the numbers of the less common species, the following terms have been used:

Very rare	less than 10 records
Rare	10-24 records
Scarce	25-50 records

The systematic list follows the sequence and scientific nomenclature of Dr. K. H. Voous (1977) "List of Recent Holarctic Bird Species".

Abbreviations used in the text are :

A.S.N.H.	Annals of Scottish Natural History
B.B.	British Birds
B.B.R.C.	British Birds Rarities Committee
B.T.O.	British Trust for Ornithology
F.I.B.O.B.	Fair Isle Bird Observatory Bulletin
O.B.R.	Orkney Bird Report
S.B.	Scottish Birds
S.N.	Scottish Naturalist
S.N.E.P.	Scottish Naturalist Extra Publication
1971 B.O.U. List	British Ornithologists' Union list "The Status of Birds in Britain and Ireland, 1971".

DIVERS : Gaviidae

Red-throated Diver
Rain Goose, Loom

Gavia stellata

Fairly common but localised breeding species, a few birds winter.

The fact that several hill lochs in Orkney are called "Loomachun", the Old Norse for "Tarn of the Diver", would seem to indicate that this species was present in Viking times.

Numbers were low at the end of the 19th century, when only four pairs were known to be breeding on Hoy (Buckley and Harvie-Brown, 1891). It has increased, especially during the last 50 years, and at least 90 pairs now breed. This increase is shown by the following counts :—

	Lack 1941	Balfour 1968	1980-82
Mainland	Several pairs	12-15 pairs	c25 pairs
Hoy	Several pairs	Not known	c40-45 pairs
Eday	2 pairs	6-8 pairs	10 pairs
Rousay	1 pair	2-4 pairs	12 pairs
Stronsay	1 pair	1 pair	2 pairs
Shapinsay	Not known	1 pair	Not known

During the period 1974-1982 breeding has also been recorded on the islands of Fara and Linga Holm.

The first birds arrive on their nesting lochs in early March and eggs can be found from May until August. Young fledge from the second week of July, with the peak fledging period occurring in the middle of August, but a few young may not leave their breeding lochs until the last week of September.

The favoured nesting sites are hill lochans, although some pairs breed on larger areas of water such as the Loch of Harray. More than one pair nest on some lochs, with a maximum of 8 pairs on a loch in the North Isles. During the breeding season, gatherings of up to 28 adult birds have been recorded at one site.

Monitoring of some breeding lochs on the Orkney Mainland during the last 10 years has shown a decline in the number of young reared, mainly due to human disturbance (Booth, 1982).

There are records for December and January from Deerness,

Eynhallow Sound, Inganess Bay, the Loch of Stenness, Roseness (Holm), Scapa Flow and Wide Firth, all of single birds, except for two at Scapa on 13th December 1980.

Young birds ringed in Orkney have been recovered during the periods:

> April to September from Essex, Caithness, Grampian and Highland Regions, Isle of Skye, Outer Hebrides and Shetland.
>
> October to March from Fife and Banff.

One young bird ringed in Shetland was recovered in Orkney in November of the same year.

Black-throated Diver
Gavia arctica

Passage migrant, small numbers winter.

This species was considered to be scarce by Buckley and Harvie-Brown (1891), while Balfour (1972) described it as an irregular passage visitor, the numbers always small.

During the period 1974-1982 it has been a regular visitor in small numbers, with the maximum recorded being 20 at Echnaloch Bay on 3rd May 1982. Although it has been noted throughout the year, the majority of sightings occur in May, September and October. Scapa Flow is a favoured area, especially Echnaloch and Waulkmill Bays, but this diver can sometimes be seen inland on the larger lochs.

Despite claims that this species has bred in Orkney, there are no authenticated records.

Great Northern Diver   Immer Goose
Gavia immer

Common winter visitor, with a few birds present in summer.

The Great Northern Diver was described by Buckley and Harvie-Brown (1891) as a common winter visitor, and there has been no change in status.

It is usually found in sheltered bays and sounds, with Scapa

J.F.H.

Flow and the area around Gairsay holding the largest numbers of wintering birds.

In early 1975 it was estimated that the total Orkney wintering population was over 450 birds. Of these, 200 were in Scapa Flow and 160 north of Gairsay (Lea, 1980). In spring a gathering of birds has been noted in Clestrain Sound with over 100 on 6th April 1908 (A.S.N.H. 1908:185). More recently the maximum seen was 81 on 8th May 1977.

Birds in full breeding plumage are recorded regularly during the summer months.

White-billed Diver

Gavia adamsii

Very rare.

There is only one record, a bird seen in Rousay Sound on 20th April 1976 (B.B. 70:412).

GREBES : Podicipedidae

Little Grebe   Dabchick; Little Footy Arse

Tachybaptus ruficollis

Scarce resident.

This species was found breeding on South Ronaldsay by Low (1813), while Buckley and Harvie-Brown (1891) stated that it was

resident and not uncommon and mentioned that it bred on the
Loch of Skaill, Mainland and Bea Loch, Sanday. Lack (1943) listed
several pairs on the Mainland, two or three on Stronsay, five or
more on Sanday and one on Westray. Balfour (1968) indicated that
a decline had occurred on the Mainland.

Although possibly under-recorded as a breeding species, there
may have been a slight decline in all areas. During the period 1974-
1982 breeding has been recorded from:

Burray	Echnaloch
Mainland	Loch of Bosquoy, Loch of Graemeshall
Sanday	Bea Loch
South Ronaldsay	Liddle Loch
Westray	Loch of Burness, Loch of Saintear

Apart from the above lochs, wintering birds have been
reported from North Ronaldsay, Rousay and several sites on
the Mainland where, at the Brig o' Waithe, small numbers are seen
regularly, with a maximum of 8 on 19th February 1981.

Great Crested Grebe

Podiceps cristatus

Very rare.

Buckley and Harvie-Brown (1891) mentioned a dead specimen,
near Melsetter, in 1829 and, quoting one of their correspondents,
stated that this species was occasionally seen in winter in the sound
between Hoy and Graemsay. Omond (1925) noted it as a rare
visitor, sometimes seen in autumn and winter.

The only dated records are:

1938	1 Loch of Harray, 16th October.
1974	2 Firth, 20th March, 2 off Birsay, 19th October.
1975	1 Holm Sound, 5th November.
1977	Singles on Loch of Boardhouse, 15th June and Loch of Hundland, 16th June, were presumed to be the same bird.
1979	1 North Ronaldsay, 23rd February to 7th March.

Red-necked Grebe

Podiceps grisegena

Scarce migrant; may occasionally winter.

Baikie and Heddle (1848) considered this species not uncommon in winter; Balfour (1972) stated that it was rather scarce, perhaps an irregular winter and passage visitor.

From 1972-1982 there are 22 records, the majority from Scapa Flow, with others from Deer Sound, North Tankerness, Skaill in Sandwick and Wyre Sound. These records are of single birds, apart from three seen at Echnaloch Bay on 28th November 1976, two there on 12th March 1977 and two off Flotta on 6th October 1979.

Monthly distribution of sightings 1972-1982

J	F	M	A	M	J	J	A	S	O	N	D
0	2	5	3	0	0	1	2	3	3	2	1

Slavonian Grebe

Podiceps auritus

Regular winter visitor and passage migrant; a few birds may be present throughout the year.

Buckley and Harvie-Brown (1891) recorded that this species had been seen in spring, autumn and winter. Balfour (1972) considered it to be mainly a winter and passage visitor in limited numbers.

Scapa Flow is an important wintering area where, in February 1975, it was estimated that there were approximately 60 birds (Lea, 1980). The Slavonian Grebe is also found in sheltered sea areas and on fresh-water lochs, groups of 5 to 20 birds being not uncommon. In most years during the summer months, birds are seen in full breeding plumage and occasionally in suitable breeding habitat.

Balfour (1968) gave a possible, but undated, breeding record at Quanterness; this may be the one referred to by Buckley and Harvie-Brown.

Black-necked Grebe
Podiceps nigricollis
Very rare.

There is only one record of this species, that of a bird obtained in 1873 (Buckley and Harvie-Brown, 1891).

ALBATROSSES : Diomedeidae

Black-browed Albatross
Diomedea melanophris
Very rare.

There are only two authenticated records:

1969   1 off Hoy, 13th August (B.B. 63:269, S.B. 6:26-27).
1975   1 adult Scapa Flow, 21st August (B.B. 69:327).

The 1933 record (Balfour, 1972) is not mentioned in the B.O.U. List 1971 and, without further details, cannot be included.

An albatross, not identified specifically, was seen 20 miles north-west of Orkney on 18th July 1894 (A.S.N.H. 1895:57).

PETRELS AND SHEARWATERS: Procellariidae

Fulmar   Mallimack
Fulmarus glacialis
Resident and numerous breeding species.

The Fulmar was obviously uncommon during the 19th century, as Buckley and Harvie-Brown (1891) mentioned only a

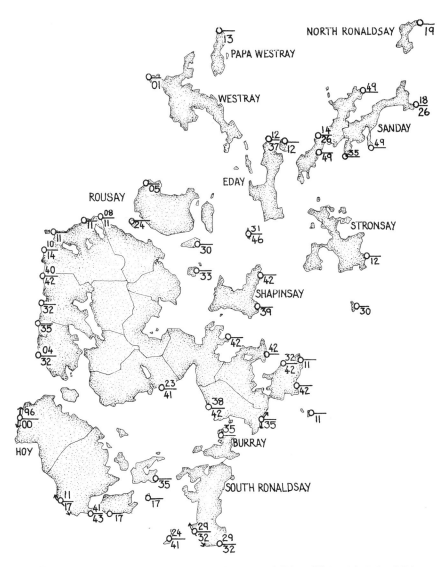

THE SPREAD OF THE FULMAR IN ORKNEY 1896–1949,
(after Fisher 1952).
UPPER DATES SHOW WHEN BIRDS WERE FIRST SEEN
PROSPECTING; LOWER DATES, WHEN PROVED BREEDING.
HOWEVER, BREEDING MAY HAVE OCCURRED EARLIER.

few occurrences. Breeding was first recorded on Hoy in 1900. In 1908 there was a colony at Costa Head and a small colony was found on the cliffs north of Marwick Head in 1910. By 1911 it was plentiful on Hoy, with hundreds of pairs between The Kame and The Old Man of Hoy. Further south, on the west coast of Hoy, where it was first noted in 1908, it had increased enormously (S.N. 1912).

Lack (1943) stated that it had increased rapidly and was common on every suitable island, while Balfour (1968) said that it had further increased and was widespread around almost all the coasts. Cramp (1974) suggested that the largest recorded increase of Fulmars between 1959 and 1969-70 anywhere in Britain had taken place in Orkney, where the population apparently leapt from 13,917 occupied sites to 47,304 (240%). However, many colonies were not counted in 1959, so these figures may have over-estimated the rate of increase.

Regular monitoring at selected cliff colonies has shown that the number of apparently occupied nests increased by 11% during the period 1976-1980 and the number of individuals by 30% during the same period (Wanless, French, Harris and Langslow, 1982).

Blue phase birds are recorded regularly, with most sightings being of single birds, although 20 were noted off Hoy on 5th November 1979 and 10 in the Pentland Firth on 10th November 1981. They are occasionally seen paired with pale phase birds and one has been present at Rackwick, Hoy from 1972.

Breeding birds may be found occupying sites on all types of cliffs and some inland rock outcrops. Other sites used are sand dunes, peat banks, at the foot of stone dykes, ruined buildings and, if undisturbed, flat ground. First eggs are usually found between 12th and 17th May.

This species has been the subject of a special study by Aberdeen University on the island of Eynhallow since 1950. It has been found that the lifespan of the Fulmar is about 40 years (Dunnet, Ollason and Anderson, 1983).

Birds ringed as pulli in Orkney have been recovered in the following countries:
Denmark (9), Faeroes (4), France (3), Germany (1), Greenland (3), Holland (1), Iceland (2), Ireland (3), Newfoundland (3), Norway (2), Nova Scotia (1), Russia (1).

Birds ringed in Spitzbergen, Sula Sgeir and Shetland have been recovered in Orkney.

A breeding Fulmar was captured in August in the North Sea, 466 kms from its chick on Eynhallow (Dunnet and Ollason, 1982).

Cory's Shearwater
Calonectris diomedea

Very rare.

There are just two records:

1970	1 off Hoy, 24th September (B.B.64:32, S.B. 6:330).
1982	1 off Brough of Birsay, 27th August (B.B.76:479).

Great Shearwater
Puffinus gravis

Very rare.

There are three authenticated records, all of single birds:

1973	Off Hoy, 19th September.
1980	8 miles N.N.W. of Sule Stack, 2nd August.
1981	North Ronaldsay, 30th October.

The 1971 record given by Balfour (1972) is not mentioned in the *Scottish Bird Reports* and cannot be included.

Sooty Shearwater
Puffinus griseus

Regular autumn passage migrant.

The first mention of this species was by Omond (1925) who noted it as a rare visitor. The increased interest in sea watching during recent years has shown it to be regular, sometimes in quite large numbers. All sightings have been in the late summer and autumn, the extreme dates being 1st July and 16th November.

The main passage takes place during August, September and early October. The largest numbers have been seen off North Ronaldsay, the Brough of Birsay and Auskerry, although sightings are regularly reported from the Pentland Firth, Scapa Flow and around the other North Isles.

Exceptional numbers were noted off North Ronaldsay between 7th and 28th September 1969, with a maximum of 800-1,000 on 22nd September.

Manx Shearwater   Lyre or Lyrie
Puffinus puffinus

Uncommon and local breeding species; passage migrant.

The Manx Shearwater has declined as a breeding species during the last two centuries. Low (1813) stated that the young were much sought after as delicacies and that "the country people salt them down for winter provision and boil them with cabbage". Baikie and Heddle (1848) considered this species to be migratory and noted that, although not numerous, it arrived in February and March and remained until autumn. Breeding was thought to be confined to Papa Westray, Westray and Waas (probably Walls).

Buckley and Harvie-Brown (1891) quoted Moodie-Heddle as having found it breeding at Rothiesholm Head, Stronsay and at several places on Hoy. They were of the opinion, however, that a decline had occurred on Hoy and considered rats to be a possible cause.

Serle (1934) said that there were certainly three nesting colonies occupied on Hoy and one of the sites was fully two miles from the sea. Lack (1943), who thought that the species was abundant in the 18th century, considered it to have greatly decreased. However, it is possible that there was some confusion by earlier writers with its name of Lyre and that of Lyer for the Puffin, so that it may have been wrongly recorded as abundant.

Balfour (1972) acknowledged that the status was not well known but noted that there appeared to have been a gradual decline since before 1925. The only known breeding places are now on Hoy, although evening rafts of from 10 to 20 birds have been recorded from the North Isles each summer. A colony found by von U. Böker (1964) was estimated to be from 15 to 20 pairs and there is another one of possibly up to 100 pairs. Rafts of birds are seen regularly off Rackwick, Hoy in the evenings of June and July, with counts of 500 on 24th June 1972 and 1,000 on 9th July 1973, but in 1981 the maximum was 150 on 21st July. Eggs have been found on 22nd May and young, still with down, on 12th September.

Red-throated Diver on nest

On passage the Manx Shearwater has been recorded from the
Pentland Firth, the North Isles, especially North Ronaldsay, and
from the Brough of Birsay, where it is noted regularly during
September, with a maximum of 40 on 9th September 1980. The
extreme dates for North Ronaldsay are 5th May and 20th October.

A bird ringed as full grown on the island of Rhum, off the
west coast of Scotland, in September 1958, was recovered in April
1963 in Orkney.

STORM PETRELS : Hydrobatidae

Storm Petrel   Storm Finch

Hydrobates pelagicus

Summer resident.

This species was recorded as breeding on Hunda and many
other smaller Orkney holms by Low (1813). Buckley and Harvie-
Brown (1891), however, stated that it had almost deserted Hunda,
but bred not uncommonly in various other places.

The largest known colonies are on Auskerry and Sule Skerry,
while breeding has been confirmed on Pentland Skerries, Switha,
the Green Holms, the Holm of Faray, Rusk Holm and the Holm
of Papa Westray. Churring birds have been heard on Eynhallow
and Copinsay during the breeding season and birds have been
caught on the Holm of Huip, Little Linga and Swona, all suitable
islands for nesting, especially as there are no resident cats.

Birds have been reported at sea from May to October, with
records from the Pentland Firth, Scapa Flow, Papa Westray,
Westray and North Ronaldsay.

The use of tape-recorded calls to attract birds has shown that
Storm Petrels are never very distant from much of the Orkney
coastline during the summer months, and numbers have been
caught in both North Ronaldsay and South Ronaldsay in this way.
The Storm Petrel is occasionally found inland after gales, especially
during October when the young have just fledged. The latest
recorded date is 16th November 1980, when a bird, freshly dead,
was found on Flotta.

C

Ringing has shown that not only is there movement of birds between colonies in Orkney, but also of birds between Orkney and colonies in other areas including Caithness, the Faeroes, the Flannan Isles, the Isle of Man, Shetland, the Shiants, St Kilda, Strathclyde and the Summer Isles.

A bird ringed in Orkney in July 1977 was recovered near Durban, South Africa in August 1980.

Leach's Petrel
Oceanodroma leucorhoa

Summer and autumn visitor, has bred.

This species probably occurs regularly in small numbers in Orkney waters during the summer and early autumn. The majority of records are from Sule Skerry where breeding was noted in 1933 (Robinson, 1934). Recent expeditions, using tape-recorded calls, have caught a number of birds on this island, but there has been no further proof of breeding.

Birds have been seen at sea off the Brough of Birsay, North Ronaldsay and Westray from July to October, and they have been recorded several times on North Ronaldsay. There are also reports of birds found stranded inland after gales, the latest date being 30th October.

GANNETS : Sulidae

Gannet   Solan Goose
Sula bassana

Local breeding species, present offshore throughout the year.

The only colony, which is on Sule Stack, has probably been in existence for several hundred years, as it was mentioned by Monteith (1633) and Sibbald (1710), according to Baxter and Rintoul (1953). Visits were sometimes undertaken to collect young and Low (1813) noted that the "feathers were good as they were not nearly so oily as those of other sea fowl; the birds were eaten, but were very wild and fishy tasted with a strong smell".

Sule Stack: Number of pairs of Gannets, 1904-1969
(Cramp et al, 1974)

1904	1914	1939	1949	1960	1969
4,000	4,000	3,490	2,010	2,900	4,018

A feature commented on by several visitors to Sule Stack is the number of immature and non-breeding birds that are present.

Birds are occasionally seen resting on the cliffs of Copinsay, where breeding may have taken place in about 1860 and 1911 (Aplin, 1916). In 1925 or 1926 a pair built a nest there, but one bird subsequently died (Baxter and Rintoul, 1953). During the period 1972-1982, birds have been noted on cliffs at Halcro Head, South Ronaldsay; The Standard, Costa Head and Marwick Head, Mainland.

The main passage offshore occurs in the autumn with smaller numbers in spring and summer.

A young bird ringed on the Bass Rock in July was recovered in Scapa Flow in October of the same year, while one from Shetland was found dead in Orkney four years later.

CORMORANTS : Phalacrocoracidae

Cormorant   Hibling or Great Scarf

Phalacrocorax carbo

Resident breeding species and partial migrant.

Although by no means an uncommon bird, Buckley and Harvie-Brown (1891) considered the Cormorant to be still far from numerous as a breeding species in the late 19th century. They mentioned the following colonies: Seal Skerry, North Ronaldsay; Rothiesholm, Stronsay; The Standard, Costa Head, Mainland; Calf of Eday; Rousay and Hoy. Nesting was stated to have taken place on Copinsay in 1831 and only one bird was seen there in 1884.

Cormorants have now ceased to nest at The Standard,

Rothiesholm, Rousay and Hoy, but colonies have been established at the Brough of Stronsay, Muckle Green Holm, Holm of Boray, Taing Skerry, Horse of Copinsay and Little Pentland Skerry.

Four types of nesting habitat have been identified (Balfour, Anderson and Dunnet, 1967): bare, rocky and exposed skerries (Seal Skerry and Little Skerry); shingle and stony beach (Taing Skerry); flat, grassy sward (Boray Holm) and flat cliff-top (the remaining colonies).

The number of nests has fluctuated, reaching a peak of over 600 in the 1960's and mid 1970's.

Counts of nests at Orkney Cormorant colonies

Seal Skerry, North Ronaldsay

1892	1965	1968-70	1979	1980	1981
50	50	50	32	86	74

Calf of Eday

1956	1961	1962	1963	1964	1965	1968-70	1974	1976	1981	1982
220	198	168	182	198	170	211	265	308	147	175 min.

Muckle Green Holm

1961	1968-70	1981	1982
82	58	c50	45-50

Brough of Stronsay

1959-63	1968-70	1975	1979	1981	1982
c20	15	23	10 min.	c20	26

Boray Holm

1959	1960	1961	1962	1963	1964	1965	1966	1968-70	1976	1977	1981	1982
180	54	17	21	188	202	208	172	224	119	112	40	56

Taing Skerry

1960	1961	1962	1963	1964	1965	1966	1976	1981	1982
166	190	185	43	15	0	c35	250	80	114

Horse of Copinsay

1962	1968-70	1980	1982
20-30	16	c17	6

Little Skerry

1962	1968-70	1982
c20	10	Present

A nest was noted on the Barrel of Butter on 13th March 1977 and in 1982 at least seven nests were counted (D.Pirie, pers. comm.). Four or five pairs nested on Little Green Holm in 1982, the first time that nesting had been recorded on this island. Occasionally single pairs are reported nesting on cliffs away from the main colonies and one pair has attempted to nest on the mast of a wreck off the Churchill Barriers.

An albino bird was present on the Pentland Skerries in 1975.

A substantial part of the Orkney population moves away in winter, mainly to the east coast of Scotland. Smaller numbers may cross to the west coast down the Great Glen (Balfour, Anderson and Dunnet, 1967). The most distant recoveries of Orkney-bred birds are from Merioneth, Sussex and Hampshire, while a third year bird was found in Norway. Several birds ringed in Shetland have been found in Orkney.

Shag
Scarf, Tappie Whaesie

Phalacrocorax aristotelis

Common breeding species and winter visitor.

This species was mentioned as being abundant by several earlier writers and there does not appear to be any change in status. It is found nesting on many cliffs, in caves and occasionally on low ledges. A very early clutch of eggs was reported from Sule Skerry on 24th February 1908 (A.S.N.H. 1908). Although the main laying season is April and May, young birds may still be seen in the nest in September.

A total of 3,600 pairs was found in Operation Seafarer 1968-70 (Cramp, et al, 1974).

Large gatherings occur in autumn and winter in several parts of Orkney, with 2,000+ reported from Scapa Flow in 1974 and 1,000 on the north coast of Rousay on 20th February 1977. There were 800 around Eynhallow on 6th September 1981.

The majority of recoveries of Orkney-ringed birds have been either local or on the coasts of Scotland; the furthest movements are of single birds to Yorkshire and France. There have been recoveries in Orkney of birds from the Farne Islands, Handa, the Isle of May, Shetland (including Fair Isle) and Sutherland.

HERONS AND BITTERNS:
Ardeidae

Bittern
Botaurus stellaris

Very rare.

There is one fully authenticated record, a bird shot at Voy, near Stromness on 22nd February 1934. It is now in the Stromness Museum (Balfour 1972).

Little Bittern
Ixobrychus minutus

Very rare.

There is an early record of one shot in Sanday in 1806 (Baikie and Heddle, 1848). Apart from this, there are two other records:

1909	Adult male shot at Loch of Stenness, 14th May (A.S.N.H.1909:183).
1971	A male seen at Hooking Loch, North Ronaldsay, 31st May (B.B.65:327).

Night Heron
Nycticorax nycticorax

Very rare.

There are two records:

1961	An adult at Rendall, Mainland, 1st November (B.B.65:395, S.B.2:475).
1982	An adult seen in Kirkwall, 23rd May and at Loch of Kirbister, Orphir 24th May (B.B.76:479).

Squacco Heron
Ardeola ralloides

Very rare.

A male was shot on North Ronaldsay on 7th September 1896 (A.S.N.H.1897:158).

Little Egret
Egretta garzetta

Very rare.

There are three records, all of single birds:

1961	Isbister Oyce, Rendall, from 30th July to 5th August (B.B.55:567).
1973	The Loons, Birsay, 18th-27th May (B.B.67:314).
1981	Swartmill Loch, Westray, 29th October to 24th November (B.B.75:488).

Great White Egret
Egretta alba

Very rare.

The only record is of a bird on North Ronaldsay on 28th and 29th April 1978 (B.B.73:495).

Grey Heron
Ardea cinerea

Rare breeding species and regular winter visitor.

The Heron has probably always been very local as a breeding species as no colonies were known to Low (1813). Buckley and Harvie-Brown (1891) stated that herons "are abundant all through the Orkneys in winter; indeed at any season except when breeding, when they are at present scarce". The following nesting places were mentioned by them and also A.S.N.H.1908:220:

Glims Holm
Hoy
Mainland:
  Black Craig, Stromness
  Lyre Geo
  Sandwick
Stronsay:
  Rothiesholm

It has decreased during this century, and of the above sites only Lyre Geo and Hoy are known to have been used during the last 50 years.

Lyre Geo was first occupied in about 1863 and appears to have had a maximum of 13 nests (Balfour 1972). The following are the recorded counts of nests, which were all situated on cliff ledges:

'28	'39	'48	'54	'56	'58	'61	'62	'65	'69	'70	'74	'75	'76	'77-9
6	9	5	6	5	6	6	8	6+1	2	2 prs	1	1	2	1
								Hellyan						
								Kellyan						

Counts for 1928 and 1948-1962 from *The Orcadian*, 9th June 1962.
Count for 1939 from Baxter and Rintoul (1953).
Count for 1965 from Groundwater (1974).

Unfortunately this site now seems to be deserted. Groundwater (1974) recorded nests with eggs on 16th April and small young on 9th May. Fully grown young have been noted on 28th June and nests still with young on 21st August.

The history of the Hoy site is not so well documented. Buckley and Harvie-Brown stated that the nests were amongst long heather and bracken at the edge of a cliff. This site was occupied in 1913 (Baxter and Rintoul, 1953) and again in 1974, when young were reared, but nesting probably also took place on occasions during the intervening years (Garden, 1958). On 6th July 1975, one nest had 2 fully fledged young and another held 4 eggs. Pairs were present in 1976 and 1978.

A new site was established on Hoy in 1978 and details of nesting are given below:

1978   1 nest
1980   2 nests, 3 young reared in one, the other failed.
1981   3 pairs bred successfully, rearing 9 young.
1982   4 nests, but only one was definitely known to have been successful.

As the number of breeding pairs is now very low, we are in danger of losing the Heron as a breeding species and it is hoped that this colony will be left undisturbed.

Elsewhere a nest was found with 4 eggs on the Orphir cliffs on 24th May 1953 (Clouston) and a pair nested in a willow bush in South Ronaldsay in 1976.

There is an influx of passage and wintering birds in July and August and they are widespread throughout the islands until the following April. Maximum counts include 25 seen on Glims Holm on 11th February 1968 (Clouston) and 22 on the Stromness Holms on 17th October 1976.

Eleven birds from Norway and 2 from Sweden, all ringed as young, have been recovered in Orkney between September and April. The presence between July and October 1981 of a tagged bird, which had been marked as a nestling in the Fife/East Perth area, indicates that some of our wintering birds may come from the mainland of Scotland.

Purple Heron
Ardea purpurea

Very rare.

There are two records, both of single birds:

1980　An immature on North Ronaldsay, 1st-8th September (B.B.75:489).

1982　Adult, South Ronaldsay, 2nd-5th August 1982 (B.B.76:482).

STORKS : Ciconiidae

Black Stork
Ciconia nigra

Very rare.

The one record is of a bird at Sandwick, Mainland from 7th-12th June 1972 (B.B.66:336).

White Stork
Ciconia ciconia

Very rare.

Baikie and Heddle (1848) noted a bird caught on South Ronaldsay in 1840. Since then the following sightings have been recorded, all of single birds:

1971	Burness Loch, Westray, 20th-24th May (B.B.65:327).
1972	Rousay, 6th June (died the next day). (B.B.66:336).
1977	Westray, 29th and 30th April,
	North Ronaldsay, 30th April-1st May,
	Harray, Mainland, 13th May,
	Rousay, 14th June (B.B.73:496).

The 1977 sightings probably all refer to the same bird.

IBISES AND SPOONBILLS:
Threskiornithidae

Glossy Ibis
Plegadis falcinellus

Very rare.

There are no recent records.

1857	An immature at Head of Work, near Kirkwall, shot on 17th September (Buckley and Harvie-Brown, 1891).
1903	An immature shot 1 mile west of Stromness on 19th September (A.S.N.H.1904:127).
1907	A flock of 19 or 20 arrived in Sandwick, Mainland on 24th September; by 1st October ten of these birds had been shot, they were all found to be immature birds (A.S.N.H.1908:50).

Spoonbill

Platalea leucorodia

Very rare.

The earliest record is of one shot prior to 1848 (Baikie and Heddle). Buckley and Harvie-Brown (1891) give the following records:

1859   Nine in Shapinsay, 19th October, of which five were shot. One was seen on the Peerie Sea, Kirkwall on 22nd October.

1861   One killed near Kirkwall.

1889   Four, Loch of Burness, Westray, 10th October.

The only 20th century records are of single birds:

1939   Evie, Mainland, shot, October (Baxter and Rintoul, 1953).

1975   Lyness, Hoy from 10th to 13th June.

SWANS, GEESE AND DUCKS:
Anatidae

Mute Swan
Cygnus olor

Common resident breeding species found on most of the larger islands where suitable habitat occurs.

The Mute Swan was first recorded in Orkney in the summer of 1869 when four appeared on the Loch of Skaill, Sandwick. Two of these birds were subsequently caught whilst moulting their flight feathers, a third bird was herded into a net. The fourth bird escaped to be eventually shot on the Loch of Clumley, Sandwick. The three captive birds were pinioned, but two died within a year or two. The third escaped and was shot on the Loch of Stenness. Subsequent events are confused but Fortescue (1886) states that four Mute Swans inhabited the Loch of Skaill in 1883.

Buckley and Harvie-Brown (1891) mention the Mute Swan as being found at only two locations, the Loch of Skaill, Sandwick and the Loch of Saviskaill, Rousay. The establishment of Mute Swans on certain lochs for ornamental purposes no doubt assisted the colonisation of this species in Orkney; two were placed on the Loch of Kirbister, Orphir (Omond, 1925).

By 1941 the species had increased significantly and was widely distributed with breeding recorded on Mainland, Papa Westray, Rousay, Sanday, Shapinsay and Stronsay. During the summer of that same year, 82 adult birds were seen on the Loch of Stenness and 92 on the Loch of Harray (Lack, 1943).

Balfour (1968) regarded the species as common, with 30 or more pairs said to have been breeding on the Lochs of Harray and Stenness. Thirty-six nests were counted on these two lochs in 1983.

There have been surveys of breeding birds in 1955-56 (Rawcliffe, 1958), 1978 (Ogilvie, 1981) and 1983 (in litt.) The results are tabulated below:

Year	Breeding Pairs	Comments
1955-56	26	Incomplete survey. Precise areas surveyed unknown

MEAN MONTHLY NUMBER OF MUTE SWANS, LOCHS OF HARRAY AND STENNESS, 1961-82. BASED ON MONTHLY WILDFOWL COUNT, SEPTEMBER TO MARCH.

Loch of Harray
MEAN NUMBER

Loch of Stenness
MEAN NUMBER

MONTH
SEPTEMBER
OCTOBER
NOVEMBER
DECEMBER
JANUARY
FEBRUARY
MARCH

Year	Breeding Pairs	Comments
1978	75*	Incomplete survey.
		See below for coverage
1983	67-68	Complete survey

*Extrapolated total.

Incomplete survey in 1978: Fifteen 10km squares were counted, HY 45, 44, 43, 42, 41, 40, 33, 32, 31, 30, 22, 21, 20, 62, 51.

The Lochs of Harray and Stenness support a large population of Mute Swans and winter numbers have been well documented. Monthly wildfowl counts, September-March 1962-1982, reveal average wintering numbers of 100 (maximum count 228) for the Loch of Harray and 85 (maximum count of 253) for the Loch of Stenness (see figure). Only those years in which at least six counts were completed have been used in the calculation of these averages. The numbers peaked during the 1970's and this was followed by a decline to a level similar to the 1960's. A high proportion of non-breeding birds frequent these two lochs, a feature noted by Balfour (1968).

The only complete winter census of Mute Swans in Orkney was conducted in November 1976, when 371 were counted (Booth, 1976).

The density of breeding and territorial pairs compares favourably with those of South and East England and was calculated to be 7.2 pairs per 10 km square by Ogilvie (1981). The occurrence of 5 nesting pairs, all of which reared young in 1976, at Echnaloch, Burray, an open water area 11 hectares in extent, is considered to be exceptional. Breeding birds are normally associated with loch margins and oyces.

During the period 1974-1983 nesting has been recorded on:

Boray Holm	Rousay
Burray	Sanday
East Mainland	South Ronaldsay
Egilsay	Stronsay
Holm of Scockness	West Mainland
North Ronaldsay	Westray
Papa Westray	

The first eggs have been noted on 12th April and the first young on 20th May.

Bewick's Swan

Cygnus columbianus

A scarce and irregular visitor.

First recorded on Hoy (1) in 1850 (Buckley and Harvie-Brown, 1891). All subsequent sightings are detailed below:

1885	1 Loch of Hundland, 3rd April (Buckley and Harvie-Brown, 1891).
1888	3 Loch of Harray, 1st March (Buckley and Harvie-Brown, 1891).
1917	2 Swona, 26th December (S.N.1917).
	1 dead, Graemsay, 2nd December (S.N.1918).
1962	1 Loch of Stenness, 13th February (Wildfowl Count).
1965	2 Loch of Skaill, 12th December (Wildfowl Count).
1966	5 Loch of Skaill, 16th January (Wildfowl Count).
	1 North Ronaldsay, 17th March (*Island Saga*).
1968	1 Loch of Stenness, 18th February (Groundwater, 1974).
1973	1 Graemeshall Loch, 18th February.
1976	1 Sanday, 6th and 13th November.

Whooper Swan

Cygnus cygnus

Common winter and passage visitor.

The Whooper Swan regularly bred in Orkney until some time before 1775. Fea (1775) said that they used to breed on several small holms in the Loch of Stenness. Neill (1806) provided additional information and stated "till within these twenty years (as I was told in Orkney) a few pairs regularly remained during the summer on the islets of the great lake of Stenness and there produced their broods". Shirreff (1814) added that several pairs used to nest on islands in the Loch of Harray until about twenty years before the date of writing. All three writers were of the opinion that the demise of the Whooper Swan as a breeding species was attributable to theft of the eggs, some of which were "sold southwards" (Fea, 1775), and general harassment. The species was also known as a winter and passage visitor.

Significant numbers of Whooper Swans continue to frequent Orkney, both as passage migrants and winter residents. During the period 1973-1982, the earliest date of arrival was 6th September and the latest 8th October. Most birds appear to depart during the last few weeks of April and early May, with the 24th May being the last recorded date. Summering birds are regular in very small numbers and these are frequently injured or immature.

During the period September to May, the numbers of Whooper Swans in Orkney undergo monthly fluctuations:

Combined total numbers of Whooper Swans seen by all observers each month, 1982

J	F	M	A	M	J	J	A	S	O	N	D
166	150	568	248	17	0	0	2	13	1,797	1,813	175

Similar trends were observed during the winter of 1980-81 and are thought to be typical. The main influx of birds occurs during October, with numbers subsequently dropping during December and January as Swans emigrate. A secondary influx occurs during March, presumably due to the northward passage of birds that have wintered on the British mainland. These monthly fluctuations in numbers may be related to changes in the birds' feeding ecology (Reynolds, 1981).

Surveys of the mid-November population have been undertaken and the results are tabulated below:

Date	Total
1976 (13th/14th November)	479
1979 (mid-November)	450
1981 (7th/8th November)	600
1982 (13th/14th November)	638

In order to place these figures in context, a national survey of Whooper Swans in Britain and Ireland (excluding Shetland) in mid-November 1979 produced 6,713 birds (Brazil and Kirk, 1981). At certain times, therefore, Orkney supports approximately 7% of the wintering Whooper Swan population of the British Isles.

It is assumed that the Orkney birds derive from Icelandic breeding grounds. One of 46 Whooper Swans, fitted with neck

Kestrel at ground nest

collars in Iceland in July 1980, was subsequently observed in Orkney in 1982. The detailed movements of this bird are:

> July 1980: caught and fitted with neck-collar, Lake Myvatn, Iceland.
>
> 16th-18th November 1980: seen Welney, Norfolk.
>
> 8th November 1981: seen Killiminster, Caithness.
>
> 28th January-21st February 1982: seen Mainland, Orkney.

Bean Goose
Anser fabalis

Scarce and irregular winter visitor.

According to Baikie and Heddle (1848), this species was observed occasionally in early winter, although it was not mentioned by Buckley and Harvie-Brown (1891). Since 1945 there have been sightings involving 23 birds; the largest flock was 8 birds, in Holm on 18th March 1982. Two in Papa Westray on 13th June 1982 was unusual.

Monthly distribution of sightings, 1945-1982

J	F	M	A	M	J	J	A	S	O	N	D
2	1	3	1	0	1	0	0	0	2	1	0

Pink-footed Goose
Anser brachyrhynchus

Passage migrant and scarce winter visitor.

This species appears to have been scarce in the 19th century. Baikie and Heddle (1848) made no mention of it and Buckley and Harvie-Brown (1891) quoted only three records.

The Pink-footed Goose is now a regular and, in some years, common passage migrant. The first autumn migrants arrive in Orkney in September, the earliest sighting being 4th September 1983. Most birds do not stay but continue south and during September and October flocks can be seen passing overhead, sometimes in the company of Greylag Geese. The total numbers vary annually, but the scale of the movement can be impressive,

Oystercatcher

e.g. 1,000+ observed on passage during the day in the East Mainland on 5th October 1980.

Very few birds appear to remain through the winter.

Monthly distribution of sightings, 1974-1982

J	F	M	A	M	J	J	A	S	O	N	D
1	0	1	2	7	0	0	0	29	22	5	1

Small numbers occur in spring with most birds being seen during May.

White-fronted Goose
Anser albifrons

Regular spring and autumn passage migrant; small numbers resident in winter.

Nineteenth century references are somewhat contradictory concerning the status of the White-fronted Goose in Orkney. The species is variously referred to as an occasional winter visitor (Baikie and Heddle, 1848) and the commonest of all geese in Orkney (Buckley and Harvie-Brown, 1891). The latter commented on the highly localised nature of wintering flocks, the largest they recorded being 50 birds.

Winter flocks are now regular and remain localised at traditional sites in both the East and West Mainland. Wintering numbers have fluctuated during the past decade but have probably never exceeded 100 birds. The largest reported feeding flock was 100 birds seen at Holm on 13th April 1958.

Monthly distribution of sightings, 1973-1982

J	F	M	A	M	J	J	A	S	O	N	D
2	7	18	15	0	0	0	0	0	22	18	8

The Loch of Tankerness would appear to have declined in importance as a regular wintering site. During the period 1963-1967, the average of the three highest monthly winter wildfowl counts was 50. The corresponding figure for the period 1970-1979 (exclusive of 1971) was 21.

In contrast, the parish of Holm (various localities) would appear to have increased in importance as a spring feeding site in recent years.

Large numbers pass through Orkney on migration, frequently

occurring in mixed flocks with other grey geese. The main autumn passage occurs during October, with the earliest migrants in the period 1972-1982 having been recorded on the 2nd October. Spring passage occurs during March, continues into April and is normally complete by the end of that month.

Even during the late 1800's, White-fronted Geese were apparently feeding on reclaimed pasture and cereal stubble (Baikie and Heddle, 1848) and this habit continues. Flocks will occasionally be seen feeding on marshy ground.

Wintering birds appear to belong to the Greenland race *A.a.flavirostris*, although birds of the nominate race *A.a.albifrons* have occasionally been observed (Balfour, 1972).

In 1956, on 29th October, a White-fronted Goose was recovered in Orkney and was found to have been ringed on 29th July 1955 as a juvenile in Greenland.

Greylag Goose

Anser anser

Common passage migrant; local winter resident in small numbers.

Historical references are conflicting concerning the status of this species during the 19th century. Baikie and Heddle (1848) noted that the species visited Orkney every winter, but not in great numbers. Buckley and Harvie-Brown (1891) referred to the Greylag as being "a very rare bird in Orkney". Omond (1925) added to the confusion by stating that it was common in snowy winters in the late 1800's but is "now hardly ever seen".

Balfour (1972) considered this goose to be a common passage visitor, with small numbers occasionally wintering.

The main autumn passage begins in late September although small numbers have been recorded in late August to early September. In some years passage is prolonged, with flocks seen throughout October until early November. On days of heavy passage, hundreds and sometimes thousands of birds pass through Orkney on a broad front, but comparatively few ever make landfall here.

The over-wintering of a small flock in Orkney, in the Loch of Harray area, would appear to have become a regular feature since the time of Balfour (1972) and the size of the flock has increased

MEAN ANNUAL NUMBER OF GREYLAG GEESE, LOCH OF HARRAY, 1962-83, BASED ON MONTHLY WILDFOWL COUNT, SEPTEMBER TO MARCH. ONLY YEARS WITH AT LEAST 6 COUNTS INCLUDED.

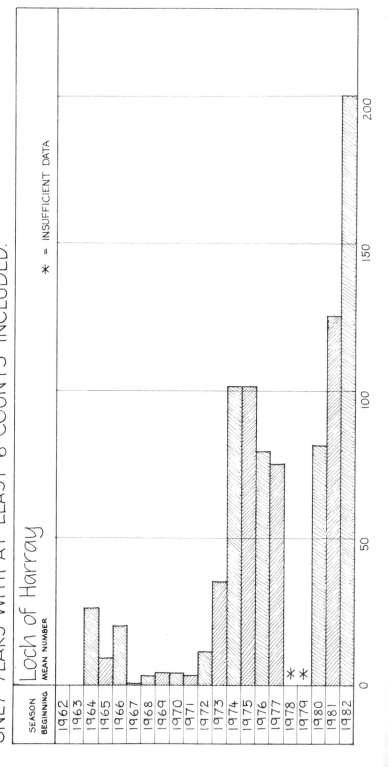

* = INSUFFICIENT DATA

Loch of Harray

(see figure). The maximum number of birds recorded in this wintering flock was 525 on 13th December 1982.

The wintering birds have generally left by the middle of May but there are occasional sightings of individuals or small flocks during the summer.

Single birds ringed in Iceland in June and July have been recovered in Orkney in April and November.

Snow Goose

Anser caerulescens

Rare and irregular visitor.

Historical texts make no reference to this species. All available sightings are detailed below:

1967	1 North Ronaldsay, 12th-13th May (Groundwater, 1974).
1968	4 white and 4 blue phase Lesser Snow Geese (A.c.caerulescens) 18th-19th May, Stenness.
1971	1 North Ronaldsay, 13th May
	6 (all white) Harray Lodge, 16th November.
1974	2 Deerness, 1st November.
1980	1 blue phase bird, Kirkwall, 11th-28th May.

Due to the occurrence of full winged Snow Geese in wildfowl collections, it is often difficult to establish if the birds are truly wild. It is quite possible that some of the birds observed come from the North American populations.

Canada Goose

Branta canadensis

Scarce visitor.

Only 19 records involving 82 birds have been reported during the period 1883-1982. The largest recorded flock consisted of 23 birds.

Monthly distribution of sightings, 1883-1982

J	F	M	A	M	J	J	A	S	O	N	D
0	0	2	2	0	5	4	2	1	4	2	1

In 1982, a family party of two adults and three juveniles remained on Shapinsay from August to December.

An individual of one of the smaller races of the Canada Goose, thought to be *B.c.minima,* was observed with a flock of Barnacle Geese, of probable Greenland stock, in South Walls, Hoy in March 1982. The bird was possibly a genuine wild vagrant from North America.

Barnacle Goose
Branta leucopsis

Regular passage visitor and winter resident in small numbers.

Baikie and Heddle (1848) knew this species as a regular winter visitor which remained until spring, when numbers increased due to the influx of returning migrants. Buckley and Harvie-Brown (1891) stated that the species was not common on Mainland, although possibly a regular visitor to some of the North Isles.

Balfour (1972) stated that Barnacle Geese "occasionally wintered". Clouston (personal diaries) recorded a flock of approximately 300 wintering on an island in Scapa Flow during the winter of 1965/66.

Small flocks are regularly observed on autumn passage, which takes place during late September and early October, the earliest recorded date being 24th September 1978 (1974-1982).

The wintering Scapa Flow flock would appear to have become a regular feature during the past decade, although it is possible that it may previously have escaped notice. Several of the Scapa Flow islands are visited by the geese and the few counts available during the period 1975-1982 have ranged from 140 to 500.

The spring passage involving a very small number of birds is usually complete by the end of May, the last recorded date being 25th May. Single birds on 24th-26th June and 2nd-11th July 1981 are the only summer records.

In East Mainland, on 10th May 1975, a Barnacle Goose was found on a nest with one egg. The bird appeared to be attached to a flock of domestic geese.

The apparent absence of colour ringed birds within the Scapa Flow flock suggests that the birds originate from the Greenland Barnacle Goose population. In contrast, it is likely that most of the birds observed on passage come from the Spitzbergen breeding stock, as indicated by ringing recoveries. On 3rd October 1981, in West Mainland, two colour ringed birds were seen and found to have been ringed in Spitzbergen during the summer. Another Spitzbergen bird, ringed on 18th July 1977, was recovered in Orkney in January or February 1978.

Brent Goose
Branta bernicla

Scarce passage visitor.

This species would appear to have declined during the present century. Fea (1775) regarded the Brent or "Horie Goose" to be sufficiently numerous to merit commercial exploitation by the local inhabitants. He stated that these geese commonly fed on extensive sand-flat areas where "there grows a species of long grass upon the surface", presumably Eel grass (Zostera). He considered them to be particularly abundant in Deer Sound from autumn until spring and "the most delicious eating"; they were apparently sold in Kirkwall for 4d or 6d each.

Pennant (1789) mentioned this species in Orkney, as does the Statistical Account of Scotland (1791-1799). Baikie and Heddle (1848) stated that Brent Geese were regular winter visitors, arriving in October and remaining until spring, in such areas as Deer Sound, Hoy Sound and parts of the North Isles.

Buckley and Harvie-Brown (1891) also noted the Brent Goose as being a common but local species on Mainland and name Deer Sound, Mainland and Catasand, Sanday as favoured haunts.

Monthly sightings of Brent Geese, 1845-1982

J	F	M	A	M	J	J	A	S	O	N	D
3	1	3	2	5	0	1	1	4	12	1+	0

Most sightings occur during passage in the months of May and October, although numbers today are small and sightings widely scattered over the islands. What appeared to be traditional wintering sites have been abandoned since the late 19th century. During the period 1972-1982, the largest recorded flock was 9 birds in Deerness from 28th April to 7th May, 1975.

Both light and dark forms occur and Balfour (1972) stated that pale-bellied birds were the more commonly seen. However, closer examination of the limited records available (1949-1982) suggests that the forms occur in roughly equal proportions (52 light, 65 dark).

Ruddy Shelduck

Tadorna ferruginea

There are only three records, all of which probably refer to escapes:

1909	Female, Sule Skerry 18th June (S.N.1909:274).
1932	1 Sanday, 4th May, in Stromness Museum (Balfour, 1972).
1966	Pair Burray, 4th May (Balfour, 1972).

Shelduck   Sly-goose

Tadorna tadorna

Fairly common breeding species, small numbers winter.

The breeding status of the Shelduck would appear to have changed little since the time of Low (1813), who regarded it as a common species which left Orkney during the winter months. Buckley and Harvie-Brown (1891) also stated that this species was abundant, especially in the North Isles and they referred to overwintering birds. During the period 1974-1982 breeding has been recorded on:

Copinsay	Papa Westray
Eday	Rousay
Egilsay	Sanday
Hoy	South Ronaldsay
Mainland	Stronsay
North Ronaldsay	Westray

Shelduck can be seen in every month of the year. However, seasonal fluctuations do occur.

Monthly distribution of sightings, 1973-1982

J	F	M	A	M	J	J	A	S	O	N	D
24	48	55	30	48	30	8	15	5	4	7	22

An increase in numbers occurs from December to March, but during April birds become less conspicuous, presumably due to dispersal to breeding areas. The increased number of sightings recorded in May is largely of adult birds with broods. The adult birds begin to depart in July and the majority have left Orkney by the end of August; later sightings frequently refer to juvenile birds.

Most birds nest in burrows in sand dunes and earthy banks, but nests amongst heather are occasionally recorded. A breeding population of up to 80 pairs has been estimated (Eggeling, 1983, pers.comm.).

A pullus ringed in Lothian in 1979 was subsequently recovered in Orkney in August 1981.

Mandarin Duck

Aix galericulata

Very rare.

A pair on Bridesness Loch, North Ronaldsay on 8th May 1979 is the only record. These birds may have been escapes.

Wigeon

Anas penelope

Common winter and passage visitor; breeds in small numbers.

The first record of breeding was in 1871 (Gray, 1871) but the date and precise location were not specified. The only breeding place known to Buckley and Harvie-Brown (1891) was on Hoy, where they were said to breed annually. Briggs (1894) collected Wigeon eggs on Sanday in May 1893 and referred to pairs or odd drakes during May and June in North Ronaldsay, although no nests were found in the latter island.

Lack (1943) stated that several pairs bred regularly on Mainland and quoted G. T. Arthur who had known nests on Mainland for at least twenty years, during which time the numbers had increased.

Balfour (1972) referred to a small but widespread and increasing population. Since 1974 breeding has been recorded on Mainland, Sanday, South Ronaldsay, Stronsay and Westray and has been suspected elsewhere, e.g. North Ronaldsay. At one Mainland site, nine pairs were present in 1981. Breeding typically occurs close to small, open water sites from sea level up to approximately 160 metres. A moorland nest found in Kingsdale, Firth in 1976, and very distant from any open water, is considered to be unusual.

The first broods are normally seen during the last week in May, the earliest date during the period 1974-1982 being 11th May.

This species has always been known in Orkney as a common winter visitor and there has been no change in status. Flocks are found in both fresh and salt water habitats throughout the islands.

The flocks begin to appear in September, with further arrivals during October. The Lochs of Harray, Stenness and Tankerness are important wintering areas. Wintering numbers at all three sites appear to have increased slightly during the period 1962-1983 (Wildfowl Count data), although conspicuous annual fluctuations occur. Individual flocks tend to be small and scattered around the periphery of the lochs, where they can frequently be seen grazing on improved agricultural pasture. Peak counts include a total of 1,665 on the Loch of Harray, October 1973 (numerous small flocks) and 850-900 on Gairsay, October 1981 (one flock). Departure from the wintering areas occurs during April and continues into May.

Of eight ringing recoveries, six birds were from the Icelandic breeding grounds and one each from the Russian and Finnish breeding areas. Two birds, ringed whilst wintering in continental Europe, were recovered in subsequent years in Orkney in winter.

American Wigeon

Anas americana

Very rare.

There are only two records of this North American species:

1980   1 male Stenness, 13th May (B.B.75:490)
1982   1 male Birsay, 3rd May (B.B.76:485)

Gadwall

Anas strepera

Scarce passage and winter visitor, rare and irregular breeding species.

Baikie and Heddle (1848) stated that the Gadwall was irregular in occurrence. Buckley and Harvie-Brown (1891) considered it to be an occasional winter visitor to the Loch of Skaill and also mentioned a flock of six to eight on the Loch of Harray on 4th December 1880.

Omond (1925) referred to the Gadwall as a rare winter visitor and a female in his possession, shot at Waulkmill Bay on 16th January 1924, was the first he had seen.

Monthly distribution of sightings, 1970-1982

J	F	M	A	M	J	J	A	S	O	N	D
1	2	2	5	15	10	10	3	8	14	2	2

Clearly the species has increased as a passage and summer visitor. Autumn influxes of note include a maximum of 38 at the Loch of Skaill, Sandwick between 28th September and 4th October 1975 and 23 at the same site on 9th October 1976.

The Gadwall has also become an irregular breeding species. The first breeding record was from Sanday in 1969, since when there are the following reports:

Mainland:	1976	1 pair bred Sandwick
	1977	1 pair bred Sandwick
North Ronaldsay:	1977	1 pair possibly bred
	1979	1 pair bred
	1980	1 pair suspected breeding
	1981	At least 1 pair bred
	1982	2 pairs present, breeding not confirmed.

Shallow, nutrient-rich, open water with much peripheral or partly emergent vegetation is chosen for nesting.

Teal

Anas crecca

Widespread breeding species in small numbers; common winter visitor and passage migrant.

The status of the Teal does not appear to have changed. It was known as a breeding species to both Baikie and Heddle (1848) and Buckley and Harvie-Brown (1891) and the former commented on the influx of wintering birds.

Lack (1943) stated that Teal were to be found breeding on all the main islands except Cava, Fara, Flotta and North Hoy. During the period 1974-1982, breeding has been recorded on Gairsay, Mainland (at least seven sites), North Ronaldsay, Papa Westray, Rousay, Stronsay and Swona. Breeding is likely to have occurred on other islands but remains undocumented.

Nesting occurs amongst dense cover, adjacent to open water bodies of variable size, from sea level up to 250 metres. For the period 1974-1982, the earliest recorded date for the sighting of young was 13th May.

It is sometimes difficult to distinguish the first autumn arrivals from birds which have remained throughout the summer. A general increase in numbers is noted in mid August. Immigration becomes increasingly conspicuous during September and October, with peak counts of 240 on the Loch of Brockan, Rendall, 8th September 1981 and 330 on the Loch of Skaill, Sandwick, 25th October 1982. Typical seasonal fluctuations in wintering numbers are shown in the following table:

Mean monthly counts

	Sept.	Oct.	Nov.	Dec.	Jan.	Feb.	Mar.	
Loch of Harray	20	31	31	16	45	52	13	*
Loch of Stenness	32	70	52	33	46	53	32	*
Loch of Skaill	3	43	19	19	45	27	15	+

* Based on Wildfowl Count data 1961/62 - 1982/83
+ Based on Wildfowl Count data 1961/62 - 1975/76, 1980/81 - 1982/83.

Wintering birds are scattered throughout the islands and, particularly during cold weather, frequent the seashore, e.g. 341 were counted on the shores of North Scapa Flow on 11th January 1982. These birds begin to leave Orkney in March and the movement continues into April.

Ringing recoveries may indicate the origin of some of these migrant birds. An adult male, ringed in Russia in July, was recovered in Orkney in January of the following year. Two birds ringed in Iceland during the summer have been recovered in Orkney in November and December, while two ringed in Essex in October and November have been found in Orkney in December and August.

Green-winged Teal

Anas crecca carolinensis

Very rare.

Drakes showing the characteristics of this North American race have been recorded on only two occasions:

1973   1 on Eynhallow, 2nd November (B.B.67:316)
1976   1 Loch of Bosquoy, Mainland, 13th and 14th February (B.B.70:416)

Mallard   Stock Duck

Anas platyrhynchos

Common breeding species and winter visitor.

This species appears always to have been common in Orkney and the comments made by Briggs (1893) are typical — "a goodly number sit about the Seal Skerry all day coming on land after dark to feed. Many pairs breed here in reeds and fields but their eggs are most systematically taken by the natives." Both Baikie and Heddle (1848) and Buckley and Harvie-Brown (1891) referred to the greatly increased numbers during winter due to the presence of migrant birds. Autumn migrants begin arriving in August and depart during March and April. Typical patterns of winter attendance are shown in the following table:

Mean monthly counts, 1961/62 to 1982/83

	Sept.	Oct.	Nov.	Dec.	Jan.	Feb.	Mar.
Lochs of Harray and Stenness	34	128	151	167	189	176	76
Loch of Boardhouse	26	85	61	62	89	77	20
Loch of Skaill	22	75	61	62	57	49	27

Wintering numbers on the Lochs of Harray and Stenness and the Loch of Boardhouse appear to peak in January and on the Loch of Skaill in October. The three former lochs may attract Mallard from alternative sites within Orkney during mid-winter and this may explain the observed trends.

Mean annual wintering numbers for the Lochs of Harray, Stenness and Boardhouse for the period 1961/62 - 1982/83 peaked during the latter half of the 1960's. Numbers subsequently declined throughout the 1970's and only recently has there been a hint of recovery to former levels. Maximum counts of 700 (November 1966) and 562 (February 1969) were recorded on the Lochs of Harray and Stenness respectively.

Wintering birds frequent a variety of habitats, including open fresh water, marsh, offshore islands and seashore. There was a peak count of 407 on the shores of North Scapa Flow on the 11th January 1982.

During the present century, Lack (1943) stated that the species was common and breeding on all the main islands. Balfour (1968, 1972) confirmed this and added that the Mallard appeared to have increased.

Documented breeding data is scarce; during the period 1973-82 breeding was recorded on Flotta, Hoy, Mainland, North Ronaldsay, Papa Westray, Rousay and Sanday. Nesting areas are extremely diverse, ranging from lowland marsh, with dense populations (e.g. 30 pairs, The Loons, Birsay 1981), to moorland with isolated nests.

During the period 1973-1982, the earliest recorded date for the sighting of young was 22nd April.

The following ringing recoveries indicate the possible origins of some of the birds wintering in Orkney. A pullus ringed in Iceland in 1958 was recovered in Orkney in December 1962; an adult male from Russia, ringed in July, was found the following autumn in Orkney and two adult males, ringed in Norway in March and July, were recovered in Orkney in December and January.

Pintail

Anas acuta

Scarce but regular breeding species; winter and passage visitor in small numbers.

Baikie and Heddle (1848) provided information on the status of the Pintail and referred to it as a winter visitor "pretty abundant in many parts of Orkney but especially in Sanday". Buckley and Harvie-Brown (1891) considered it to be rare on Mainland but recorded Sanday as a wintering area. None of these earlier authors mentioned the Pintail as a breeding species. Noble (1908), however, stated that "a few nest in a certain spot in Orkney". Hale and Aldworth (1910) found several nests with eggs on Sanday and also caught several young. They stated that the species had probably nested for at least the two or three preceding years. Baxter (Baxter and Rintoul, 1953) saw a female with young at the north end of Sanday in 1927.

Lack (1943), quoting G. T. Arthur, said that several pairs bred regularly on Mainland. Lack observed two females with young on Stronsay and a single male on North Ronaldsay in mid-June 1941. Baxter and Rintoul (1953) referred to the species as a regular breeder in fair numbers. Balfour (1972) considered the Pintail to be a very scarce but annual breeder and a winter and passage visitor in small numbers. Clearly the Pintail has increased in Orkney during the present century and, during the period 1973-1982, breeding has been recorded on Mainland (several sites, few of them regular), Sanday, Stronsay, and North Ronaldsay. Sanday appears to have declined in importance as a nesting area, the last recorded breeding having occured in 1973.

Breeding sites are usually near shallow, open water areas with adjacent marsh vegetation. Exceptionally, single pairs nest in moorland several kilometres from open water. At the most important Mainland site, up to nine pairs are thought to have been present during the breeding season in 1981.

During the period 1973-1982, the earliest recorded date for the sighting of young birds was 10th May.

Monthly distribution of sightings, 1973-1982

J	F	M	A	M	J	J	A	S	O	N	D
7	14	32	36	56	18	17	12	7	22	12	11

Maximum counts during the period 1971-1982 include:

25 Brig of Brodgar, 8th Mar. 1971
56 Stronsay, 1st Oct. 1975 (in three groups of 10, 44 and 2)
26 North Loch, Sanday, 10th Nov. 1980 and 8th Feb. 1982
21+ The Loons, Birsay, 14th Aug. 1982

The increased sightings during October are likely to reflect an influx of migrant birds, perhaps from Icelandic breeding grounds, as indicated by the recovery in Orkney in October of a pullus ringed in Iceland in July of the same year. An adult bird ringed in March 1933 in Cumberland was recovered in Orkney in October 1933.

Garganey
Anas querquedula

Scarce passage visitor.

Baikie and Heddle (1848) referred to the Garganey as a rare species which appeared mainly in spring. Buckley and Harvie-Brown (1891) confirmed this status and mentioned one killed in Sanday in 1820.

During the period 1975-1982, birds have been seen annually with the exception of 1977 and 1982. The species remains scarce with no more than three individuals being reported in any one year. However, Baxter and Rintoul (1953) recorded 5 seen on North Ronaldsay on 5th July 1938. The extreme dates are 27th April and 25th September.

Monthly distribution of sightings, 1971-1982

Apr.	May	June	July	Aug.	Sept.
2	4	1	1	1	4

There is an unconfirmed breeding record from G. T. Arthur of a female with two young on a loch in North Ronaldsay on 20th July 1943 (Balfour, 1972).

Blue-winged Teal

Anas discors

Very rare.

There are only three records of this American species:

1966   Male, North Ronaldsay, 10th Nov. (B.B.60:314)
1973   Two males shot, Stronsay, 5th Sept. (B.B.67:316)
1979   Male, Woodwick, Evie, 2nd to 4th May (B.B.73:499)

Although definite wild birds have occurred in the British Isles, the possibility that some records may refer to escapes cannot be ruled out.

Shoveler

Anas clypeata

Local breeding species in small numbers; passage visitor and uncommon winter resident.

Birds in breeding plumage would appear to have been a rare sight, according to Baikie and Heddle (1848), although they did suggest that "red-breasted" birds were not infrequently encountered. These were presumably non-breeding males, in supplementary plumage, recorded during autumn passage. They also noted a male bird shot in Sanday on 24th May 1833.

Buckley and Harvie-Brown (1891) mentioned several having been shot in the North Isles, especially Sanday, although clearly the bird was uncommon. Breeding was first recorded in 1891, when four pairs were seen on a small loch on Sanday. One nest was found and more than thirty young subsequently seen (Harvey, 1892). Two pairs bred on Mill Loch, North Ronaldsay in 1892 (Briggs, 1893) where birds may have been present in 1891 and four nests were found on Sanday in 1893 (Briggs, 1894).

Clearly the Shoveler was becoming established as a breeding species. Hale and Aldworth (1910) stated that "a few pairs nest in Orkney". They ringed young birds but provided no information on location.

Lack (1943), quoting G. T. Arthur, said that breeding occurred regularly on Mainland. He observed broods on Stronsay and

E

Westray and also recorded birds on North Ronaldsay, Sanday, Shapinsay and South Ronaldsay. Balfour (1968) stated that the Shoveler, as a breeding species, occurred mainly on some of the North Isles and was scarce on the Mainland.

During the period 1974-1982, breeding has been recorded on North Ronaldsay, Papa Westray, Sanday, Stronsay, West Mainland (3 sites) and Westray. Precise numbers are difficult to ascertain but a maximum of 15 pairs is thought to be a reasonable estimate based on data for this period. Small shallow-water areas are preferred for breeding and the earliest recorded date for the sighting of broods is 15th May.

Monthly distribution of sightings 1973-1982

J	F	M	A	M	J	J	A	S	O	N	D
8	9	11	28	52	30	16	10	14	16	13	9

The small wintering population appears to be confined to some of the North Isles, in particular North Ronaldsay and Sanday, and consists of less than forty birds. Maximum counts include 58 on North Ronaldsay on 8th October and 40 there on 15th October 1979. Forty were observed flying south over North Ronaldsay on 8th October 1977 and 38 flying south-east on 1st November 1978.

An adult ringed on 26th March 1965 in Belgium was recovered on 25th April 1965 in Orkney.

Pochard

Aythya ferina

Common winter resident and passage visitor; has bred.

The status of this species does not appear to have changed significantly during the past hundred years. Baikie and Heddle (1848) and Buckley and Harvie-Brown (1891) referred to the Pochard as a common and regular winter visitor, appearing in large numbers in some years. Moodie-Heddle reported the species breeding on Hoy in 1895 and 1896 (Buckley, 1896).

H. W. Robinson (Baxter and Rintoul, 1953) considered it to be very common in winter and nesting in Orkney. In 1927, Baxter observed Pochard breeding on Bea Loch, Sanday and saw many on a loch at the north end of the island, where they were said to breed. Thirty-four males, a few ducks and well-grown young were

MEAN ANNUAL NUMBER OF POCHARD, LOCHS OF HARRAY AND BOARDHOUSE 1962-83
BASED ON MONTHLY WILDFOWL COUNT, SEPTEMBER TO MARCH.
ONLY YEARS WITH AT LEAST 6 COUNTS INCLUDED.

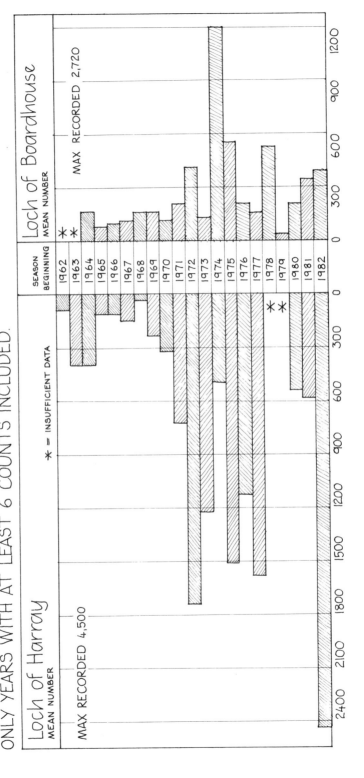

also seen during the same year on the Loch of Kirbister, Mainland (Baxter and Rintoul, 1953). Lack (1943), quoting G. T. Arthur, stated that a number of pairs had bred on Mainland for at least twenty years. Lack observed four males and one female on Sanday and one pair on Stronsay and considered the species to be increasing.

Balfour (1968) refered to the Pochard as being a scarce breeding species, confined mainly to the North Isles. During the period 1973 to 1982, breeding has been recorded in only two years:

1973   Possible juvenile seen, Bea Loch, Sanday.

1975   Female with 2 young seen on a small loch near Lowrie's Water, Evie, in mid-July.
        Family party observed making downstream, Harray, 12th July.

1980   Female exhibiting distraction display, 27th May, The Loons, Birsay.

As a breeding species, the Pochard would appear to have declined in recent years. This duck remains an important winter visitor and considerable numbers frequent Orkney's lochs during the months of September to March. The Lochs of Harray and Boardhouse support nationally significant wintering populations and the combined average annual numbers for the two lochs for the period 1964-1983 are shown in the figure. Wintering numbers appear to have increased since the 1960's. Male birds predominate in the winter flocks. These start to build up at the end of July and early August and the Loch of Tankerness, East Mainland, is especially important at this time, with peak counts of 400 on 31st July 1973, 200-300 on 17th July 1975 and 400 on 12th August 1981. The main influx of birds occurs during October, with most birds having left the islands by April. Maximum counts include 4,500 on the Loch of Harray, February 1983 and 2,720 on the Loch of Boardhouse, November 1974.

Ferruginous Duck (White-eyed Pochard)

Aythya nyroca

Very rare.

Although mentioned by Baikie and Heddle (1848), Buckley

and Harvie-Brown (1891) and Omond (1925), none of these early records has gained general acceptance.

The first authenticated sighting was of a male, seen at Birsay on 24th May 1981. The possibility that this bird was an escape cannot be ruled out.

Tufted Duck

Aythya fuligula

Common winter visitor, breeds in small numbers.

Nineteenth-century references mentioned the Tufted Duck as being a common winter visitor (Baikie and Heddle, 1848; Buckley and Harvie-Brown, 1891). The first reference to breeding was given by Millais who, in 1888, is said to have discovered a nest on the Loch of Stenness (Baxter and Rintoul, 1953). Buckley (1896) quoted Moodie-Heddle who recorded nesting on Hoy in 1895.

In 1910, several pairs were seen and two nests with eggs discovered at undisclosed locations by Hale and Aldworth (1910), who also commented that Tufted Duck were increasing as a breeding species.

Lack (1943) noticed the same trend and, quoting G. T. Arthur, referred to a number of pairs breeding regularly on Mainland. Lack also saw three broods on Sanday.

Balfour (1968) stated that the Tufted Duck was fairly widespread, although not numerous, as a breeding species. The same situation exists today, with breeding having been recorded on Mainland, Papa Westray, Rousay, Sanday, Shapinsay, Stronsay and Westray during the period 1968-1982.

In late September and October there is a significant influx of wintering birds, at least some of which probably originate from Icelandic breeding grounds.

The figure shows the mean annual numbers of wintering Tufted Duck on the Loch of Harray, based on monthly wildfowl counts, September-March 1962-1983. Wintering numbers appear to have increased since the early 1960's and peaked during the winter of 1973/74.

One bird, ringed as a chick in July 1930 in Iceland, was recovered in Orkney in January 1932.

MEAN ANNUAL NUMBER OF TUFTED DUCK, LOCH OF HARRAY, 1962-83
BASED ON MONTHLY WILDFOWL COUNT, SEPTEMBER TO MARCH
ONLY YEARS WITH AT LEAST 6 COUNTS INCLUDED.

Loch of Harray
MEAN NUMBER

MAX RECORDED 2600

Scaup

Aythya marila

Regular winter visitor and occasional breeding species.

Baikie and Heddle (1848) recorded this species as a winter visitor, which chiefly frequented salt water or lochs near the sea. Buckley and Harvie-Brown (1891) regarded this duck as a very common winter visitor, appearing in hundreds on the Loch of Stenness, with smaller flocks occurring elsewhere. They also observed that very few occurred on the Loch of Harray. Briggs (1893) stated that the Scaup was occasionally shot on North Ronaldsay, but that it was by no means plentiful.

The largest wintering flocks now occur on the Lochs of Harray and Stenness, with birds arriving in October and departing in March. The figure shows the mean annual numbers of Scaup wintering on the Lochs of Harray and Stenness, September-March 1962-1983. During this period the maximum numbers recorded in any month were 386 and 380 respectively. It can be seen from the figure that the wintering population of Scaup has declined during the past twenty years. In addition, throughout the 1960's, the Loch of Stenness can be seen to have supported almost the entire wintering population. As Buckley and Harvie-Brown commented, very few occurred on the Loch of Harray. The situation then changed very abruptly during the 1970's with the Loch of Harray assuming the greater importance. The reason why Scaup should suddenly leave the brackish Loch of Stenness in favour of the essentially fresh water of the Loch of Harray is not understood.

The Scaup occasionally breeds in Orkney and details are given below:

1954-1959 Up to 2 pairs bred, Papa Westray (Balfour, 1968)
1965 Female with 4 young observed, North Ronaldsay (Walker, 1967)
1969 Female with 3 young on pool, West Mainland (Balfour et al, 1972)
1973 Female with 2 young, West Mainland, 11th July
1978 Pair with 7-8 young, West Mainland, late June
1979 Pair with 2 young, West Mainland, 27th and 28th July

MEAN ANNUAL NUMBER OF SCAUP, LOCHS OF HARRAY AND STENNESS 1962-83, BASED ON MONTHLY WILDFOWL COUNT, SEPTEMBER TO MARCH. ONLY YEARS WITH AT LEAST 6 COUNTS INCLUDED.

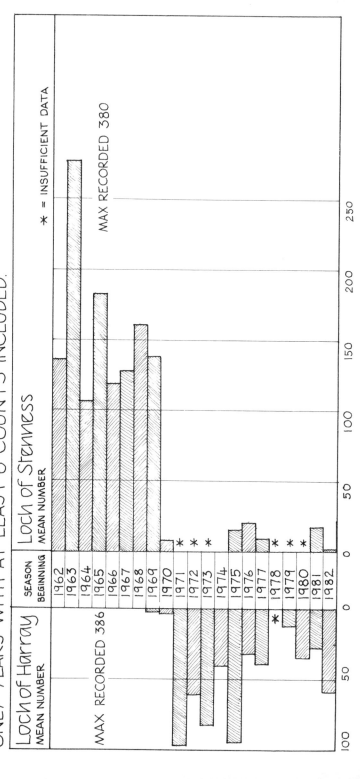

Records of small numbers of summering, but apparently non-breeding, birds are regular.

An indication of the origin of our wintering Scaup is provided by two birds, ringed in Iceland in June 1933 and July 1948, which were subsequently recovered in Orkney in December 1933 and March 1955 respectively.

Eider   Dunter

Somateria mollissima

Common resident breeding species and possible winter visitor.

Eiders were said to have bred on Sule Skerry in 1582 (Buchanan, 1793). Subsequently the species appears to have bred in small numbers but was known mainly as a winter visitor (Barry, 1805). By the late 1800's, the Eider was increasing as a breeding species and was becoming very common in many of the islands, probably due to protection. Eider eggs were a "favourite food of the crofter and fisher classes" and Eynhallow appears to have been a popular collecting site. Prior to 1884, few broods had been observed in the vicinity of the island, but by 1887, following protection under new ownership, 200 Eider nests were found on Eynhallow (Buckley and Harvie-Brown, 1891).

Omond (1925) stated that Eiders were very common and breeding extensively. This was confirmed by Baxter during visits to Orkney in the period 1927-1948 (Baxter and Rintoul, 1953). On Eynhallow 136 nests were counted in 1928, 185 in 1930 and 207 in 1933 (Robertson, 1934). The island continues to provide nest sites for some 200 pairs (Dunnet, 1975).

Lack (1943) commented that Eiders were common on all the main islands and indicated that no decline appeared to have occurred since the 19th century increases. Balfour (1968) considered the species to have decreased slightly, although still common and widespread as a breeding bird. There has been no obvious change in status.

Recent breeding data is sparse. The species continues to nest on Sule Skerry, 11 nests being recorded there on 25th May 1975. In 1981 there were 28 nests on Sweyn Holm on 21st May and 58 nests on Holm of Papa Westray on 27th May. During the period 1973-1982, the earliest date on which young have been seen is 24th May.

Flocks of up to 400 moulting birds can be seen from June to September, although small parties of about 20 birds are more frequently recorded. Some of the larger flocks contain mainly adult males, whilst many of the smaller ones are composed of sub-adult males and brown plumaged birds (Hope Jones and Kinnear, 1979; Dunnet, 1983).

There may be some link between the Orkney and Shetland moulting Eider populations and it has been suggested that mainly adult males gradually leave Orkney each summer to moult in Shetland waters. Such a movement would explain the observed annual fluctuations in both Shetland and Orkney (Hope Jones and Kinnear, 1979).

Scapa Flow supports an important wintering population. This area was regularly counted during the period 1974-1978.

Mean Monthly Counts of Eiders, Scapa Flow,
1974-1978 (Lea, 1980)

J	F	M	A	M	J	J	A	S	O	N	D
1112	1494	1279	910	992	no count	729	974	979	1124	966

The above figures are based on the totals of mean monthly counts; details of count areas are given in Appendix 1.

The Orkney wintering Eider population has been estimated to total about 6,000 birds (Lea, 1980). Peak counts include 1,400 off Gairsay on 20th March and 650 off Eynhallow on 6th September 1981.

A young bird, ringed in July 1968 in Aberdeenshire, was recovered in Orkney in July 1980.

King Eider
Somateria spectabilis

Rare.

Baikie and Heddle (1848) mentioned a statement by Bullock that a nest with 6 eggs had been found on Papa Westray in June 1812. Buckley and Harvie-Brown (1891) noted the possible breeding of a King Eider on the Holm of Papa Westray in two consecutive years, some time in the 1870's. These records have not been authenticated. This species was regarded by early writers as an occasional visitor.

All dated records are given below:

1884   Adult male shot, March (Buckley and Harvie-Brown, 1891)
1906   1, February (Witherby, 1939)
1925   1, 19th January, now in Stromness Museum (Balfour, 1972)
1930   A pair in Kirkwall Bay in winter (Balfour, 1972)
1933   1, June (Witherby, 1939)
1975   1 male, Longhope, 8th February (B.B.69:331)
1978   1 male, North Ronaldsay, 19th Oct. (B.B.73:501)
1982   1 female near Kirkwall Harbour, 10th December to 6th February 1983 (B.B.76:488)

Steller's Eider

Polysticta stelleri

Very rare.

All records are given below:

1947   1 adult male and 1 immature male, 5th-19th January, Wide Firth (B.B.40:253)
1949   1 male, Sandside Bay, Deerness, 13th November (S.N.1950:57)
1974   1 immature male, Westray, 25th October-14th November (B.B.68:313)
1976   Female, North Ronaldsay, 16th-17th April (B.B.70:417)
1978   Male between Westray and Papa Westray, 14th July (B.B.74:464)
1979   Male, Papa Westray, 2nd-19th June (B.B.73:501)
1980   Male, Papa Westray, 29th April-late August (B.B.74:464)
1981   Male, 7th May-24th June, Papa Westray and Westray (B.B.75:495)
1982   Male, Papa Westray, 30th April-1st July. Observed displaying to Eiders (B.B.76:495)

The 1978-1982 records may all refer to the same bird.

[Harlequin Duck]
Histrionicus histrionicus

Baikie and Heddle (1848) referred to an undated record of a young female shot in Orkney. Buckley and Harvie-Brown (1891) expressed doubts concerning the authenticity of this record.

Balfour (1972) considered the Harlequin Duck to be a very rare visitor and recorded a full plumaged male off Papa Westray, seen by G.T. Arthur and A. Wood, in June 1937. There is no mention of this record in the B.O.U. list 1971 and without further details it cannot be included in the Orkney list.

Long-tailed Duck   Calloo
Clangula hyemalis

Common winter visitor; has bred.

The status of this species would appear to have changed little since the early 19th century.

The Orkney wintering population totals about 6,000 birds, equivalent to 30% of the British wintering population. A substantial number winter in Scapa Flow; in February 1975 it was estimated that 2,400 birds were present and this is thought to be a typical winter maximum (Lea, 1980). Seasonal fluctuations in numbers are shown in the following table of mean monthly counts:

Wintering Long-tailed Duck, Scapa Flow, 1974-1978 (Lea, 1980)

J	F	M	A	M	J	J	A	S	O	N	D
1212	1679	1380	1271	312	No count	1	1	626	1110	1141

See Appendix 1 for count areas.

Within Scapa Flow, the birds feed during daylight hours in shallow water ten metres deep, but occasionally up to twenty metres. Before dusk the birds move to deeper water, where they roost in small parties, scattered over a wide area (Hope Jones, 1979). These nocturnal gatherings, being located close to the Flotta Oil Terminal, are very vulnerable to oil spillage. To date, however, the birds have escaped serious pollution.

Other important wintering areas include the shallow sounds surrounding the island of Wyre. Small numbers also winter on some of the fresh water and brackish lochs. On the Loch of Stenness, wintering numbers appear to have increased since 1962, with a peak being reached in the mid 1970's.

The autumn influx of birds begins in late September to early October, the earliest recorded arrival, 1972-1982, being 29th September. Spring departure commences during April and continues into May, most birds having left by the end of the month. A flock of 24, last noted in Widewall Bay, South Ronaldsay on 17th June 1981, was exceptional.

Pre-migration gatherings regularly occur, e.g. 450-500 in Wyre Sound on 26th April and 500 off North Ronaldsay on 29th April 1980.

Summering individuals are regularly recorded and occasionally apparently paired birds remain throughout the summer. Baxter and Rintoul (1953) quoted H. W. Robinson, who noted summering pairs on the Loch of Stenness in 1905 and 1906 and commented "hardly a summer passes but one or two pairs remain behind".

The first authenticated nesting record for Orkney was in 1911 (Aplin) when a clutch of eggs and some down were taken. Breeding probably also occurred in 1912 and 1926 (Baxter and Rintoul, 1953).

When a boy, G.T. Arthur (1950) found a nest in Orkney although date and location are unspecified.

Common Scoter

Melanitta nigra

Scarce winter and passage visitor; has bred.

Presumably the "Black Scoter" of Baikie and Heddle (1848) which was known to them as a winter visitor, "though less common than the Velvet Scoter".

This species was clearly uncommon and Buckley and Harvie-Brown (1891) referred to it as a rare bird, a few of which frequented Swanbister Bay, Orphir in winter, but never more than 6 or 8 in a flock.

During the early 20th century, Baxter and Rintoul (1953) were of the opinion that the species had increased slightly as a winter visitor. They stated that a large flock was seen off the south end of Graemsay during the first week of March 1908 and also noted large numbers seen by George Waterston around sheltered parts of the coast in November 1943.

Common Scoter bred in Orkney for a very brief period, and were first recorded in 1927 when a female with three half-grown young was seen at Finstown, Mainland in early August (Baxter, 1928). G. T. Arthur apparently recorded a brood on Mainland some years before 1941 (Lack, 1943).

In 1941 eleven pairs were recorded on a freshwater loch in June on the island of Eday and courtship was in progress. On a subsequent visit, one female was seen with 3 newly hatched young and, although breeding was proved for only one pair, it was suspected that 11 pairs bred or attempted to breed. Breeding was suggested to have been regular at this site for several years (Lack, 1943).

The site on Eday continued to be frequented by Common Scoter during the breeding season for several years and the information is summarised below:

> 1954   1 pair Loch of Doomy and 1 pair Loch of London, 10th and 11th July; 11 males and 3 females also seen in Fersness Bay. Conclusive proof of breeding lacking, although some may have bred or attempted to breed (Balfour, unpublished)
>
> 1955   Duck with 4 newly hatched young, Loch of Doomy, 3rd July (Balfour, unpublished)
>
> 1957   2 pairs Loch of Doomy, 24th May (Balfour, unpublished)
>
> 1958   2 pairs Loch of London, 16th May (Balfour, unpublished)

Breeding has not been confirmed since 1955 and has not been suspected since 1958. The days of the Common Scoter as an Orkney breeding species were very brief and this duck is unlikely to breed again at the Eday site. In the early 1970's the Loch of Doomy was drained.

Monthly distribution of sightings, 1974-1982

J	F	M	A	M	J	J	A	S	O	N	D
7	3	0	4	9	1	4	2	3	8	6	1

Birds are occasionally present in summer and one pair remained on Swona during the summer of 1969 (Balfour, 1972). Passage movements are indicated by peaks in sightings during May and October. Numbers are generally small and frequently consist of isolated individuals or small flocks. Maximum counts during the period 1974-1982 are: 50 in Sound of Eday, 27th January 1975 and 25 at Echnaloch, 5th May 1980.

Surf Scoter
Melanitta perspicillata

Very rare.

The statement by Baikie and Heddle (1848) that Surf Scoter appeared in small flocks during winter seems unlikely; Buckley and Harvie-Brown (1891) also expressed doubt concerning this statement. They gave several records and concluded that "the Surf Scoter can scarcely be called a very rare bird in the Orkneys".

All documented records are given below:

1845	3 seen between St Mary's, Holm and St Margaret's Hope, South Ronaldsay, March.
1847	1 in September, Longhope, Hoy.
1857	4 Longhope, Hoy, 16th October.
1866	Adult male, shot Swanbister, Orpir, March.
1872	1 obtained off Hoy.
1875	1 near Rysa Little, February.
1876	1 male near Rysa Little, February.
1880	1 adult male near Rysa Little, 23rd October.
1884	1 male near Rysa Little, 20th November. (All Buckley and Harvie-Brown, 1891).
1905	Adult male Stromness, 14th-21st December (Baxter and Rintoul, 1953).
1962	Male Echnaloch Bay, 21st October (B.B.56:398; S.B.2:306)
1980	1 Echnaloch Bay, 4th-6th May (B.B.74:464)

Monthly distribution of sightings, 1845-1980

J	F	M	A	M	J	J	A	S	O	N	D
0	2	2	0	1	0	0	0	1	3	1	1

Robinson (1905) knew of six Surf Scoters shot and identified during the previous fourteen years. It is possible that this species was more commonly seen during the late 1800's than it is today.

This North American species frequently associates with flocks of Velvet Scoter.

Velvet Scoter

Melanitta fusca

Regular winter and passage visitor.

Both Baikie and Heddle (1848) and Buckley and Harvie-Brown (1891) indicated that this species was a common winter visitor in many parts of the islands, particularly in Damsay Sound and adjacent waters.

Small wintering flocks are regular, although occasionally larger concentrations can be seen. Baxter and Rintoul (1953) quoted a record of "several hundred" in Inganess Bay on 6th January 1917 and 110 were seen there on 31st August 1981. Usually birds are dispersed over wide areas such as Wide Firth, Eynhallow Sound and Fara Sound.

Monthly distribution of sightings, 1973-1982

J	F	M	A	M	J	J	A	S	O	N	D
7	9	10	15	11	3	1	4	9	13	9	12

The earliest date for a presumed autumn migrant during the period 1973-1982 is 6th August. Spring passage and departure of Orkney wintering birds occur during April and May.

In 1975 the estimated total wintering population in Orkney was 350, with up to 100 present in Scapa Flow (Lea, 1980).

Sightings in summer are not unusual and were mentioned by Buckley and Harvie-Brown (1891). Five were seen off Finstown on 12th June 1907 and G. T. Arthur, on several occasions, noted adults on fresh-water lochs during the summer (Baxter and Rintoul, 1953). More recently three birds were seen at Waulkmill Bay during the period 3rd-14th June 1982.

Although there are no authenticated records of breeding, A. Wood was confident that Velvet Scoter bred on Sweyn Holm in 1914 (Balfour, 1968).

[Bufflehead]
Bucephala albeola

One specimen was said to have been obtained in Orkney in 1841 (Baikie and Heddle, 1848), although the evidence is unsatisfactory. As no Orkney records are mentioned by Baxter and Rintoul (1953) or given in the B.O.U. list (1971), this species cannot be included in the Orkney list.

[Barrow's Goldeneye]
Bucephala islandica

Although Robinson (1905) reported this species as having visited Orkney, records of Barrow's Goldeneye are not mentioned elsewhere. In the absence of any confirmed sightings, this species cannot be included in the Orkney list.

Goldeneye
Bucephala clangula

Common winter visitor.

Although not wintering in large numbers, Goldeneye are widespread throughout the islands, as they were during the time of Baikie and Heddle (1848) and Buckley and Harvie-Brown (1891).

The main influx of birds occurs during October and fresh water, brackish and marine habitats are utilised. The Lochs of Harray and Stenness constitute one of the more important wintering areas in Orkney and analysis of wildfowl count data for the period 1962/63-1982/83 indicates that the wintering population has increased both here and at other lochs (see figure). It is of interest that Groundwater (1974) stated that "the increase in the past 6 years or so has been said to be spectacular".

Maximum winter counts include 172 Loch of Harray (February 1983); 230 (February 1974) and 296 (January 1981) Loch of Stenness.

Most wintering birds leave Orkney during April, but a small number of summering, non-breeding individuals remain each year.

F

MEAN ANNUAL NUMBER OF GOLDENEYE, LOCHS OF HARRAY AND STENNESS 1962-83
BASED ON MONTHLY WILDFOWL COUNT, SEPTEMBER TO MARCH.
ONLY YEARS WITH AT LEAST 6 COUNTS INCLUDED

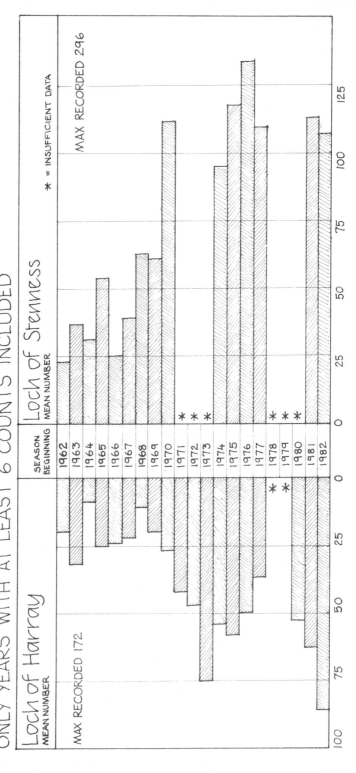

Loch of Harray
MEAN NUMBER

MAX RECORDED 172

Loch of Stenness
MEAN NUMBER

MAX RECORDED 296

✳ = INSUFFICIENT DATA

SEASON
BEGINNING

1962
1963
1964
1965
1966
1967
1968
1969
1970
1971
1972
1973
1974
1975
1976
1977
1978
1979
1980
1981
1982

Smew

Mergus albellus

Rare visitor.

The general lack of historical information suggests that this species has always been rare. Buckley and Harvie-Brown (1891) mention a male killed on Hoy in 1870, in addition to birds killed on the same island in the 1850's. Briggs (1893) observed a Smew on North Ronaldsay on 1st September 1892.

The 20th century records are:

1958	Male, Loch of Stenness, March-April
1966	1 North Ronaldsay, 19th September
1968	Male, Swartmill Loch, Westray, March
1974	1 North Loch, Sanday, 2nd March
	1 Brig o' Waithe, Stenness, 11th April
1976	Male, North Ronaldsay, 5th November
1978	1 Loch of Skaill, Mainland, 3rd December
1980	1 North Ronaldsay, 19th October-1st November
1981	1 Loch of Stenness, 15th-16th December
1982	1 Loch of Harray, 7th and 8th March; possibly the same bird Loch of Clumly, Sandwick, 2nd April
	1 Loch of Skaill, 26th November and 4th December
	Probably a different bird, Loch of Harray, 13th December

The species appears to have become fairly regular in recent years.

Red-breasted Merganser

Sawbill

Mergus serrator

Common breeding resident and winter visitor.

Dunn (1837) considered the Red-breasted Merganser to be plentiful, as did Buckley and Harvie-Brown (1891) who reported breeding on most islands and holms. Lack (1943) found the species to be common on all the main islands and although remaining common, Balfour (1968) thought that a slight decline had occurred in the breeding population.

During the period 1973-1982, confirmed breeding has only been reported from Papa Westray, Sanday and Mainland. The species is likely to be under-recorded because of its relative abundance and inconspicuous breeding habits. In the absence of any firm data, it is not possible to comment on trends in the breeding population.

The earliest sighting of young birds during the period 1973-1982 is 6th July, with most broods being seen from the second week of July onwards. Occasionally females have been recorded with exceptionally large broods, e.g. 30, 25 and 20, and these are likely to be a consequence of either brood amalgamation or several females laying in one nest.

The largest flocks are usually recorded during the flightless period; maximum counts include 87 in Hunda Sound on 30th September 1978 and 80 on Echnaloch on 28th August 1981.

Lea (1980) estimated that the total wintering population in Scapa Flow in February 1975 was approximately 350 and suggested that this may be a normal winter maximum. Examination of count data for Scapa Flow during the period 1974-1978 would indicate a resident population, whose numbers are augmented in autumn by birds from elsewhere which subsequently depart during April.

Mean Monthly Counts of Red-breasted Mergansers, Scapa Flow, 1974-1978 (Lea, 1980)

J	F	M	A	M	J	J	A	S	O	N	D
246	242	249	165	166	No count	118	161	232	270	196

See Appendix 1 for details of count areas.

Goosander

Mergus merganser

Scarce passage and winter visitor.

This species appears never to have been common in Orkney. During the period 1900-1982 there have been 31 sightings involving a minimum of 32 birds.

Monthly distribution of sightings, 1900-1983

J	F	M	A	M	J	J	A	S	O	N	D
8	5	3	2	1	1	0	1	0	3	3	4

The Goosander has been recorded annually from 1979-1982 and all sightings refer to either single or paired birds.

On 7th May 1981 a female Goosander was observed displaying to a male Red-breasted Merganser.

Ruddy Duck

Oxyura jamaicensis

Very rare.

The only record is of a pair that were present on St Mary's Loch, Holm from 3rd-6th May 1980.

KITES, VULTURES, HARRIERS, HAWKS, BUZZARDS, EAGLES: Accipitridae

Honey Buzzard

Pernis apivorus

Rare passage migrant.

The only 19th century record is of one, undated, noted by Crichton (1866). During the period 1963-1982 there have been 20 sightings, each of single birds, with extreme dates being 30th April and 29th September. Between 1972 and 1982 it has been recorded annually except for 1975 and 1978.

Monthly distribution of sightings, 1963-1982

April	May	June	July	August	September
1	6	4	3	1	5

Black Kite
Milvus migrans

Very rare.

There are four records:

1966	1 Harray, 18th and 19th May (B.B.60:315, S.B.4:295)
1968	1 Rousay, 15th May (B.B.62:466;S.B.6:38)
1970	1 North Ronaldsay, 28th September (B.B.64:348, S.B.6:331)
1975	1 Eday, 3rd May (B.B.69:333)

Red Kite
Milvus milvus

Very rare.

Buckley and Harvie-Brown (1891) gave only two records, both from Sanday:

1877	1 shot, 24th April
1878	1 shot

White-tailed Eagle   Erne
Haliaeetus albicilla

Very rare visitor; formerly bred.

The history of the White-tailed Eagle in Orkney is well documented by Buckley and Harvie-Brown (1891). In 1684 Sibbald noted that there were many Ernes on the east side of the Mainland

and also on the island of Hoy. Wallace (1700) spoke of them as being plentiful and Low (1813) mentioned several pairs on Hoy, as well as ones at Mull Head in Deerness and on Switha.

Baikie and Heddle (1848) listed three nesting sites on Hoy and one each on Eday, Costa Head (Mainland) and South Ronaldsay, but stated that at the time of writing only two sites, both on Hoy, were occupied. By 1860 only one pair was nesting on Hoy and probably the last breeding attempt was in 1873, although reports of birds from various parts of the islands continued until about 1888.

Baxter and Rintoul (1953) recorded that the British Museum had a clutch of eggs taken from Hoy in 1877, while Love (1983) noted that an egg was collected there in 1911. It has not been possible to confirm these dates.

The only recent occurrences are of single birds:

1976   Immature bird, Hoy, 6th May (B.B.71:496)
1982   North Ronaldsay, 15 April (in litt.)

A wing-tagged bird, one of those released as part of the re-introduction programme on Rhum, was observed on several occasions during 1983.

Marsh Harrier

Circus aeruginosus

Rare passage migrant.

This species was said by Baikie and Heddle (1848) to be an occasional visitor to Orkney, but Buckley and Harvie-Brown (1891) gave only one authenticated record, that of a bird shot on Hoy on 28th November 1883.

All available 20th century records are listed:

1944   1 shot Sanday, 6th April. This bird was ringed as a nestling on 13th June 1941 in Denmark (Baxter and Rintoul, 1953)
1965   1 male, North Ronaldsay, early October *(Island Saga)*
1977   1 Stronsay, 2nd June
1978   Single birds, North Ronaldsay, 16th April and Birsay 22nd May and 14th June

1979	1 Stenness, 27th August
1980	1 juvenile, North Ronaldsay, 23rd September
1981	Single birds, Birsay, 19th May; Loch of Banks, Sandwick 21st May; Orphir, 5th June; Loch of Banks, 29th June; Holm 17th and 19th September. 1 found dead, Deerness, 27th May

Hen Harrier

Gos-haak, Kattakally

Circus cyaneus

Fairly common but localised breeding species, passage migrant and winter resident.

Baikie and Heddle (1848) stated that it was "one of our most common hawks", whilst Buckley and Harvie-Brown (1891) thought that it was probably the commonest hawk throughout the islands. Persecution during the early part of the 20th century much reduced its numbers but protection in the 1930's and the cessation of gamekeeping allowed a build-up of breeding birds during the 1940's. Since 1950 the rate of increase has been slower, with females greatly outnumbering males in the breeding population and polygyny has been widespread (Balfour and Cadbury, 1975).

In the period 1972-1982, annual totals of nests have varied between 45 and 90 on Mainland, 5-12 on Rousay, 3-4 on Hoy and one occasionally on Eday (Picozzi, unpublished).

First eggs are laid in late April and there is evidence to suggest that high fledging success is associated with good weather in June. A nest with 10 eggs (Picozzi, 1983) being incubated by 2 females sitting side by side, was recorded in 1981. Main prey items identified have been Orkney Vole, Skylark, Meadow Pipit, Starling, young Rabbits and Wader chicks (Balfour and Cadbury, 1975). From September to April communal roosts occur in well vegetated marshy areas on low ground, with a maximum of 22 birds having been recorded at the largest roost. About 12 roosting sites have been located (Picozzi and Cuthbert, 1982).

Some Orkney birds remain in winter, but many disperse to eastern Scotland, also to East Anglia, southern Ireland and the Continent. Young birds ringed in Orkney have been recovered in the breeding season on the Scottish mainland and there is evidence of immigration into the Orkney breeding population (Balfour and

Cadbury, 1975). Outside the breeding season, birds have been reported from many of the islands.

[Montagu's Harrier]
Circus pygargus

Although said by Baxter and Rintoul (1953) to have occurred in Orkney, there are no authenticated records.

Goshawk
Accipiter gentilis

Very rare visitor.

Early records of this species are unreliable, due to confusion with the Hen Harrier and Peregrine.

There are seven authenticated occurrences:

1968	Female collided with wires, Finstown, 14th May
1974	1 shot, Shapinsay, probably May. This bird had jesses and was obviously an escaped falconer's bird.
1976	1 Cottascarth, Rendall, 12th April
1977	1 Loch of Banks, Sandwick, 15th December
1978	1 Cottascarth, 24th Feb.; 1 Aikerness, Evie, 20th May
1981	A first year female, North Ronaldsay, 6th May was found dying, covered with Fulmar oil, 12th July

Sparrowhawk
Accipiter nisus

Regular passage migrant; has bred; a few birds may winter.

The status of this species during the 19th century is not clear, owing to confusion with the Kestrel and the Merlin. Buckley and Harvie-Brown (1891) gave one definite breeding record, in 1886 at Muddiesdale Plantation near Kirkwall, when an adult and 4 young were shot. Breeding took place at Binscarth, near Finstown for a few years from about 1911 (Balfour, unpublished). Lack (1943), quoting G. T. Arthur, stated that two or three pairs bred regularly on Mainland, however Balfour (1968) indicated that breeding was irregular after the 1930's and that there was no record of nesting since about 1943.

During the period 1974-1982, there has been at least one breeding attempt, in 1978, but the young died just after hatching. A pair successfully reared four young in 1983.

It has been noted regularly on spring and autumn passage, with peak sightings occurring in May and October. Wintering birds may be found in suitable areas where there is tree cover, such as Binscarth, Hoy and Orphir.

Monthly distribution of sightings, 1972-1982

J	F	M	A	M	J	J	A	S	O	N	D
8	9	4	17	27	2	3	5	9	24	14	8

A bird ringed as a nestling in Caithness was controlled in Orkney during November of the following year.

Common Buzzard

Buteo buteo

Very rare breeding species and rare passage migrant.

Only four occurrences were given by Buckley and Harvie-Brown (1891) who considered it to be a rare visitor. Balfour (1972) stated that it was extremely rare up to about 1955 and that one or two pairs had been resident and bred since about 1961. An account of possible nesting from 1961-1965 and proved nesting in 1966 is given by Balfour (1967). Two pairs probably attempted to breed from 1966-1972, while a single pair nested in 1973, 1974, 1976, 1981 and possibly also in some of the intervening years. All nests, were situated on inland crags.

Away from the breeding area it still remains a rare visitor; one wintered in Firth, Mainland in 1964.

Monthly distribution of sightings, 1973-1982
(excluding breeding area)

J	F	M	A	M	J	J	A	S	O	N	D
1	2	2	2	1	1	1	5	6	2	0	0

Rough-legged Buzzard

Buteo lagopus

Scarce passage migrant and winter visitor.

Buckley and Harvie-Brown (1891) gave two records from Rousay during the 19th century. Balfour (1972) mentioned the Rough-legged Buzzard as occurring most frequently in April, May, October and November and suggested that it was more numerous during the 1930's and 1940's. From 1973-1982 it has been recorded annually except in 1974 and 1980.

Monthly distribution of sightings, 1973-1982

J	F	M	A	M	J	J	A	S	O	N	D
3	1	6	14	5	0	1	0	0	6	2	4

At least one bird wintered in the Rendall-Birsay moor area, Mainland in 1982/83.

Golden Eagle

Aquila chrysaëtos

Very rare breeding species and occasional visitor.

Stated by Baikie and Heddle (1848) to be "much more rare than formerly", Buckley and Harvie-Brown (1891) were of the opinion that the Golden Eagle had probably always been confined to the island of Hoy and that never more than one pair had nested during the early 19th century. They recorded that the last breeding attempt was in 1844, although nesting may have occurred subsequently as Balfour (unpublished) mentioned a nest found in about 1890.

In 1966 a pair again became established and between 1967 and 1982 successful breeding has been proved on 11 occasions. Mountain Hare and Red Grouse are the main prey items, but Fulmars have also been recorded (Lea and Bourne, 1974. B.B.68:293).

Sightings of single birds, mainly immature, have been noted during the period 1974-1982 from Mainland and Rousay. In 1977 one was seen regularly on Rousay from 16th January, but it was found in mid-July of that year coated with Fulmar oil and unable to fly; it subsequently died.

OSPREYS : Pandionidae

Osprey
Pandion haliaetus

Scarce passage migrant.

Noted as very rare by Buckley and Harvie-Brown (1891), the Osprey appears to have occurred more frequently in recent years. During the period 1974-1982 the extreme dates are 13th April and 27th October.

Monthly distribution of sightings, 1974-1982

Apr.	May	June	July	Aug.	Sept.	Oct.
1	9	3	1	1	0	2

FALCONS : Falconidae

Kestrel   Moosie Haak, Wind Cuffer
Falco tinnunculus

Fairly common resident but decreasing; passage migrant.

Early writers recorded the Kestrel as a common species, and Lack (1943) noted that, although clearly scarcer than in former times, it was still not uncommon. According to Balfour (1968) it increased in the early 1940's but numbers had decreased slightly by the late 1960's. This decline has continued and several nesting sites used in the 1970's are no longer occupied.

During the period 1972-1982 nesting has been reported from the following islands:

Eday	Rousay	South Ronaldsay
Hoy (c4 pairs, 1974)	Sanday (3 pairs)	Stronsay
Mainland	Shapinsay	Westray

The majority of nests are on sea cliffs but buildings, quarries, inland cliffs and steep banks are used. Ground nesting among heather was first noticed in 1945 (Balfour, 1955) and became widespread by the mid 1950's when at least nineteen territories were known, but probably only half this number are now occupied.

Eggs are usually laid in the last week of April and early May but a nest with 6 eggs was found on 24th April. Fledging occurs from the last week of June.

There is some evidence of spring and autumn passage with sightings at these times, usually of single birds, reported from North Ronaldsay, Papa Westray, Pentland Skerries and Sule Skerry.

Birds ringed as nestlings in Orkney have been recovered as follows:

France	1	Scotland	7
Germany	1	Shetland	1
Holland	2	Southern England	2
Northern England	2		

Red-footed Falcon

Falco vespertinus

Very rare visitor.

There are five records of single birds:

1962	Female near Stromness, Mainland, 8th May (B.B.56:399; S.B.2:422).
1967	Immature, Firth and Rendall, Mainland, 11th August to 10th September (B.B.61:338).
1973	Adult male, South Ronaldsay, 25th May (dead), now in Royal Scottish Museum (B.B. 76:490).
1977	Immature, Papa Westray, 18th August (B.B.73:502).
1981	First year male, Westness, Rousay, 30th May - 4th June (B.B.75:496).

Merlin

Falco columbarius

Rare breeding species and passage migrant.

This species was very common, according to Baikie and

Heddle (1848) but Buckley and Harvie-Brown (1891) believed that it had become rarer and noted nesting on Hoy, Mainland, Papa Westray and Rousay. Lack (1943) considered that the species had not declined any further since the 19th century, due largely to protection. He found nesting pairs on Flotta, Hoy, Mainland, Rousay and South Ronaldsay. Balfour (1968) thought that there were perhaps 25 pairs breeding annually between 1955 and 1960 and that a slight decline had occurred over the last few years. Numbers then remained fairly stable until the late 1970's when a further decrease was noted, together with signs of pesticide contamination such as eggshell thinning and poor breeding success. In 1983, out of 11 pairs which attempted to nest, only 5 pairs successfully reared young (E. R. Meek, in prep.).

The majority of clutches are laid in mid-May and young fledge after the first week of July. During the period 1974-1982, nesting has been recorded on Eday, Hoy, Mainland, Rousay and Stronsay. The main species found as prey items at nests in 1983 were Meadow Pipit, Skylark and House Sparrow (E. R. Meek, in prep.).

There is a noticeable increase in sightings in autumn due to the dispersal of young and an influx of migrant birds. During the winter months some birds are still to be found near their nesting territories, but Merlins can be seen in a variety of habitats, even venturing into town gardens.

Birds ringed as nestlings in Orkney have been recovered as follows:

France	1
Scotland	3
West Germany	1

Three birds ringed in Shetland, including one from Fair Isle, have been recovered in Orkney. One of these, ringed as a nestling in Shetland in 1977, was trapped as a breeding adult at a nest in Orkney in 1981, suggesting that there is some interchange between the Orkney and Shetland breeding populations.

Hobby
Falco subbuteo

Very rare passage migrant.

Buckley and Harvie-Brown (1891) were doubtful if this species had ever been seen in Orkney. There are seven records, all of single birds:

1957	Rendall, Mainland, 26th June (F.I.B.O.B. 3:197; S.B.1:31).
1959	Melsetter, Hoy, 12th May (Balfour, 1972).
1974	Stenness, Mainland, 3rd June.
1979	Berstane, St Ola, Mainland, 30th July and 3rd August.
1980	St Ola, Mainland, 4th June.
1981	North Ronaldsay, 3rd June.
1982	Papa Westray, 17th and 18th August.

Gyrfalcon
Falco rusticolus

Rare visitor.

There are twelve known records, all of single birds:

1832	Shot, 30th March, probably Sanday (Baikie and Heddle, 1848).
1874	Orphir, Mainland (Icelandic) (Omond, 1925).
1887	13th October *The Field*, 22nd October, 1887: 611, given as 15th October by Buckley and Harvie-Brown, (1891).
1903	Female, trapped Orphir, Mainland, 23rd March (Gyr) (A.S.N.H.1903:185, 1904:211).

1906	Female near Harray, Mainland, 14th March (Icelandic) (S.N.1920:182).
1913	Female, Sule Skerry, 22nd April (Greenland) (S.N.E.P.No.3, 1913:68).
1920	Adult female, Sule Skerry, 26th February (Greenland) (S.N.1920:154).
1921	Male, Sule Skerry, 19th January (Icelandic) (S.N.1922:72).
1947	April (S.B.4:371).
1949	August (S.B.4:371).
1966	Burrien Hill, Mainland, 13th May (Gyr) (B.B.60:316, S.B.4:371).
1967	North Ronaldsay, 23rd November-24th December (B.B.61:338).

Peregrine
Falco peregrinus

Rare breeding species; passage migrant.

Wallace (1700) recorded 25 nesting sites of the Peregrine, although he did not say whether all these sites were occupied in any one year. The only indication of status given by Buckley and Harvie-Brown (1891) was from Ranken, who thought that this species was still fairly plentiful in Orkney. Subsequently a decline must have occurred, as by 1919 there were apparently not more than 6 occupied eyries (Groundwater, 1974).

The situation appeared to improve during the next two decades, although G. T. Arthur in 1945 was perhaps a little optimistic in suggesting that 25 pairs were breeding (Groundwater, 1974).

Balfour (1968, 1972) noted that there were at least a dozen pairs in 1959 and that breeding success in 1964 and 1965 was low, with fewer pairs attempting to nest. The low breeding success during the 1960's was attributed to persistent toxic chemical contamination. In 1971 it was estimated that there were between 11 and 16 pairs. A survey in 1981 showed that little change had occurred and of a maximum of 16 pairs which attempted to nest, only nine produced young. Several pairs continued to show signs of organo-chlorine contamination and one Fulmar-oiled bird was recorded.

During the winter months Peregrines can be seen in the vicinity of their nesting territories, but they are also frequently noted over other areas such as farmland.

The majority of nests are on sea cliffs but occasionally inland crags are used. Eggs have been recorded as early as 27th March, but most clutches are laid during the first two weeks of April. Fledged young have been noted on 13th June, but young from a repeat laying may not fledge until the end of July.

In the 1981 survey, twenty-seven bird species were recorded as prey items, ranging in size from Pipits to a Pintail Duck, with Rock Doves, Auks, Kittiwakes and Starlings the most frequently taken.

GROUSE : Tetraonidae

Red Grouse   Muir-hen

Lagopus lagopus

Fairly common breeding species, in suitable habitat.

The Red Grouse was common in Orkney in the late 17th century, according to Wallace (1700), but there had been a decrease in numbers by 1795, probably due to land reclamation (Old Statistical Account). Buckley and Harvie-Brown (1891) recorded breeding on Burray, Cava, Eday, Fara, Flotta, Hoy, Mainland, Rousay and Rysa Little. They noted that in the severe winter of 1879/80, birds were seen to cross the Pentland Firth from Scrabster to Hoy.

Lack (1943) stated that this species had been extinct on Eday since 1918 and during a brief visit it was not seen on Shapinsay, where it had been present in 1910. He found it to be rather scarce on Cava, Fara, Flotta, Hoy and Mainland, but common on Rousay, where protected. Balfour (1972) listed it as not very numerous and indicated that it was much more common between 1920 and 1940. During the period 1972 to 1982, Red Grouse have been found breeding on Cava, Fara, Flotta, Gairsay, Hoy, Mainland and Rousay and during the winter months have been

G

noted in several other islands. The largest single flock of 40 birds was seen in Orphir on 18th September, 1980.

Ptarmigan
Lagopus mutus

Extinct, formerly bred.

This species was found only on Hoy, and the last birds were shot about 1831 (Buckley and Harvie-Brown, 1891).

Black Grouse
Tetrao tetrix

Introduced, extinct.

An introduction was attempted in about 1859 but failed (Buckley and Harvie-Brown, 1891). The two records given by Balfour (1972) must be considered doubtful in view of possible additional introductions.

PARTRIDGES AND PHEASANTS:
Phasianidae

Red-legged Partridge
Alectoris rufa

Introduced, extinct.

An introduction near Kirkwall in 1840 failed (Buckley and Harvie-Brown, 1891).

Grey Partridge
Perdix perdix

Introduced, extinct.

Several introductions were mentioned by Buckley and Harvie-Brown (1891) but all of them eventually failed. Balfour (1972) recorded it as a scarce irregular visitor with single birds having occurred from time to time. Groundwater (1974) gave two dated records, both of single birds, at Yesnaby on 11th March 1954 and Stromness on 15th November 1967. In view of attempted introductions, it must be considered doubtful if any of these records refer to genuine wild birds.

About 30 hand-reared birds were released on Shapinsay in 1976 and at least one pair bred successfully; it is not known if breeding occurred in subsequent years.

Quail
Coturnix coturnix

Rare irregular breeding species and scarce passage migrant.

There are several breeding records given by Buckley and Harvie-Brown (1891) and Lack (1943). More recently, nesting was suspected at Rendall and Stenness, Mainland in 1953 and young were seen on Rousay in 1958 (Balfour, 1968) and at Firth, Mainland in 1982.

Between 1976 and 1982, there have been 19 records of either sightings or calling birds, from Mainland (Evie, Rendall, Stenness, St Ola), North Ronaldsay, Papa Westray, Sanday and Shapinsay, with extreme dates being 22nd April and 9th November.

Monthly distribution of records, 1976-1982

April	May	June	July	Aug.	Sept.	Oct.	Nov.
1	3	6	3	3	1	1	1

Pheasant
Phasianus colchicus

Introduced, now resident and breeding on several islands.

The first introduction, according to Buckley and Harvie-Brown (1891), was in 1859 when eggs were brought from Dumfriesshire, but this attempt failed. Since then there have been numerous introductions. Lack (1943) stated that it was doing well on Rousay and one was seen on Shapinsay, where it was introduced in 1905. Balfour (1968) recorded breeding on Shapinsay and at St Margaret's Hope, South Ronaldsay. It is now well established in several parts of Mainland and breeding has also been reported from Hoy, Rousay, Shapinsay and South Ronaldsay.

RAILS, CRAKES AND COOTS: Rallidae

Water Rail
Rallus aquaticus

Winter visitor and passage migrant; has bred.

Despite claims by earlier writers that the Water Rail bred in Orkney, Buckley and Harvie-Brown (1891) could find no authentic evidence of a nest ever having been taken. Omond (1925) noted it as fairly common all the year round, while Lack (1943), quoting G. T. Arthur, said that "a few pairs bred on Mainland". The only recent breeding record is from St Ola in 1968 (Balfour, 1972).

During the period 1972-1982, this species has been recorded in every month except June, from many areas, the majority of sightings occurring from October to December. Birds regularly winter in the St Ola area.

Spotted Crake
Porzana porzana

Very rare.

This species was mentioned by Baikie and Heddle (1848) as

having "been observed, though rarely, in Sanday". There are only four dated records:

1884   1 shot, North Ronaldsay, 8th September (A.S.N.H. 1893:75).

1892   1 shot and another seen, North Ronaldsay, 27th September (A.S.N.H.1893:75).

1968   1 heard calling, Rothiesholm, Stronsay, in late May (Balfour, 1972).

1981   1 Birsay, 22nd April.

Corncrake
Crex crex

Local summer resident, decreasing.

The Corncrake was an abundant summer visitor to Orkney in the 19th century, according to Buckley and Harvie-Brown (1891), and this was still the case when Lack (1943) visited the islands, although he mentioned that G. T. Arthur considered it had decreased. Lack found it on almost all the cultivated islands where there were cornfields or areas of long grass.

Balfour (1968) stated that it had decreased considerably and that few nested in cultivated or grass fields, but appeared to nest more frequently in areas of rush and nettle. In 1972 he noted it as still breeding in most islands, but most commonly in the North Isles.

The decrease continues and it is absent from many of the areas where it was formerly common. A complete survey carried out in

1979 found 102-104 calling males (Cadbury, 1980), distributed as follows:

Burray	1	Papa Westray	6
Copinsay	1	Rousay	1
Eday	2	Sanday	6
Egilsay	1	Shapinsay	5
Flotta	4	Sth Ronaldsay	5 - 6
Graemsay	3	South Walls	2
Hoy	4	Stronsay	6
Mainland	38	Westray	11-12
North Ronaldsay	5	Wyre	1

Recent records of successful breeding are few. In 1980 the only young seen were on North Ronaldsay. In 1981 a single brood was seen on Papa Westray and three broods were found there in 1982.

Groundwater (1974), in a series of first calling dates from 1923 to 1970, gives extremes of 3rd March and 3rd May. During the period 1973-1982, the extreme dates were 16th April and 15th May. The last date for a sighting in autumn was 20th September.

Buckley and Harvie-Brown (1891) received many accounts of this species being found in winter.

Moorhen   Water-hen

Gallinula chloropus

Fairly common breeding species; passage migrant.

This species was by no means abundant in the 19th century, but scattered throughout most of the islands where suitable habitat was to be found (Buckley and Harvie-Brown, 1891). It may then have increased, as Lack (1943) found it widely distributed and Balfour (1972) noted it as common. More recently, loss of habitat due to drainage and land reclamation may have led to a slight decline in some areas.

During the period 1974-1982, breeding has been reported from Flotta, Gairsay, Mainland, North Ronaldsay, Papa Westray, Sanday, South Ronaldsay and Westray.

In winter, small flocks have been noted with maximum counts of 27 at Crantit Ponds, St Ola on 7th February 1981 and 20 at Voy, Sandwick on 29th November 1981.

There are the following ringing recoveries of full grown birds:

Ringed	Recovered
Holland, December 1934	Orkney, May 1939
Denmark, September 1962	Orkney, November 1962

Coot   Snaith, Snysen

Fulica atra

Local breeding species and winter visitor.

The Coot was a common species where there was suitable habitat, according to Buckley and Harvie-Brown (1891). Lack (1943) found it on all low-lying reedy waters, but Balfour (1968) noted that it had decreased, especially on the Mainland, since about 1930 and was common only in a few of the North Isles.

Between 1974 and 1982 breeding has been reported from:

Egilsay
Mainland:
    Dounby
    Graemeshall, Holm
    The Loons, Birsay
    Loch of Banks, Sandwick
    The Shunan, Harray
North Ronaldsay
(max. 14 pairs in 1979)

Papa Westray (2 pairs)
Sanday
South Ronaldsay:
    Lochs of Aikers, Liddle
    and Lythe
    Moss of Dale
Stronsay (min. 4 pairs in 1977)
Westray (4 pairs)

It has probably increased as a winter visitor this century, as Buckley and Harvie-Brown (1891) only mentioned small flocks of from six to twelve birds on the Loch of Harray in winter. Counts of over 100 have been reported regularly from this loch in recent years. The main wintering flocks are to be found on the Lochs of Bosquoy, Harray and Stenness.

Peak counts, 1974-1982

Loch of Bosquoy	Loch of Harray	Loch of Stenness
10th October, 1980	7th December, 1976	19th December 1981
160	470	151

Other peak counts were 70 Loch of Burness, Westray on 1st October 1975 and 60 at Graemeshall, Holm on 28th December 1981.

CRANES : Gruidae

Crane
Grus grus

Rare visitor.

Baxter and Rintoul (1953) considered that all old records of Cranes in Scotland were unreliable due to confusion with Herons. The following are the 20th century records:

1903	1 Pentland Skerries, 1st and 2nd May, then shot (A.S.N.H.1903:186).
1955	1 Birsay, 17th May (Balfour, 1972; S.B.6:128).
1969	1 Stronsay, 20th May-29th May (B.B.63:274). 1 Loch of Swannay, 20th August-6th September (B.B.63:274).
1971	1 Papa Westray, 23rd May; Westray, 24th May-29th May; Wideford Hill, 3rd June (B.B.65:331).
1978	2 Deerness, early May to mid-September (B.B.72:518).
1980	2 Stenness, 13th April (B.B.74:465).
1982	1 Birsay, 20th April (B.B.76:491). 1 Firth, 4th May (B.B.76:491).

BUSTARDS : Otididae

Great Bustard
Otis tarda

Very rare.

There are three records:

1876	A female, weighing 9¾lbs, was shot at Holland, Stronsay on 29th March (Tudor, 1881).
1892	A female at Housebay, Stronsay, 8th February, now in Royal Scottish Museum (A.S.N.H. 1892:138).

1924 An immature female, Sanday, 4th January. This bird was caught at Newark Farm and kept alive until 20th February, when it died (Baxter and Rintoul, 1953).

OYSTERCATCHERS: Haematopodidae

Oystercatcher   Skeldro, Chaldro
Haematopus ostralegus

Common breeding species, passage migrant; present throughout the year.

All writers agree this is a very common species and Dunn (1837) noted that in severe winters comparatively few remained. Lack (1943) found it an abundant breeding bird. Balfour (1972) stated that it had greatly increased since about the 1930's when it began to nest inland on cultivated fields and dry hill ground, as well as on the coast.

The Oystercatcher nests in a variety of habitats, including sandy and shingle sea and loch shores, moorland, waste ground, cultivated fields, stone dykes and, in the case of one pair, the roof of a building. During the period 1974-1982, a pair was seen on territory as early as 4th February and the earliest date for chicks was 15th May. Breeding counts include:

Auskerry, 12 pairs 1980, 1981
Calf of Eday, min. 17 pairs, 1982
Cava, 9 pairs, 1980
Fara, 25 pairs, 1976
Flotta, 30-50 pairs, 1981
Gairsay, 26 pairs, 1981

Papa Westray:
North Hill, 104 pairs, 1982
Pentland Skerries, 8 pairs, 1982
Rousay: 1981 (Lea 1982)
Central moorland, 62 pairs
Brings & Quandale, 82 pairs
Faraclett, 17 pairs;
Switha, 10 pairs, 1977

Although recorded in every month, numbers fall during the

winter and birds start returning in February, the increase continuing through to May. Autumn passage occurs mainly in September.

Partial Wader Survey, January 1983
(Martin and Summers, 1983) Appendix II

Burray	Hoy Group	Mainland	Sanday	S Ronaldsay	Westray
66	329	874	315	366	219

Total counted: 2,169.

Ringing recoveries show that many of the Orkney breeding population winter in south-west Britain and Ireland, but three have been recovered in France and one in Spain. Full grown birds ringed in south-west and west Britain and Ireland from August through to the following June, have been recovered in Orkney during the summer. Young birds from Faeroes and Shetland have also been recovered in Orkney.

STILTS AND AVOCETS:
Recurvirostridae

Black-winged Stilt
Himantopus himantopus

Very rare.

There is only one record of this species, that of two birds shot at Lopness, Sanday in 1814 (Baikie and Heddle, 1848).

Avocet
Recurvirostra avosetta

Very rare.

Although Yarrell (1843) claimed that the Avocet occurred in Orkney, the only authenticated records are:

1934   June (Baxter and Rintoul, 1953).

1965   1 North Ronaldsay, 5th May (S.B.3:371).
1974   2 The Ouse, Westray, 8th May.
1975   1 Toab, East Mainland, 6th July.
1980   1 North Ronaldsay, 30th March-1st April.

COURSERS AND PRATINCOLES: Glareolidae

Collared Pratincole
Glareola pratincola

Very rare.

There is only one authenticated record, that of a single bird in South Ronaldsay on 6th October 1963 (B.B.59:300).

Omond (1925) stated that a bird shot by Bullock in Orkney was the second British record of this species. In fact the bird was shot not in Orkney but in Unst, Shetland in 1812 (Baxter and Rintoul, 1953).

PLOVERS : Charadriidae

Ringed Plover   Sand Lark, Sinloo
Charadrius hiaticula

Recorded throughout the year, probably decreasing as a breeding species; passage and winter visitor.

Baxter and Rintoul (1953) mentioned that, according to Sibbald in 1684, it bred at Cross and Burness and that it "abounded in Evie and Rendall". Low (1813) stated that the Ringed Plover was very common, especially in winter when vast flocks were found in all the sandy bays of the county. Serle (1934) found only a few pairs breeding on Hoy as there were few suitable nesting localities. Lack (1943) found it common on all suitable shores, breeding occasionally on moorland and ploughed land near the sea and the edges of inland lochs. Balfour (1972) recorded that it bred in smallish numbers and had decreased slightly.

The Ringed Plover is basically a bird of the sea coast and usually nests on sandy or pebbly shores, maritime heath and machair. Inland nesting on the Mainland is only common round lochs. The nest, which is normally in the open, may be occasionally under a stone and in 1913, Laidlaw found 4 pairs nesting this way on Auskerry (S.N.1913:212). In 1976 two nests were found in gravel on a peat track, high up on a hill in Orphir.

Birds may be seen on territory by the end of February. During the period 1974-1982, the earliest date for a full clutch is 9th April, but unfledged young have been noted as late as August.

The only breeding counts are:

Cava, 1 pair, 1980	Pentland Skerries, at least 3
Gairsay, 10 pairs, 1981	pairs, 1982
Papa Westray:	Rousay:
North Hill 7 pairs, 1981	Central moorland, 11 pairs,
9 pairs, 1982	1981 (Lea, 1982).

Flocks may be found in sandy bays throughout the winter and not infrequently as many as 100 birds can be seen. At times of high water birds feed in fields near the shore.

Peak flock counts are 110 Peerie Sea, Kirkwall, 17th January 1976 and c100 Scapa Beach, St Ola, October 1977 — February 1978.

Partial Wader Survey, January 1983
(Martin and Summers, 1983) Appendix II

Burray	Hoy Group	Mainland	Sanday	S. Ronaldsay	Westray
38	112	565	279	40	136

Total counted: 1,170.

Baxter and Rintoul (1953) noted that the Arctic form *C.h.tundrae* had been recorded in Orkney.

A bird ringed in August 1953 in Ross-shire was recovered in Orkney in April 1960, and a young bird from Shetland was controlled in Orkney in December of the same year.

Greater Sand Plover

Charadrius leschenaultii

Very rare.

The only record is of a bird at Deerness from 9th-16th June 1979 (B.B.74:467; O.B.R.1981:59).

Dotterel

Charadrius morinellus

Very rare.

Baikie and Heddle (1848) stated that this bird "appears in September and October, remains during the winter and leaves in the spring". They mentioned that a large flock appeared in South Ronaldsay in May 1830.

There is one breeding record, in 1850, when a nest with 3 eggs was found in Hoy (Bree, 1850).

The only other sightings are:

1857	8 shot out of a flock, Burray, 25th May (Buckley and Harvie-Brown, 1891).
1976	1 North Ronaldsay, 5th October.
1977	3 South Ronaldsay, 4th May.
1978	1 North Ronaldsay, 20th May.

Balfour (1972) said there was suggestive evidence of breeding on Mainland in 1935. Two boys took 3 eggs from a plover-type nest on the top of a hill. The bird was said to be very tame and the eggs were smaller than those of a Lapwing.

Lesser Golden Plover

Pluvialis dominica

Very rare.

The only record is of one shot near the Loch of Stenness on 26th November 1887. It was in a flock of Golden Plover (Buckley and Harvie-Brown, 1891).

Golden Plover
Pliver

Pluvialis apricaria

Uncommon and declining breeding species, passage migrant and winter visitor.

The Golden Plover was described by writers in the early part of the 19th century as common, with flocks of thousands appearing in autumn and winter. In severe weather, however, many left and moved south. Buckley and Harvie-Brown (1891) said it was less numerous than it had been and gave land reclamation and increased shooting as two of the possible causes for the decline. Lack (1943) found it "abundant on Rousay, fairly common on Hoy and Eday, a number of pairs on Mainland, a few pairs found breeding on South Ronaldsay, South Walls (1), Shapinsay, Sanday, Stronsay and Papa Westray (1)". The Golden Plover has obviously declined during the period 1930-1980. Nethersole-Thomson (1971) found 4 nests in 10 acres on Mainland in 1932 and Balfour (unpublished) records 6-10 pairs on the Burrien Hill-Ward of Redland area, Firth in 1954. There have been about two breeding pairs only in that area from 1974-1982. Balfour (1972) stated that the species was much reduced in numbers since the 1930's, but still bred in scattered pairs over the higher moors. At the present time, flocks are common during passage and in winter, but the breeding numbers appear to be still decreasing.

During the breeding season, the Golden Plover is widely, but thinly, distributed over moorland. Display has been recorded on 13th February and the first eggs found on 13th April. A late clutch was found hatching on 12th July. During the period 1974-1982, breeding has been recorded from:

Eday	Fara	Gairsay	Hoy
Mainland	Rousay	S. Ronaldsay	Stronsay

The only breeding counts are:
Gairsay, 2 pairs, 1981 and 1982
Hoy, min. 24 pairs, 1974
Rousay: Central moorland 19 pairs, 1981 (Lea, 1982)

Large flocks are seen on both spring and autumn migration. During spring there is a marked rise in numbers about mid-February and again in mid-April, when some of the birds show characters of the Northern race. The first of the autumn flocks are noted in mid-July, then numbers increase greatly in late September and October. Some of the birds stay on as winter residents but, in severe frost and snowy conditions, numbers can fall rapidly.

Peak counts include 3,000 at Sandwick, in September 1981 and 2,500 at St Ola, on 12th December 1981, while flocks of 2,000 birds have been recorded at St Ola on 7th November 1976; Hatston, Mainland on 11th November 1982 and Tankerness on 13th December 1981.

During the winter of 1977/78 the following counts of wintering flocks were obtained (Booth, 1978):

Locality	26th/27th Nov.	31st Dec./ 1st Jan.	4th/5th Feb.
Eday	200	0	0
West Mainland	1,027	1,755	941
East Mainland and South Ronaldsay	329	1,003	5
North Ronaldsay	678	249	764
Papa Westray	8	150	85
Rousay	12	200	0
Sanday	808	215	0
Westray	1,500	530	220
Totals	4,562	4,092	2,015

Partial Wader Survey, January 1983,
(Martin and Summers, 1983) Appendix II

Burray	Hoy Group	Mainland	Sanday	S. Ronaldsay	Westray
300	36	1,239	477	54	1,247

Total counted: 3,353.

Young birds ringed in Caithness and Sutherland have been recovered in Orkney in December of the same year. A full grown bird ringed in Holland in March was found in Orkney in December of the same year.

Grey Plover
Pluvialis squatarola

Passage migrant.

Baikie and Heddle (1848) gave the first written record of this species, two in September 1822. The Grey Plover was regarded as a

scarce autumn migrant and occasional winter visitor by both
Buckley and Harvie-Brown (1891) and Baxter and Rintoul (1953).
Balfour (1972) described it as a regular passage migrant in very
small numbers.

During the period 1970-1982, this species has been recorded in
every month, although it is most numerous on spring and autumn
passage.

Monthly distribution of sightings, 1970-1982

J	F	M	A	M	J	J	A	S	O	N	D
6	2	3	6	10	3	3	2	25	41	11	6

The majority of sightings are of 1-6 birds, but there are peak
counts of 45 at Deer Sound, Mainland in November 1975 and 27
on Sanday on 7th May 1982, many of the latter being in breeding
plumage.

Partial Wader Survey, January 1983, (Martin and Summers, 1983) Appendix II

Mainland	Sanday	Westray
4	14	4

Total counted: 22

Sociable Plover

Chettusia gregaria

Very rare.

There are only three records, all of single birds:
  1926   First winter female, shot North Ronaldsay, 3rd
            November (S.N.1927:157).
  1949   Rendall, Mainland, early December (S.B.5:467).
  1969   Carrick, Eday, 15th January (B.B.63:275; S.B.6:85).

Lapwing   Teeick, Teeo

Vanellus vanellus

Common breeding species and passage migrant; recorded throughout the year.

Dunn (1837) said the Lapwing was a rare bird in Orkney, with only a few pairs visiting in the summer. Baikie and Heddle (1848) stated that they appeared "in great abundance" in March, immediately paired and bred, stayed until the end of October, most migrating southwards, but some spending the winter here. Buckley and Harvie-Brown (1891) recorded that summer residents only were known until about 1870, but then the numbers increased. After the 1890's numbers started to fall, due to the taking of eggs and adult birds. Lack (1943) recorded that "since the special Act of Parliament to protect it, the Lapwing has been increasing rapidly (D. J. Robertson, 1935; G. T. Arthur)". Balfour (1972) said that, although still a reasonably common breeder, it had been probably three to four times as numerous about the 1920's and 1930's and earlier.

Today the Lapwing is still regarded as a common bird, but numbers have been reduced due, in part, to the severe winter of 1981-82, but the greatest impact has probably been from the destruction of habitat and changes in farming methods.

Favoured breeding habitat is very rough pasture with damp, rushy areas, but low moorland, where the soil is easily accessible, and ploughed fields are also commonly used.

During the period 1974-1982, birds have been seen on territory by 25th February. The first full clutch was laid by 28th March and flying young were seen in early June.

Counts of breeding pairs include:

> Auskerry, 1 pair, 1981
> Cava, 2 pairs, 1980
> Gairsay, 22 pairs, 1981
> Mainland:
> > The Loons, Birsay, c103 pairs, 1981
> > Durkadale, 2 pairs, 1982
> Papa Westray:
> > North Hill, 12-13 pairs, 1981
> > 14 pairs, 1982
> Pentland Skerries, 2 pairs, 1982
> Rousay:
> > Central moorland, 45 pairs, 1981 (Lea, 1982)

By early June, unpaired birds and failed breeders have started to flock and these flocks gradually enlarge as other adults and flying young join them. Birds on autumn passage arrive in

H

September, but October and November see the large autumn flocks. On 19th November 1979 a flock of 6,000-7,000 Lapwing was seen leaving the Marwick area and flying towards the south west.

In December there are often considerable numbers which, in severe frosty weather or if the ground is snow-covered, can disappear almost overnight. Peak winter flock count was c2,000 at Tankerness on 13th December 1980.

Returning birds start arriving in early February and numbers build up towards the end of that month and into March.

Partial Wader Survey, January 1983
(Martin and Summers, 1983) Appendix 11

Burray	Hoy Group	Mainland	Sanday	S. Ronaldsay	Westray
150	455	2080	111	480	79

Total counted: 3,355.

From the ringing recoveries, it is evident that some of our breeding population moves in a south-westerly direction, Ireland being an important wintering area, with some going as far as France. A pullus ringed in Norway was found a year later in Orkney.

SANDPIPERS, STINTS, GODWITS, CURLEWS, SNIPE, PHALAROPES: Scolopacidae

Knot

Calidris canutus

Passage migrant, usually in small numbers.

Baikie and Heddle (1848), Buckley and Harvie-Brown (1891) and Omond (1925) all gave only a few occurrences. Baxter and Rintoul (1953) described it as "not very abundant and only occasionally seen in the winter". Balfour (1972) noted this species as a regular passage visitor, usually occurring in small parties and, more rarely, in large flocks.

Although recorded throughout the year, during the period 1974-1982, it was most numerous on spring and autumn passage.

Monthly distribution of sightings, 1974-1982

J	F	M	A	M	J	J	A	S	O	N	D
5	2	7	4	18	2	18	54	63	23	11	12

Most sightings are of 1-20 birds, but flocks of 100 have been seen on several occasions. On 14th August 1964 a flock of 220 was seen on North Ronaldsay *(Island Saga)*.

It is not unusual for birds in full breeding plumage to be seen in summer.

Partial Wader Survey, January 1983
(Martin and Summers, 1983) Appendix II

Mainland

18

Sanderling
Calidris alba

Passage migrant recorded in every month; some birds winter in the North Isles.

Early writers regarded this as a somewhat rare species but Baxter and Rintoul (1953) thought that it probably occurred regularly. Balfour (1972) considered the Sanderling to be a regular passage visitor, usually in small numbers and generally in early autumn.

Although there are records in every month for the period 1974-1982, sightings increase during the spring passage in May and to an even greater extent in the autumn, from the end of July to October.

Monthly distribution of sightings, 1974-1982

J	F	M	A	M	J	J	A	S	O	N	D
5	7	4	4	21	17	27	33	57	17	10	6

Some birds winter, mainly in the North Isles, and North Ronaldsay usually has a significant population, with a peak count of 110 in January 1978. There were 300 on North Ronaldsay on

7th October 1976 and 223 birds at the north end of Sanday on 29th November 1981.

Partial Wader Survey, January 1983
(Martin and Summers, 1983) Appendix II

	Sanday	Westray
	472	177

Total counted: 649.

Little Stint
Calidris minuta

Scarce but regular passage migrant.

There were only a few 19th century records until Briggs (1893) recorded about 80 on North Ronaldsay on 26th August 1892. Balfour (1972) considered this species to be a regular passage visitor in very small numbers. During the period 1972-1982, it has been recorded annually with all sightings occurring between May and October. The majority of reports are of single birds, but there were up to 16 on North Ronaldsay from 10th September to 4th October 1978, 9 at Sandwick, West Mainland on 27th September 1980 and 9 on North Ronaldsay on 6th and 7th October 1976.

Distribution of sightings in fortnightly periods, 1972-1982

May 16th- May 29th	May 30th- June 12th	June 13th- June 26th	June 27th- July 10th	July 11th- July 24th	July 25th- Aug. 7th
1	2	1	1	0	6

Aug. 8th- Aug. 21st	Aug. 22nd- Sept. 4th	Sept. 5th- Sept. 18th	Sept. 19th- Oct. 2nd	Oct. 3rd- Oct. 16th
2	6	18	15	10

Extreme dates for the above periods are 29th May and 7th October.

Temminck's Stint
Calidris temminckii

Very rare.

There are only two records, both of single birds:

1964	North Ronaldsay, 21st May *(Island Saga)*.
1981	Papa Westray, 22nd June.

White-rumped Sandpiper
Calidris fuscicollis

Very rare.

There are five records, all of single birds:

1969	North Ronaldsay, 31st October (B.B.63:277).
1970	Tankerness, 11th-12th October (B.B.64:351).
1973	Sanday, 23rd July (B.B.67:323).
	Deerness, 28th October (B.B.67:323).
1978	North Ronaldsay, 2nd-4th October (B.B.73:507).

Pectoral Sandpiper
Calidris melanotos

Very rare.

There are the following authenticated records, all of single birds:

1889	Westray, 26th August, shot (Buckley and Harvie-Brown, 1891).
1971	North Ronaldsay, 6th and 7th September (Balfour, 1972).
1980	Rennibister, Firth, 1st October.
1981	Tankerness, 26th August-2nd September.
	Birsay, 17th September.
1983	Loch of Banks, Sandwick, 18th September.

Curlew Sandpiper
Calidris ferruginea

Scarce passage migrant, most often recorded in autumn.

Briggs (1893) recorded birds of this species on North Ronaldsay from the end of August to early October 1892 and said it was the first time he had seen them there. Balfour (1972) stated that it was a scarce passage visitor, occuring most frequently in August and September.

From 1971-1982 it has been recorded annually, except in 1973 and 1974. The extreme dates in spring are 12th May and 1st June and in autumn, 21st July and 9th November, with most sightings between 28th August and 29th September.

Monthly distribution of sightings, 1971-1982

May	June	July	August	Sept.	Oct.	Nov.
4	1	1	5	13	1	1

The majority of sightings in the above period are of 1-3 birds, but 4 were recorded at Stenness on 29th August 1982. There are records of 8 birds at Rendall on 10th September 1969 and 10 at Eynhallow on 24th May 1956 (Balfour unpublished).

Purple Sandpiper
Calidris maritima

Regular winter visitor.

All the writers from the time of Dunn (1837) described this species as very numerous and Buckley and Harvie-Brown (1891) believed it was the most abundant of all the small waders in the winter. Balfour (1972) said it was a regular passage and winter visitor, usually in small flocks.

Purple Sandpipers have been recorded in every month during the period 1974-1982. In spring there is a build-up of numbers in April and May, with peak flock counts of 750 at the north end of Sanday on 22nd May 1979 and 550 on North Ronaldsay on 2nd May 1982. There are occasional sightings throughout the summer, but the main return passage in the autumn occurs from mid-October.

Peak winter flock counts include:

Mainland:

Evie Bay,	250	14th November 1978
Newark, Deerness	250	23rd February 1982
North Ronaldsay	320	8th February 1981
Papa Westray	490	mid-January 1981

A partial survey of Mainland and South Ronaldsay between 12th and 27th December 1980 obtained the following counts, with a total of 710 birds:

Mainland:

Bay of Ireland	3	Marwick	2
Birsay	135	Scapa	40
Deerness	90	Stromness	183
Evie	76	Weyland Bay	34
Lamb Holm	6		
Total	569		

South Ronaldsay:

Burwick	62	Sandwick	15
Hoxa	6	Widewall	33
Newark	25		
Total:	141		

Partial Wader Survey, January 1983
(Martin and Summers, 1983) Appendix II

Hoy group	Mainland	Sanday	S Ronaldsay	Westray
135	995	1,242	106	1,072

Total counted: 3,550.

Dunlin   Plover page

Calidris alpina

Local breeding species in small numbers; regular passage migrant and winter visitor.

Dunn (1837) described the Dunlin as plentiful and breeding in Orkney. He noted the change of winter plumage which had led some to believe it was a different species. Buckley and Harvie-Brown (1891) stated ". . . they are abundant. Found on every island and holm, breeding everywhere throughout the Orkneys". They also said the Dunlin was commoner in the summer, with only a few remaining during the winter. Omond (1925) refused to mention the localities where this species bred, as there was a great demand by egg-collectors for clutches. Lack (1943) thought it had decreased markedly, except on Sanday, but G. T. Arthur said that on Mainland, thanks to protection, it had been increasing. In 1927, Baxter found them well distributed throughout the islands (Baxter and Rintoul, 1953). Balfour (1972) noted it as a regular breeding species in small numbers, widely scattered.

In the breeding season, the Dunlin may be found in grassy marshes and also on moorland, close to water, from sea level to over 1,000 feet.

Trilling birds have been heard on 3rd May and fledged young seen on 7th July.

During the period 1974-1982, breeding pairs and displaying birds on territory have been reported from:

Auskerry	Papa Westray:
Fara, 4 pairs, 1974	North Hill, 5 pairs, 1974
Flotta	3-4 pairs, 1981
Gairsay	Sanday
Hoy, 24+ pairs, 1974	South Ronaldsay
Mainland:	Stronsay
The Loons, Birsay,	Westray
10-15 pairs, 1975	
Evie	
Orphir	
Stenness	

As a breeding species, it is obvious that the Dunlin has declined considerably. In 1954, there were 12-15 pairs near the Ring of Brodgar, Stenness (Balfour, unpublished). The area has been reclaimed and there are now only 2 or 3 pairs present.

In the spring, there is evidence of passage in May with flocks of over 400 birds reported from Sanday and 200 from Papa Westray. The autumn movements begin in late July and continue into October. Flocks in winter may be found on sandy beaches, loch margins and often feeding in grass fields close to the shore.

**Peak Winter Counts, 22nd November-10th February,
Scapa Beach, Mainland, 1974-1982**

1974	1975	1976	1977	1978
400	750	450	400	370

	1979	1980	1981	1982
	500	300	350	120

**Partial Wader Survey, January 1983
(Martin and Summers, 1983) Appendix II**

Mainland	Sanday	S. Ronaldsay	Westray
333	1,228	100	250

Total counted: 1,911.

A juvenile ringed at the Wash in August 1968 was recovered in Orkney in June 1975. A full grown bird, ringed in Norway in September, was found in Orkney in October of the same year and an adult, ringed in Sweden in August, was found in Orkney in January of the following year.

Buff-breasted Sandpiper

Tryngites subruficollis

Very rare.

The only record is of a single bird in Sandwick, Mainland, 25th-26th June 1976 (B.B.70:423).

Ruff

Philomachus pugnax

Passage migrant.

According to Baikie and Heddle (1848), the Ruff was often seen in Orkney, most of the sightings occurring on Sanday and usually during September. Buckley and Harvie-Brown (1891) thought it was a rare bird and Omond (1925) gave only one record. Baxter and Rintoul (1953) stated that it was fairly regular, but that the numbers varied greatly. Balfour (1972) regarded it as a regular passage visitor in small numbers, usually in autumn, but occasional breeding-plumaged birds occurred in spring and summer.

During the period 1974-1982, the Ruff has been recorded annually on passage, being more numerous in the autumn. There are only a few spring sightings with the extreme dates of 28th March and 10th June. Most reports involve 1-2 birds, but 3 were seen at Deerness on 14th April 1982 and 3 at Birsay on 20th April 1976.

In autumn, a single bird has been noted on 9th July, but the extreme dates for the main passage are 25th July and 24th October, with the majority of sightings occurring in August and September. A peak count of 55 was reported from Sanday on 17th September 1981. There are late records of a single bird on 30th November 1982 and two were seen on 25th December 1981.

Jack Snipe

Lymnocryptes minimus

Passage migrant in small numbers; winter visitor.

Early writers considered this species to be not uncommon, while Balfour (1972) said it occurred in limited numbers and was a regular passage and winter visitor.

Monthly distribution of sightings, 1969-1982

J	F	M	A	M	J	J	A	S	O	N	D
5	9	8	5	0	0	1	0	6	53	13	9

Most sightings are of single birds, but 2-5 are occasionally recorded and there are peak counts of 12+ on 17th October and 6+ on 21st October 1976 from North Ronaldsay. A bird ringed in Orkney in October was recovered in Moray the following February.

Snipe
Horse-gowk

Gallinago gallinago

Widespread breeding species; probable passage migrant and winter visitor.

All the early writers stated that this species was very numerous, but Buckley and Harvie-Brown (1891) thought that numbers had declined considerably, probably due to the severe winters of 1878-79 and 1880-81. The drainage of breeding and feeding grounds and the increased number of guns were contributory factors. According to Lack (1943) the Snipe was breeding commonly on all the main islands and he thought that the decrease had not continued. He noted that Meinhertzhagen (1939) ascribed the Orkney birds to the Faeroe form (G.g.faeroeensis). Baxter and Rintoul (1953) found them plentiful in many places and Balfour (1972) said they bred commonly on most of the islands.

The Snipe is widespread as a breeding species, being found on marshland, wet meadows and moorland. Drumming has been reported as early as 10th February and Groundwater (1974) records a nest found on 19th March. The earliest date for flying young is 25th May but unfledged young can still be found in August.

During the period 1974-1982, it has obviously been under-recorded and the only breeding counts available are:

Auskerry	10 pairs, 1977, 1981
Cava	2 pairs, 1980
Gairsay	8-11 pairs, 1981
North Fara	c 4 pairs, 1981
Pentland Skerries	3 nests, 1982
Rousay:	
Central moorland	5 pairs, 1981 (Lea, 1982)

The numbers of Snipe increase during the autumn, especially from August to October. Peak counts from North Ronaldsay are:

Many hundreds	15th October, 1976
300	24th and 25th October, 1981
115	15th August, 1977

Briggs (1893) recorded it as most plentiful on North Ronaldsay in the latter half of November and most of December, 1892, but in 1893 (Briggs, 1894) it was most numerous in August.

In cold weather, it is often found feeding on the shore. In the very severe winter of 1981/82, many were seen feeding at roadside ditches.

Partial Wader Survey, January 1983
(Martin and Summers 1983) Appendix II

Hoy group	Mainland	Sanday	S. Ronaldsay	Westray
13	79	53	1	61

Total counted: 207.

Great Snipe
Gallinago media

Very rare.

The only records are:

1863	1 shot, Shapinsay, September (Buckley and Harvie-Brown, 1891). Buckley and Harvie-Brown also mention two or three killed on Hoy (no dates given) and one shot near Skaill, Sandwick in either 1864 or 1865.
1901	2 Stronsay, 25th September (A.S.N.H.1902:54).
1905	2 Stronsay, 12th September (A.S.N.H.1906:54).

The 1959 record given by Balfour (1972) is not mentioned in B.B.R.C. reports and cannot be included.

Dowitcher species

Limnodromus scolopaceus or L.griseus

Very rare.

The only occurrence is of one on North Ronaldsay, 4th April, 1970. (B.B.64:349).

Woodcock

Scolopax rusticola

Passage migrant, winter visitor; has bred.

Both Low (1813) and Dunn (1837) considered the Woodcock to be a transient visitor, merely resting on passage, but Baikie and Heddle (1848) said that some remained until spring. Buckley and Harvie-Brown (1891) noted that, at times, large numbers arrived, especially on Hoy. Balfour (1972) stated that this species was a regular passage and winter visitor; usually single birds were seen, but up to a dozen could occur.

The following are records of known and probable breeding:

1888	At least 2 nests at Trumland, Rousay (Buckley and Harvie-Brown, 1891)
1896	A chick from Orkney is mentioned in the British Museum Catalogue (Baxter and Rintoul, 1953).
1923	A nest found on Rousay on 5th July (Omond, 1925).

Lack (1943) said that G. T. Arthur found young once on the Mainland, but no date is given.

1963	An injury-feigning adult on Eday on 20th June, but no young could be found in the dense undergrowth (Balfour, 1972).

It is difficult to distinguish the spring passage because of the presence of wintering birds, but during the period 1974-1982, there was a peak count of 12 on North Ronaldsay on 28th March, 1980 and the last reported date was 14th May. There were sightings of single birds in June and July and the first autumn record was on 13th August. The main movements occurred in October and

November, with a maximum of 30-40 birds at Berriedale, Hoy on 28th October 1976. There were sightings of 1-3 birds from many areas between December and March.

Monthly distribution of sightings, 1974-1982

J	F	M	A	M	J	J	A	S	O	N	D
24	14	17	9	9	1	1	2	3	36	35	37

A bird ringed in February 1977 in Orkney was found in Angus in January 1979.

Black-tailed Godwit

Limosa limosa

Passage migrant in small numbers; has bred.

This species has always been regarded as rather rare. Baxter and Rintoul (1953) said that, although breeding was suspected in 1910, 1911 and 1914, when birds were seen in June, there was no satisfactory proof. Balfour (1972) gave the first proven record of breeding on Sanday in 1956.

The only other records of proved or possible breeding are:

1973   Pair displaying, Birsay, 20th-27th May.

1974   Pair defending territory, West Mainland, 6th June. They were seen the following day, but there was no evidence of territorial defence. No proof of breeding.

1975   2 pairs bred. One pair was at the West Mainland site where territory was defended in 1974. They were first noted on 21st June, and on 17th August well grown young were found. The second pair bred on Sanday. On 23rd July, a pair with one young, just able to fly, were seen.

1976   Birds were present at the West Mainland site in June, but on 29th June one, a female, was found dead. There was no evidence of breeding.

Since then, apart from 1978 and 1982, birds have been at the known breeding sites, but no further nesting has taken place.

Monthly distribution of sightings, 1971-1982

J	F	M	A	M	J	J	A	S	O	N	D
1	2	1	5	19	9	5	17	22	4	0	3

The sightings are usually of 1-5 birds, but 10 were seen at Stenness on 23rd August 1977 and 11 at Rendall on 23rd September 1981.

Bar-tailed Godwit

Limosa lapponica

Regular winter visitor and passage migrant; recorded throughout the year.

Early writers regarded this species as a rare winter visitor. Baxter and Rintoul (1953) said it was not very common in Orkney, but that it did occur on migration and, occasionally, in winter. Balfour (1972) described it as a regular passage visitor, almost always found on sandy or muddy beaches.

Although there are sightings for every month, the main passage is in the autumn. Catasand, Sanday; St Peter's Pool, Deerness; Mill Sands, Tankerness and Scapa Beach are favoured localities.

Sanday provides some of the largest flock numbers and it often supports non-breeding flocks in the summer. There was a flock of about 200, in non-breeding plumage, present there during the summer of 1975.

Peak December counts, Scapa Beach, 1974-1981

1974	1975	1976	1977	1978	1979	1980	1981
60	No count	8	10	No count	27	34	69

Partial Wader Survey, January 1983
(Martin and Summers, 1983) Appendix II

Mainland	Sanday	S. Ronaldsay	Westray
54	777	22	1

Total counted: 854.

Whimbrel

Numenius phaeopus

Rare breeding species; passage migrant.

Dunn (1837) remarked that the Whimbrel was as numerous as the Curlew, but later writers did not agree with this. Buckley and Harvie-Brown (1891) thought they had never been numerous and were declining as a breeding species. They gave the following breeding records:

1831	Salmon in *London's Magazine* said Whimbrel bred sparingly in marshy places between the hills of Hoy, but when he was there on 3rd June, the eggs had hatched (Salmon, 1831).
1868	One or two pairs with young in Walls, Hoy.
1887	A pair which evidently had young at Melsetter, Hoy, but no breeding in 1888.
1889	Known to have bred on Hoy.

In 1900 a pair bred near Finstown (A.S.N.H.1900:245). The record given by Omond (1925) was probably this one. Lack (1943) found none breeding, but recorded that G. T. Arthur said there were two breeding records since 1918; neither of these was confirmed.

Balfour (1968) knew of no further instances of breeding, but later recorded that 3 pairs bred on Eday in 1968 and a pair on Mainland in 1970 (Balfour, 1972).

All details of known and possible breeding, since 1968, are given below:

1968	3 pairs bred Eday (Balfour, 1972). In S.B.5:322, this is given as "at least 2 pairs Eday 27th June behaved as if they had young".
1969	No breeding—area devastated by fire.
1970	1 pair bred Mainland.
1971	1 pair summered in Orkney.
1972	Present in 2 areas in June, but no proof of breeding.
1973	Present during breeding season.
1974	2 pairs bred Eday, both rearing young.
1975	2 pairs bred at same site.

Snipe

1976	3 pairs bred Eday. Another pair held territory but probably did not breed.
1977	2 pairs bred, each rearing 3 young, Eday. Territorial birds on Westray and Sanday, but no evidence of breeding.
1978	Bred at usual site, Eday.
1979	Pair held territory, West Mainland, but no proof of breeding.
1980	Bred, Eday.
1981	Minimum of 5 pairs bred, Eday.
1982	Probably 6-7 pairs bred, Eday.

During the period 1974-1982, birds have been recorded regularly from April to October, with the extreme dates being 17th April and 20th October. The main spring passage is in May, with a peak count of 13 on North Ronaldsay on 12th May 1981. In autumn, the main movements are recorded in August, with a maximum of 14 on Copinsay on 7th August 1975.

Curlew Whaup

Numenius arquata

Common breeding species, passage migrant and winter visitor.

Heppleston (1981) reviewed the history of this species in Orkney. As early as 1700, Pennant said that the Curlew was common in Orkney and it was regarded as such until Buckley and Harvie-Brown (1891) stated that it was scarce during the breeding season. In 1885, one nest was found at Hobbister and it was not known to have bred in the parish before; it was known to breed on Hoy and, in 1886, "several breeding pairs" were seen, with eggs or young. Omond (1925) said it was again a common species. Lack (1943) found it breeding on Mainland, Hoy, Rousay, Westray, one pair each on Eday and Stronsay and several pairs on North Ronaldsay. Migrants and non-breeding flocks were seen on all the other islands. From previous records and the statements of D. J. Robertson (1935) and G. T. Arthur, it was evident that the Curlew had increased over the past 50 years. Baxter and Rintoul (1953) and Balfour (1972) agreed about the increase and Balfour described it as one of our commonest moorland breeding birds.

The Curlew nests on moorland, where it is widely distributed,

I

but it also nests in damp, rushy areas and sometimes in agricultural grassland.

During the period 1974-1982, birds have been reported holding territory on 11th February. First eggs have been found on 18th April, while young, still unable to fly, have been seen as late as 4th August.

Counts of breeding pairs include:

Auskerry	1 pair, 1981	Papa Westray:
Cava	1 pair, 1980	North Hill 6 pairs, 1981
Gairsay	9 pairs, 1981	Pentland
Mainland:		Skerries 2 pairs, 1982
Durkadale	11 pairs, 1982	Rousay: (Lea, 1982)
The Loons,	44 pairs, 1981	Central Moorland
Birsay		145 pairs, 1982
N. Ronaldsay	6 pairs, 1980 and 1981	Stronsay c51 pairs, 1979

Local flocks start forming in early June and by mid-July over 1,000 were seen in Birsay in 1981 and c2,000 on 28th August 1981 at Sands of Evie and adjacent fields.

There is an increase in numbers in October and many birds stay on to winter. Peak winter counts include 1,500 at Quanterness, St Ola on 18th January 1976.

Partial Wader Survey, January 1983
(Martin and Summers, 1983) Appendix II

Burray	Hoy group	Mainland	Sanday	S. Ronaldsay	Westray
379	1,419	11,440	762	2,779	746

Total counted: 17,525.

A leucistic bird has been reported in the Rendall-Firth area since 1968 (Groundwater, 1974). In 1979 possibly the same bird nested in Firth.

A young bird, ringed in Sweden in June 1964, was found in Orkney in December 1974 and one, ringed in Finland in 1965, was recovered in Orkney in September 1974. Young birds ringed in Orkney have been found in Caithness the following January and Co. Antrim the following August.

Spotted Redshank
Tringa erythropus

Scarce passage migrant.

The only 19th century record was given by Baxter and Rintoul (1953). Balfour (1972) described it as a regular passage visitor in small numbers.

During the period 1974-1982, it has been reported annually, with most records in the autumn. There is only one spring record, that of a single bird at Birsay on 27th May 1979. In the autumn the extreme dates are 26th July and 2nd October.

Fortnightly distribution of sightings, July-October, 1974-1982

July 26th- Aug. 8th	Aug. 9th- Aug. 22nd	Aug. 23rd- Sept. 5th	Sept. 6th- Sept. 19th	Sept. 20th- Oct. 3rd
6	9	3	3	4

Most of the sightings are of single birds, but there were 3 in St Ola on 9th August 1980, 2 on Hoy on 26th July 1980 and 2 in Deerness on 13th and 16th August and 6th September 1981.

There are two late records, both of single birds, on North Ronaldsay on 14th October 1969 and Orphir on 5th November 1968.

Redshank
Tringa totanus

Common breeding species, passage migrant and winter visitor.

This species has long been known in Orkney, Sibbald (1684) being the first to mention it (Baxter and Rintoul, 1953). Lack (1943) thought it safe to conclude that the Redshank was much commoner than it had been a hundred years before, as both Low (1813) and Baikie and Heddle (1848) stated that it nested "in retired marshy spots". Also Buckley and Harvie-Brown (1891) considered it to be very common, so the main increase had probably occurred before the writing of their book. Lack also mentioned that Briggs (1893) said only a few pairs bred on North Ronaldsay, but that it was now common. Balfour (1972) stated that it was a common breeding species.

The Redshank nests mainly in grassy marshes, with tufts of rushes and coarse grass, but occasionally on moorland several hundred feet above sea level, as on Rousay (Lack, 1943).

For the period of 1974-1982, the earliest recorded date for display was 16th March and young, a few days old, were seen on 16th May. There are few breeding counts, but these include:

Cava	2 pairs, 1980
Gairsay	min. 22 pairs, 1981
Mainland:	
The Loons, Birsay	30 pairs, 1981
North Fara	2-3 pairs, 1982
Rousay: (Lea, 1982)	
Central moorland	10 pairs, 1981
Brings & Quandale	3 pairs, 1981
Faraclett	2 pairs, 1981

The Redshank is one of the under-recorded species, but from the information available there appears to be a small spring passage in March and April and a larger autumn passage from July to September.

Peak counts include:

Spring	180 Widewall, South Ronaldsay, 22nd April 1982	
Autumn	336 Deer Sound, 5th September 1976	
Winter	450 Deer Sound, 2nd November 1975.	

Partial Wader Survey, January 1983
(Martin and Summers, 1983) Appendix II

Burray	Hoy group	Mainland	Sanday	S. Ronaldsay	Westray
34	662	2,630	742	610	815

Total counted: 5,493.

Young birds ringed in Iceland have been recovered in Orkney in October and December of the same year, while another was recovered four years later in April. An adult bird, ringed in Lancashire in October 1970, was found in Orkney in June 1972 and a young bird from Orkney was recovered 4 months later in Invergordon.

Marsh Sandpiper
Tringa stagnatilis

Very rare.

There is only one record, that of a single bird at Bridesness Loch, North Ronaldsay on 23rd August 1979 (B.B.73:509).

Greenshank
Tringa nebularia

Regular spring and autumn passage migrant in small numbers; has bred.

Early writers regarded the Greenshank as an occasional visitor to Orkney, but Balfour (1972) recorded it as a regular passage visitor in both spring and autumn and listed two breeding records:

    1926 Heddle Hill, Firth
    1951 Hoy

Since 1974 this species has been recorded annually with extreme dates of 13th March and 22nd October. A late record, of a single bird, was on 12th December 1972 at Stenness.

Monthly distribution of sightings, 1974-1982

Mar.	Apr.	May	June	July	Aug.	Sept.	Oct.
5	10	17	3	19	75	46	46

The majority of sightings are of 1-4 birds, with a peak count of 14 on North Ronaldsay on 12th August 1980.

Green Sandpiper
Tringa ochropus

Passage migrant in small numbers.

Baxter and Rintoul (1953) mentioned autumn records at several sites and Balfour (1972) described this species as a passage visitor, probably regular but in small numbers, most usual in autumn. There has been no change in status.

Annual sightings, 1974-1982

1974	1975	1976	1977	1978	1979	1980	1981	1982
0	5	0	7	4	0	21	9	11

In spring, there are 7 sightings which fall between 6th May and 7th June. In autumn, the extreme dates are 13th July and 22nd September. The majority of sightings are of single birds but 3 were recorded on 10th August and 9th September 1980, 23rd May and 4th September 1982.

Fortnightly distribution of sightings, Autumn, 1974-1982

July 11th- July 24th	July 25th- Aug. 7th	Aug. 8th- Aug. 21st	Aug. 22nd- Sept. 4th	Sept. 5th- Sept. 18th	Sept. 19th- Oct. 2nd
1	10	24	8	4	3

Wood Sandpiper
Tringa glareola

Rare passage migrant.

Only two records were mentioned by Baxter and Rintoul (1953) and Balfour (1972) described it as a rather scarce passage visitor in both spring and autumn.

There have been 1-4 records annually between 1973 and 1982, except for 1978 and 1982, when there were no reported sightings. In spring, during the same period, there are 3 records, all between 20th and 24th May. In autumn, the extreme dates are 1st August and 1st October.

Fortnightly distribution of Sightings, Autumn, 1973-1982

Aug. 1st- Aug. 14th	Aug. 15th- Aug. 28th	Aug. 29th- Sept. 11th	Sept. 12th- Sept. 25th	Sept. 26th- Oct. 9th
2	5	1	2	1

All sightings are of single birds, except for 2 on Stronsay on 20th August 1977.

Common Sandpiper

Boondie

Actitis hypoleucos

Scarce breeding species, regular passage migrant.

Baikie and Heddle (1848) said that this species was "an occasional visitant", but a note, left by Heddle at a later date, showed that he became aware that it bred here. Buckley and Harvie-Brown (1891) saw the Common Sandpiper on several occasions on Hoy, Rousay and Mainland and recorded a nest at Swanbister, Orphir. Omond (1925) saw a few pairs every season. Lack (1943) stated that a very few bred on Mainland (G. T. Arthur), three pairs in the north of Hoy and at least ten pairs round Muckle and Peerie Water, Rousay. There were no breeding pairs found elsewhere. Lack also reported that, according to G. T. Arthur, in the last twenty years this species had greatly decreased on Mainland, where formerly it was common. Balfour (1972) recorded it as a rather scarce breeder, but "in the first third of this century it was a pretty common breeder". There has been no change in status.

For the period 1973-1982, breeding pairs have been reported from:

Hoy: Rackwick
     Sandy Loch
Mainland: Loch of Boardhouse
          Loch of Hundland, Birsay
          Loch of Kirbister, Orphir
          Loch of Swannay, Birsay
          Loch of Wasdale, Firth
Rousay:
     Central moorland, 4 pairs 1981 (Lea, 1982).

The earliest date for display was 6th May and a nest with a full clutch was found on 25th May. The last reported date on which adult and young were seen together was 23rd July.

Sightings are usually of single birds, with a maximum of 7 on 12th May, 1982 at the Loch of Swannay. The extreme dates are 25th April and 26th October. A single bird was seen at Evie on 19th December 1979, a late date.

Turnstone   Stoney-putter
Arenaria interpres

Common passage and winter visitor; some present throughout the summer.

Low (1813) knew this species as a winter visitor, as did Baikie and Heddle (1848), who mentioned that a few occasionally remained during the summer. Buckley and Harvie-Brown (1891) wrote that, although common, like all small waders, numbers were falling. In August 1928, Baxter reported a great many on Papa Westray and small numbers on other islands (Baxter and Rintoul, 1953). Balfour (1972) said that breeding had not been suspected although a few stayed throughout the summer. He described the Turnstone as a common passage and winter visitor.

This species is usually found on the shore, but it can be seen feeding, often with other waders, in grass fields.

Although there is no record of breeding, during the period 1974-1982, there have been several instances of birds singing and displaying in May and June and there is one report of birds scraping on one of the North Isles. In 1974, from the end of June to early July, a female, in full breeding plumage, held territory on Papa Westray and on 24th July of the same year, a female with a juvenile was seen on Westray.

A few birds are recorded regularly in summer, with a maximum of 50 at Westayre, Sanday on 18th June 1979, but some areas report that they have no Turnstones from mid-May to late July. Numbers build up from August to October, but tend to fall during the winter months. Large flocks are again seen during the spring passage in April and May, with a peak flock count of 750 at Riv, Sanday on 22nd May 1979.

Partial Wader Survey, January 1983,
(Martin and Summers, 1983)
Appendix II

Burray	Hoy group	Mainland	Sanday	S. Ronaldsay	Westray
33	276	1,901	1,141	255	579

Total counted: 4,185.

Wilson's Phalarope
Phalaropus tricolor

Very rare.

The only record is of a single bird at Birsay on 3rd September 1981 (B.B.76:498).

Red-necked Phalarope
Phalaropus lobatus

Scarce passage migrant; has bred.

The Red-necked Phalarope in Orkney has been well documented from the time of Pennant (1789) to the present day. It was first recorded as breeding on Sanday and North Ronaldsay in 1804. By 1831 several pairs nested on Sanday but they were greatly persecuted, eggs being taken and birds shot, until they seemed to be practically exterminated about 1870. Dunn (1837) recorded it from Sanday, Westray and Sandwick (West Mainland). The species continued to breed on Sanday and, in 1927, Baxter found 7 or 8 pairs had bred. By 1929 the birds had disappeared and Baxter and Rintoul (1953) knew of no subsequent breeding record for Sanday. Breeding in North Ronaldsay was noted in 1841 (Wilson's *Voyage round Scotland and the Isles,* 1842) and a few pairs bred in 1895. Serle (1934) saw birds at a promising locality, on the west side of Hoy, in July 1931 and, by the behaviour of one bird, judged there were young in the vicinity. Lack (1943) said that a few years previously, one or two pairs nested on Papa Westray, but they had gone (W. Traill, G. T. Arthur). In 1941, Lack found several pairs on North Ronaldsay and, on two other islands, signs of probable nesting.

There is doubt as to whether there was breeding on Sanday in 1953; on 20th June a pair behaved as if nesting, but no nest was found. In mid-July, 10 birds, 2 of which may have been juveniles, were present at a different Sanday site (Balfour, unpublished). Other known and probable breeding records:

1955   4 males, 3 females, Sanday 8th May (Clouston)

1956   1 pair with fully grown young and 1 pair probably with small young, Sanday, 19th July (Balfour, unpublished)

1961   3 pairs Sanday, one pair behaved as if nesting
        and another pair seen mating, 21st June (Balfour,
        unpublished)
1962   At least 2 pairs, Sanday, mid-June
1972   1 pair Orkney

Since 1972 there have been the following sightings:

1975   1 Papa Westray, 23rd May
        1 Stronsay, a female, seen several times, mid-July
        3 together, North Ronaldsay, 21st July
1976   1 Hoy, 22nd July
1977   1 Stronsay, 4th September
1979   1 Westray, 5th August
1981   1 North Ronaldsay, 11th-14th July
1982   2 Sanday, 18th May
        1 Westray, 13th-14th August.

Balfour (unpublished) noted that there used to be many Red-
necked Phalaropes on North Ronaldsay, but since water mills were
no longer used, water levels on lochs had been reduced.

Grey Phalarope
Phalaropus fulicarius

Rare.

Buckley and Harvie-Brown (1891) gave only 3 records
October 1881, October 1884 and July 1888.

All known 20th century records are listed:

1900   1 shot, North Ronaldsay, 15th October
1903   1 Sule Skerry, 15th February
1922   1 Birsay (Omond, 1925)
1923   1 Stenness (*The Orcadian*, 8th November 1923)
1956   1 in breeding plumage, Bay of Skaill, early June
        (Balfour, 1972)
1963   2 Pentland Skerries, 15th September
1964   1 North Ronaldsay, 16th May (*Island Saga*)
1975   1 North Ronaldsay, 21st July

1977	A remarkable series of records from North Ronaldsay, where birds were seen daily from 4th-15th September, with a peak count of 15 on 10th
1978	1 North Ronaldsay, 17th September
1980	Single birds on North Ronaldsay on 10th and 11th February and 15th September
1982	1 North Ronaldsay, 4th November

SKUAS : Stercorariidae

Pomarine Skua

Stercorarius pomarinus

Scarce passage migrant.

Baikie and Heddle (1848) gave only one record of this species and Buckley and Harvie-Brown (1891) considered it to be a very scarce bird. They believed that the report of breeding was very doubtful and that there had been some confusion with other species of skua. Balfour (1972) described the Pomarine Skua as a passage visitor in small and irregular numbers and recorded that up to ten per day were seen passing Auskerry in the last week of September 1966.

Between 1974 and 1982, there have been the following sightings, all of single birds:

1975	Eday, 12th May
	Stronsay, 13th July
1977	Hoy Sound, 24th May
	Clestrain Sound, 6th September
1978	North Ronaldsay, 6th October
1979	North Ronaldsay, 5th August
1980	Birsay, 18th September
1981	Scapa Flow, 30th April
1982	Herston, South Ronaldsay, 8th August and 2nd November
	Scapa Bay, 4th December

Arctic Skua   Skootie Allan

Stercorarius parasiticus

Common but local breeding species and passage migrant; increasing.

The Arctic Skua was probably breeding in Orkney in the 18th century as Low (1813) stated that "it continues here the whole breeding time". There seems some confusion as to the actual location of breeding pairs, even up to the time of Buckley and Harvie-Brown (1891). Dunn (1837) noted that they were "most numerous on the Calf of Eday", but in 1888 Buckley and Harvie-Brown found it limited to the parish of North Walls in Hoy, where it was abundant. They mentioned that the Arctic Skua may have formerly bred on the south end of Sanday and quote a paper by Salmon (1831) who "observed them on every island but their principal breeding places were Hoy and Eday". They then confirmed that they could obtain no certain information of this species having bred anywhere else than on Hoy.

It seems probable that a gradual expansion of the Arctic Skua's breeding range in Orkney commenced early in the 20th Century, as Wood (1916) reported a nest at Quanterness, Mainland and Omond (1925) gave its status as "not uncommon and breeding". Nesting first occurred on Papa Westray in either 1924 or 1925 (Baxter and Rintoul, 1953). Lack (1943) in 1941 found 14-18 pairs there, 1 pair on Westray and at least 60 pairs on the west side of Hoy. He quoted G. T. Arthur, who thought that it had increased.

This increase continued during the next forty years, with a spread to many of the islands, as is indicated by the counts in the table. Further details of this expansion are given by Meek, Booth, Reynolds and Ribbands (in litt.).

Due to the difficulties involved in accurately censusing breeding Arctic Skuas, earlier counts of large colonies (1941, 1961 and 1969/70) especially those on Hoy, should be interpreted as approximations only.

The islands of Shapinsay, Helliar Holm, Cava, Switha and Swona, which previously held breeding pairs in 1974, were not visited in 1982, so the actual total of breeding pairs in 1982 is probably higher than 1,034.

The only colonies to have shown a definite decrease in the period 1974-1982 are those of Spurness (Sanday) and Westray. In

Numbers of Arctic Skuas (pairs) breeding or holding territory in Orkney, 1941-1982

Island	1941[1]	1961[2]	1969[3]	1974[4]	1982[5]
North Ronaldsay	—	—	1	Present	1
Sanday	—	up to 10	9	45	25
Papa Westray	14-18	18+	24	86	95
Holm of Papa Westray	—	—	1	2	1
Westray	1	a few	64	93	45
Eday	—	6-8	11	59	101
Calf of Eday	—	—	Present	7	22
Faray (and Holm)	—	—	3	3	1
Stronsay	—	1-2	7	18	44
Linga Holm	—	—	—	—	2
Auskerry	—	—	1	3	2
Rousay	—	15-20	11	51	94
Egilsay	—	—	1	2	1
Wyre	—	2-3	3-4	3	3
Holm of Scockness	—	—	2	1	1
Eynhallow	—	1	10	10	19
Gairsay	—	2-3	3-4	19	38
Sweyn Holm	—	—	—	—	1
Shapinsay	—	—	1	7	Not counted
Helliar Holm	—	—	2	1	Not counted
Mainland	—	2-3	5	32	67
Hoy	*60+	100-150	68	237	407
South Walls	—	—	—	—	1
Fara	—	—	2	4	28
Cava	—	—	2	1	Not counted
Flotta	—	—	Present	21	26
Burray (Hunda)	—	—	—	—	2
South Ronaldsay	—	—	—	—	7
Switha	—	—	—	1	Not counted
Swona	—	—	—	1	Not counted
TOTALS	75+	157+-218+	231-233	717	1,034

Bannerman (1963) included a total of c200 for Hoy in 1961, giving Balfour as his source, but in 1968 Balfour's figures were 100-150 pairs for the 1961 count.

In 1976 there were 55 pairs on Spurness, Sanday and two pairs on Swona in 1977.

[1] Lack (1943)
[2] Cramp et al. (1974)
[3] Seafarer (Cramp et al., 1974)
[4] Booth (1974)
[5] Meek, Booth, Reynolds and Ribbands (in litt.)
* West side only counted

the former case the decline is almost certainly attributable to agricultural reclamation of moorland.

During the 1982 survey, of a total of 1,869 birds, 75.7% were found to be dark phase and 24.3% pale phase (i.e. those with pale, cream or white belly feathers).

During the period 1974-1982, birds have been noted to arrive in the middle of April, the earliest date being the 11th, and many are on territory by the second week of May. Eggs have been recorded on 20th May and the first fledged young on 11th July. The majority have left their breeding territories by mid-September but there are a number of sightings offshore in October and occasionally in November, with the latest date being 4th December.

Birds ringed as pulli in Orkney have been recovered as follows:

Ringed	Recovered
July 1970	Ghana, January 1972
June 1974	Lebanon, October 1975
July 1980	Portugal, August 1980

Long-tailed Skua
Stercorarius longicaudus

Rare passage migrant.

This species was recorded as very rare by Buckley and Harvie-Brown (1891). They gave two definite records and mentioned information given by a Mr Begg, who said that about 35 years before, a dozen or so had bred on Hoy and that he had obtained four specimens. Unfortunately, none of the specimens could be traced, so this statement was not verified. Balfour (1972) described the Long-tailed Skua as a scarce, perhaps irregular, passage visitor.

For the period 1974-1982, there have been the following authenticated records, all of single birds:

1974	Evie, 5th July
1975	Eday, 14th May
	Hoy, 8th July, seen displaying to Arctic Skua
1976	Hoy, 20th June
	Evie, 21st July
1977	Evie, 29th May
	North Ronaldsay, 16th June-12th August
1978	Hoy, 14th July
1980	North Ronaldsay, 26th May
	Birsay, 7th September
1981	Evie, 15th May
	Pentland Firth, 7th August
1982	Hoy, 28th June until at least 7th July
	Birsay, 7th September

Great Skua Bonxie

Stercorarius skua

Common but local breeding species and passage migrant; increasing.

This species was obviously rare at the beginning of the 19th century, as only two occurrences were given by Baikie and Heddle (1848), while Buckley and Harvie-Brown (1891) described it as a very uncommon visitor. Birds were first recorded on Hoy in 1908; they were seen there again in 1914 and in 1915 two pairs were found nesting (Jourdain, 1917). There were four pairs by 1918, but only three in 1922 and two in 1923 (Omond, 1925). Serle (1934) found 6 pairs, widely scattered over Hoy, in 1933 and Lack (1943) estimated that there were more than 20 pairs in 1941.

The increase continued and Balfour (1955) recorded nesting on Papa Westray prior to 1952, while breeding was first noted on Rousay in 1955 and Westray in 1958. Over 60 pairs were counted on Hoy in 1961 and by 1969 there were pairs on Auskerry, Eday,

Fara, Gairsay and Stronsay (Cramp et al., 1974). The Birsay moors, West Mainland, were colonised in 1971 (Booth, unpublished).

Surveys in 1974 and 1982 showed further increases, especially on Hoy. Breeding occurred on the East Mainland in 1979 and South Ronaldsay and the West Mainland coast, between Stromness and Yesnaby, in 1982.

Details of the surveys are given in the table, but as already stated with the Arctic Skua, care should be taken in interpreting the early Hoy counts.

Numbers of Great Skuas (pairs) breeding or holding territory in Orkney, 1941-1982

Island	1941[1]	1969[2]	1974[3]	1982[4]
Papa Westray	-	6	4	2
Westray	-	2	2 pairs present	6
Eday	-	1	1	6
Calf of Eday	-	Birds present	1	4
Stronsay	-	1	2	8
Auskerry	-	1	1	1
Rousay	-	1	5	16
Eynhallow	-	0	0	1
Gairsay	-	1	1	3
Mainland	-	0	5	25
Hoy	20+	72	462	1,573
Fara	-	1	0	6
Cava	-	1	0	Not counted
Flotta	-	0	1 pair present	0
South Ronaldsay	-	0	0	2
TOTALS	20+	87	485	1,652

[1] Lack (1943)
[2] Seafarer (Cramp et al. 1974)
[3] Booth (1974)
[4] Meek, Booth, Reynolds and Ribbands (in litt.)

During the period 1974-1982, there are January and February records of single birds from Scapa Flow and the Pentland Firth, but no reports from the breeding grounds until 28th March. The majority of birds have taken up territory by early May and the first young have been seen on 11th June. Most birds leave their nesting territories towards the end of August and early September,

Common Gull

although offshore sightings continue into October. There are only three November records and a very late bird was seen at Stromness on 26th December.

Birds ringed as pulli in Orkney have been recovered in Denmark (October), France (September, December), Norway (February), Spain (August, December) and Tunisia (June). Birds ringed as pulli in Shetland (7) and Iceland (1) have been recovered in Orkney.

GULLS : Laridae

Little Gull
Larus minutus

Scarce visitor.

The Little Gull has occurred several times in Orkney, according to Baxter and Rintoul (1953) who included a record of 10 seen together at Holm on 8th October 1899. Balfour (1972) described this species as a rather scarce passage visitor.

During the period 1972-1982, it has been recorded in 1972, 1976 and annually from 1978-1982. The majority of sightings are of single birds, but four were seen between South Ronaldsay and Swona on 14th September 1980. The extreme dates for this period are 23rd February and 14th September, with a late record of a single bird on Flotta on 29th December 1979.

Monthly distributions of sightings, 1972-1982

J	F	M	A	M	J	J	A	S	O	N	D
0	1	1	0	7	2	2	2	2	0	0	1

Sabine's Gull
Larus sabini

Very rare.

There is one record, a single bird on North Ronaldsay on 16th October 1979.

J

Cliff-nesting seabirds

Black-headed Gull   Rittock
Larus ridibundus

Widespread breeding species, passage migrant; present throughout the year.

This species was observed by Low (1813) and Dunn (1837). Buckley and Harvie-Brown (1891) recorded it as numerous, noting several colonies, the largest of which was on North Ronaldsay. Lack (1943) found it breeding commonly in suitable habitat and Balfour (1972) described it as a common and widespread species.

There has probably been no change in status, although there is relatively little information available. The Seafarer count, 1968-1970, found 4,500 pairs (Cramp et al., 1974).

The only recent breeding counts are:

North Ronaldsay	c1,000 pairs, 1978 and 1980, but fewer in 1981
Papa Westray	120 pairs, 1979
Pentland Skerries	3 pairs, 1982
Rousay:	
Brings and Quandale	120 pairs, 1981 (Lea, 1982)
Sanday	140+ pairs, 1979
Stronsay	113 pairs, 1979
Shapinsay	600 individuals at the Mill Dam, 1981

Although usually nesting in grassy marshes and amongst reeds, this species can also be found on heather moorland.

The earliest date for a bird with a full black head is 25th January and the first eggs have been found on 2nd May.

The Black-headed Gull is scarce on some of the North Isles, especially North Ronaldsay, in December and January. There is an increase in sightings of birds on North Ronaldsay in February, but the main arrival is from mid-March and on into April. An obvious decrease in numbers occurs during July and there are only occasional records there in October and November.

Peak winter counts are: 250 St Ola, 3rd December 1981 and 200+ Weyland Bay, Mainland, 9th February 1982.

Black-headed Gulls counted with the Partial Wader Survey, January 1983 (Martin and Summers, 1983). Appendix II

Burray	Hoy group	Mainland	Sanday	S. Ronaldsay	Westray
1	28	397	11	65	57

Total counted: 559

There are the following recoveries of ringed pulli:

Place and year of ringing		Date and place of recovery		
Iceland	1934	Nov.-Dec.	1935	Orkney
Shetland	1955	January	1963	Orkney
Norway	1958	April	1960	Orkney
Iceland	1967	January	1968	Orkney
Iceland	1977	April	1980	Orkney
Norway	1980	September	1980	Orkney
Orkney	1981	October	1981	Tayside
Orkney	1981	February	1982	Grampian

Common Gull   White-maa

Larus canus

Common breeding species, passage migrant and winter visitor.

This species was noted by the early writers and Buckley and Harvie-Brown (1891) described it as very abundant. Lack (1943) said it had greatly increased in recent years and Balfour (1972) recorded it as a common breeding species. There has been no change in status, although egg collecting has taken place regularly at some colonies, with reduced breeding success.

The Seafarer count, 1968-1970, found 4,850 pairs (Cramp et al., 1974), approximately 39% of the total British breeding population.

The only recent breeding counts are:

Cava	c10 pairs, 1980
Gairsay	9 pairs, 1981
Pentland Skerries	95 birds, 1982
Papa Westray	129 pairs,1982
Rousay: (Lea, 1982)	
Central moorland	669 pairs, 1981
Brings & Quandale	677 pairs, 1981
Faraclett	165 pairs, 1981

| Sanday | 250 pairs, 1979 |
| Stronsay | 200 pairs, 1979 |

The Common Gull nests in colonies in a variety of habitat, including moorland, grassy marshes and rocky beaches. Birds take up nesting territories in early March and eggs are usually found about 25th April, while the earliest date for fledged young is 25th June.

There is a marked increase in numbers during October and early November and large flocks can be seen in many areas. Peak counts include a roost flock of c7,000 at Bay of Skaill, Sandwick on 24th November 1982 and c3,000 feeding on spilt grain in a stubble field at Brodgar, Stenness on 23rd November 1982.

Common Gulls counted with the Partial Wader Survey, January 1983 (Martin and Summers, 1983). Appendix II

Burray	Hoy group	Mainland	Sanday	S. Ronaldsay	Westray
59	560	2,057	1,286	396	180

Total counted: 4,538

There are a number of recoveries of young birds, ringed in Orkney, from several areas of Scotland, as far south as Dumfries. Single birds have been found in Ireland in November, Norway in May and Wales in September. Five birds ringed as young in Shetland have been recovered from August to October and single young birds from Iceland and Russia have been found in October and November respectively in Orkney.

Lesser Black-backed Gull

Larus fuscus

Passage migrant and local breeding species.

Buckley and Harvie-Brown (1891) recorded that, although there were a few pairs scattered throughout the islands, this species was only numerous in Walls (Hoy) and Rousay. Serle (1934) described it as an abundant summer resident on Hoy, breeding on the cliffs but more usually in large colonies on the ground. Lack (1943) noted that it had increased since 1919 and bred on moorland on a number of islands, especially Hoy, where there were large colonies inland. Balfour (1968) said there had been a marked decrease from the 1940's, but that there were signs of recovery. He suggested that egg collecting and the increase in numbers of the Great Black-backed Gull, which had colonised the old territories of the Lesser Black-backed Gull, were two of the possible causes of the decline.

The Lesser Black-backed Gull remains the scarcest of the breeding gulls in Orkney and only 800 pairs were counted in Seafarer, 1968-1970 (Cramp et al., 1974). The majority of pairs are in moorland colonies, often associated with Herring Gulls. In 1973, 38 pairs nested amongst Terns on North Hill, Papa Westray.

The only recent breeding counts are:

Papa Westray:
North Hill   52 pairs, 1982
Rousay:
Central moorland   202 pairs, 1981   (Lea, 1982)
Brings & Quandale   10 pairs, 1981

The first birds arrive in February, with the earliest date for the period 1974-1982 being 3rd, and most have left by the end of September. The last sighting is of a single, immature, bird on 31st October.

There have been a number of sightings, all of single birds, of the Scandinavian form *L.f.fuscus.*

On 16th April 1964 there were scores of Lesser Black-backed Gulls in Scapa Flow and one in five was noted to be of the Scandinavian form (S.B.3:144).

Full grown birds ringed in Surrey, Warwickshire and Worcestershire, from August to February, have been recovered in Orkney during the summer. Young birds ringed in Orkney have been recovered in Cornwall, France, Scotland and Spain in October and November, and a young bird ringed in Iceland was found in September five years later, in Orkney.

Herring Gull   White-maa

Larus argentatus

Common and widespread breeding species recorded throughout the year; passage migrant.

Since the time of Low (1813) this species has been recorded as common. Balfour (1972) described it as a numerous breeding species, found commonly on coasts and small islands and also at a few inland moorland localities.

There does not appear to have been any change in status, although there is very little recorded information. First eggs have been seen on 23rd April.

The Seafarer count of 1968-1970 found 7,800 pairs (Cramp et al., 1974).

The only recent breeding counts are:

Copinsay	210 pairs, 1974
Gairsay	22 nests, 1981
Papa Westray:	
North Hill	101 individuals, 1981
	83 pairs, 1982
Rousay:	
Central moorland	207 pairs, 1981 (Lea, 1982)

Peak winter counts include 320 at Stromness Harbour on 19th December 1982.

Herring Gulls counted with the Partial Wader Survey, January 1983 (Martin and Summers, 1983). Appendix II

Burray	Hoy group	Mainland	Sanday	S. Ronaldsay	Westray
9	39	243	939	167	184

Total counted: 1,581

Young birds ringed in Orkney have been recovered in Scotland, while young birds from the Faeroes, Norway and Shetland have been recovered in Orkney.

Sightings and recoveries of full grown birds, ringed in winter from areas as far south as Yorkshire, have been reported in spring and summer from Orkney.

Iceland Gull

Larus glaucoides

Scarce and irregular winter visitor.

Buckley and Harvie-Brown (1891) described this species as "an infrequent visitant," while Balfour (1972) regarded it as an irregular winter visitor, much less common than the Glaucous Gull.

There were relatively few sightings during the period 1972-1980 and all were of single birds. 1981 and 1982 were exceptional, however, with 79 sightings. Mainly single birds were seen, but a maximum of 4, possibly 5, was reported from Stromness on 28th December 1982.

For the period 1972-1982, the extreme dates were 4th October and 7th June.

Monthly distribution of sightings, 1972-1982

J	F	M	A	M	J	J	A	S	O	N	D
9	10	17	16	17	1	0	0	0	2	4	13

The majority of records in 1981 and 1982 were from Kirkwall and Stromness Harbours.

Glaucous Gull

Larus hyperboreus

Regular winter visitor in small numbers.

The Glaucous Gull is possibly a more frequent visitor now than it was in the 19th century, as Buckley and Harvie-Brown (1891) mentioned only a few records. Balfour (1972) described this species as a regular winter visitor in very small numbers.

During the period 1974-1982, it has been recorded annually although the number of sightings has fluctuated.

Annual sightings, 1974-1982

1974	1975	1976	1977	1978	1979	1980	1981	1982
4	14	23	27	12	11	23	62	50

There are records from all parts of the Mainland and from most of the islands. The majority of sightings are of single birds, but 2 and 3 have been reported on several occasions. The maximum is 4 on North Ronaldsay on 18th and 22nd October 1980.

Monthly distribution of sightings, 1974-1982

J	F	M	A	M	J	J	A	S	O	N	D
43	11	23	28	36	11	14	3	2	19	18	14

Balfour (1972) stated that most of the birds seen were sub-adults and this has certainly been the case in 1981 and 1982.

Year	Adults	Sub-adults	Total
1981	16	46	62
1982	3	47	50

Great Black-backed Gull   Baakie
Larus marinus

Common breeding species, present throughout the year.

This species was noted by Dunn (1837) and Baikie and Heddle (1848) as widely dispersed, but not numerous. Buckley and Harvie-Brown (1891) also stated it was widely distributed and mentioned a large colony on an island in the Loch of Swannay. Lack (1943) said that the species had generally increased and Balfour (1968) recorded that it had increased greatly, ousting the Lesser Black-backed Gull in some places. He reported that there were large colonies where, 25 years previously, there were only a few pairs.

The Great Black-backed Gull can be found nesting in large and small colonies or as isolated pairs. Some of the bigger colonies are on moorland, occasionally up to 3 miles from the sea; others are on small islands. Individual pairs may be found on rock stacks and also along the cliffs.

During the period 1974-1982, birds have been noted on territory by 16th February, the first eggs on 25th April and fledged young on 12th July. The Seafarer count, 1968-70, found a total of 6,000 pairs (Cramp et al., 1974). In 1968, there were an estimated 4,000 pairs on Hoy.

There are the following counts from the main colonies:

Calf of Eday	1,150 pairs, 1974
Copinsay	450 pairs, 1974
	480 pairs, 1975
Hoy	3,400 pairs, 1974
	(including 1,750 pairs, Burn of Forse, and 1,000 pairs, Stourdale)
Stronsay:	
Rothiesholm	360 pairs, 1979
	700-800 individuals, 1982

Counts from other colonies include:

Auskerry	125 pairs, 1974
Boray Holm	30 pairs, 1981
	10 pairs, 1982
Cava	20-25 pairs, 1980
Fara	145 pairs, 1976
	c50 pairs, 1982
Faray	190 pairs, 1974
Gairsay	18 pairs, 1981
Horse of	
Copinsay	160 pairs, 1980
	c250 individuals, 1982
Rousay: (Lea, 1982)	
Brings & Quandale	114 pairs, 1981
Central Moorland	198 pairs, 1981
Swona	45 pairs, 1976

Peak winter flock count was c200 on Muckle Green Holm, 15th January, 1982.

Great Black-backed Gulls counted with the Partial Wader Survey, January 1983 (Martin and Summers, 1983). Appendix II

Burray	Hoy group	Mainland	Sanday	South Ronaldsay	Westray
5	99	193	1,046	104	330

Total counted: 1,777.

Recoveries of birds, ringed as young in Orkney, show that many move south, down the east coast of Britain as far as Essex, and there is one recovery from Sussex. A young bird, ringed in Orkney in 1973, was found in Denmark in May 1974 and one ringed in 1974 was recovered in Holland in April 1975.

Single young birds, ringed on the Isle of May and North Rona, have been found in Orkney.

Kittiwake   Kittick

Rissa tridactyla

Common breeding species, recorded throughout the year.

The Kittiwake appears to have always been a common sight on Orkney's cliffs during the spring and summer months. In 1969 the islands were thought to support approximately 128,680 pairs (Cramp et al., 1974), equivalent to 27% of the British and Irish population.

Among the largest colonies are:

West Westray	60,000-70,000 pairs (Seafarer, 1968-70, Cramp et al., 1974)
Copinsay	10,000-12,000 apparently occupied nests (R.S.P.B. 1979, unpublished)
Marwick Head	9,700 apparently occupied nests (R.S.P.B. 1979, unpublished)

Changes in the number of Kittiwake nests detected under the monitoring programme (Appendix III) are shown in the following table:

Mean numbers of Kittiwake nests in sample plots within five colonies on Mainland, Orkney, in 1976 and 1982 and the proportional change between them.

Colony	Mean number of nests		% change
	1976	1982	
Costa Head	239	217	− 9.2
Row Head	677	418	−38.3
Marwick Head	1,059	656	−38.1
Gultack	286	226	−21.0
Mull Head	863	875*	+ 1.4
Total	3,124	2,392	−23.4

Numbers at Mull Head were increasing until 1980, but have since started to decrease.

Clearly the Kittiwake is undergoing a period of decline as a breeding species in Orkney (Wanless, Reynolds and Langslow, 1982).

Concentrations of Kittiwakes will sometimes be noted on the water in the vicinity of the breeding cliffs in February, and on 24th January 1982, 100 were seen bathing in a loch in Sandwick. Birds are usually recorded on the breeding ledges for the first time in early March, the earliest date during the period 1974-1982 being 4th.

In April and May, large numbers of birds can be seen collecting nesting material from nearby cliff tops, from fresh-water lochs and from the exposed seaweed-covered rocks close to the breeding sites. The earliest date for the first eggs is 10th May. The majority of young fledge in July and by early August the nesting cliffs are almost deserted; subsequent sightings are mainly of birds at sea.

There are several recoveries of nestlings ringed in July in Orkney:

Ringed	Recovered
Orkney, 1974	Ireland, June 1978
Orkney, 1975	Greenland, August 1977
Orkney, 1978	Greenland, September 1978

An adult, ringed at Berwick in May 1957, was found in Orkney in August 1959 and one ringed in Russia in July 1969 was recovered in Orkney in January 1972. Young birds from Norway and the Farne Islands have been found in Orkney in March and August respectively.

Ivory Gull

Pagophila eburnea

Rare.

Apart from two obtained in 1832 (Baikie and Heddle, 1848), all other records are of single birds:

1849	Shot (Buckley and Harvie-Brown, 1891)
1886	Longhope, shot in December (Buckley and Harvie-Brown, 1891)
1889	Westray, shot 9th December (Buckley and Harvie-Brown, 1891) (probably an immature bird)
1895	Holm, shot 1st April (S.N.1915:116)
1916	North Ronaldsay, 8th November (S.N.1917:151)

1918   North Ronaldsay, 3rd November (S.N.1919:102)
1920   Auskerry, 20th May (S.N.1921:109)
1935   Birsay, shot 6th February (Groundwater, 1974)
1948   Sanday, found dead, 14th April (Groundwater, 1974)
1949   Kirkwall Bay, 29th April-6th May (Balfour, 1972)

TERNS : Sternidae

Gull-billed Tern
Gelochelidon nilotica

Very rare.

The only record is of one on Pentland Skerries, 7th May 1913, which was a male in an exhausted condition (S.N.1913:154).

Sandwich Tern
Sterna sandvicensis

Regular breeding species; passage migrant.

Briggs (1894) reported 16 pairs arriving and nesting on North Ronaldsay in 1893, the first satisfactory breeding record for Orkney. In 1910, none bred on North Ronaldsay, but 40-50 pairs bred on Sanday (Lack, 1943). Lack stated that in recent years, until 1941, there have been colonies, increasing in size, on both islands (G. T. Arthur and others). He said there were two colonies on North Ronaldsay and that he saw possible breeding birds on Sanday and Stronsay. Balfour (1968) gave the following details of colonies:

North Ronaldsay	300 pairs in 1962 after a few years absence c150 pairs in 1963, but none nested in 1964 and 1965 200 pairs in 1967
Sanday	340 pairs, Whitemill Point in 1958 A small number of nests in 1965

Balfour (1972) mentioned that this species nests most constantly on North Ronaldsay and Sanday, but occasionally on other islands, such as Burray, Eday, Holm of Rendall, Stronsay and Wyre.

Orkney is the most northerly regular breeding area of the Sandwich Tern. The numbers of breeding birds fluctuate from year to year and the colony sites also vary.

The only full surveys of this species were carried out in 1969 (Cramp et al., 1974) when c290 pairs were counted and in 1980 (Bullock and Gomersall, 1981) when 119 pairs were found.

Counts of colonies—1969 and 1973-1982

Location	1969	1973	1974	1975	1976	1977	1978	1979	1980	1981	1982
Auskerry		2p									
Burray	1p										
Eday									8p		
Holm of Rendall	220p	100p	Bred				150p	80-100p	20p	c10p	103n
Mirkady (Deerness)		c40p			Bred						
North Ronaldsay	37p	c40p		60p			35p	5p			
Papa Stronsay					33n						
Papa Westray										1p	2p
Pentland Skerries				14p							26n
Rousay		10-20p									
Sanday	28p	26n	16n		81n	88n			110p	91p	98n
Stronsay			Bred	60n	c50n		35n				
Swona			1p								
Westray	7p										

p = counts of pairs   n = counts of nests

In the 1980 survey, Sandwich Terns were found breeding on unimproved sheep-grazed pasture or heath and also on shingle. Colonies were located as far as 300 metres inland and up to a height of 25 metres (Bullock and Gomersall, 1981).

The first birds usually arrive at the beginning of April and most have left by the end of September, but extreme dates for the period 1974-1982 are 24th March and 11th October. Fledged young have been seen on 10th July.

Young birds ringed in Orkney have been recovered as follows:

Ringed	Recovered
June 1968	Dahomey, May 1969
July 1973	Tayside, July 1981

July 1976   Ghana, October 1977
June 1977   Durham, September 1977
June 1981   Ivory Coast, February 1982

Roseate Tern
Sterna dougallii

Very rare.

There are the following records:
    1969   Up to 3 pairs carrying fish and displaying in Arctic
             Tern colony, Sanday
    1976   1 seen on several occasions between 21st and 27th
             May, amongst nesting Common Gulls and Arctic
             Terns, Sanday
    1980   1 Pentland Skerries, 3rd July

Although listed as breeding in 1969 (Cramp et al., 1974), no
nests were found and no young seen.

Common Tern   Pickie-terno, Ritto
Sterna hirundo

Regular breeding species in small numbers; passage migrant.

The first record of the Common Tern in Orkney was of a
bird shot on the Loch of Stenness in 1860 (Crichton, 1866).
Buckley and Harvie-Brown (1891) noted that it was found nesting
in the East Mainland in 1890. Balfour (1972) described it as a
"regular migrant breeder, the numbers not large."

In the period 1974-1982, the earliest date for arrival is 27th April,
but early May is the more usual time. At the end of the breeding
season, most birds have left by mid to late August, although a late
bird was seen on 9th October.

Most information on this species has been provided by
Seafarer, 1968-1970 (Cramp et al., 1974) and the R.S.P.B. Tern
Survey, 1980 (Bullock and Gomersall, 1981), when the following
totals were obtained:

    1969   200 pairs in 11 colonies
    1980   231 pairs in 28 colonies

Counts of pairs of Common Terns, main colonies only

Location	1969	1980
Burray	86	0
Eday	c15	7
Mainland	50	113
Pentland Skerries		73
Sanday	2	21
South Ronaldsay		14
Stronsay	11	3

In the 1980 survey, it was found that the average colony size was 8 pairs and that 58% of the nests were on rough grazing, but heath and shingle were other habitats used.

A young bird ringed in August in the Firth of Forth was found a month later in Orkney.

Arctic Tern   Pickie-terno, Ritto

Sterna paradisaea

Regular breeding species in large numbers; passage migrant.

All earlier writers mentioned the Arctic Tern as being plentiful in summer. Balfour (1972) described it as a fairly common migrant breeder, not as numerous as formerly.

This species may be found nesting on shingle, sand, rough grazing, improved pasture and arable land. The colonies, which are often dense, vary much in size; some may be 20 pairs or less, while the large colonies, like that of North Hill, Papa Westray, hold several thousand pairs and cover c200 hectares. Most colonies are found from sea-level up to 10 metres, with the highest at 90 metres, and over 50% are situated within 100 metres of the sea, (Bullock and Gomersall, 1981). There are several colonies in Orkney which regularly hold more than 1,000 pairs, including Auskerry, Flotta, Hoy, Papa Westray, Pentland Skerries and Rousay. The colonies, however, may vary in size and location from year to year.

During Operation Seafarer, 1968-1970, a total of about 32,000 pairs in 100 colonies was found, but this figure was later revised to 12,300 pairs (Cramp et al., 1974). A more comprehensive survey, with better coverage and using a new census technique, was carried out in 1980 and found a total of 33,069 pairs in 215 colonies (Bullock and Gomersall, 1981). This is about 43% of the British population and just over 25% of the total European breeding population. Although it was not possible to make direct comparison of the surveys, because of the different techniques each used, there was, nevertheless, some evidence that the population had increased since 1969.

Counts of pairs of Arctic Terns

Location	1969	1980
Eday	180	669
Hoy and Graemsay	c68	1,699
Mainland	797	1,682
North Ronaldsay	950	1,537
Papa Westray	17,865	7,653
Pentland Skerries	110	3,731
Rousay	624	4,951
Sanday	c470	3,179
Shapinsay	41	169
South Ronaldsay	339	770
Stronsay	c640	2,430
Walls and Flotta	c207	2,317
Westray	9,780	2,282
Totals	32,071	33,069

Birds generally arrive in early May but during the period 1974-1982, the earliest record was 11th April. Last sightings are usually towards the end of September; a late bird was seen on 20th October 1982 in North Ronaldsay.

Counts of colonies obtained in 1982 were:

7,000 birds Pentland Skerries, 6th June
5,322 birds North Hill, Papa Westray, 28th June
1,000 birds (3 colonies), Rousay, 4th July
1,000 birds, Eynhallow, 28th May

Birds ringed in Orkney have been recovered from Cameroon, Ghana, Liberia, Morocco, Nigeria, Portugal and Senegal, showing their southward passage, along the west coast of Africa, to the southern hemisphere.

A young bird ringed in July 1980 in Estonia, U.S.S.R., was found in Orkney in August of the same year.

Arctic Tern

Bridled Tern
Sterna anaethetus

Very rare.

The only record is of an immature bird in Stromness on 6th-7th August, 1979 (B.B.73:513).

Sooty Tern
Sterna fuscata

Very rare.

There is one record, that of a single bird at Isbister, Rendall on 22nd April 1954 (1971 B.O.U.:146)

Little Tern
Sterna albifrons

Rare.

This species has not bred in Orkney, as stated by Witherby (1939). In 1928, a "good many" were reported in Papa Westray and Holm in August (Baxter and Rintoul, 1953). Balfour (1972) said the Little Tern was an irregular passage visitor with a few seen in recent years.

Other records are:

1951	3 Graemeshall, Holm, 12th September
1961	Small party, St Margaret's Hope, South Ronaldsay, 5th-8th October (Balfour, unpublished)
	2 Lamb Holm, 12th October
1967	2 North Ronaldsay, 7th May
1971	3 Waulkmill Bay, Orphir, 4th June
1976	1 Longhope, South Walls, Hoy, 12th August
1981	1 Stenness, 4th August

Woodpigeon at nest in heather

K

Black Tern

Chlidonias niger

Rare.

There are the following records:
1913	1 Auskerry, 13th October
1965	1 North Ronaldsay, 7th May
	1 Westray, 26th May
1967	4 North Ronaldsay, 9th May
1968	1 Yesnaby, Sandwick, late May
	1 Tankerness, 15th September
1971	1 North Ronaldsay, 27th August
1974	1 Loch of Harray, 18th May
	1 off Copinsay, 22nd May
1975	2 Graemshall Loch, 7th June
1979	1 Birsay, 24th June
1980	1 Firth, 15th May
1982	1 Yesnaby, Sandwick, 12th July
	2 Deerness, 5th August

White-winged Black Tern

Chlidonias leucopterus

Very rare.

There are two records, both of single birds:
1966	Adult, North Ronaldsay, 11th-13th June (B.B.60:321;S.B.4:373)
1976	Adult, North Ronaldsay, 24th-26th May (B.B.71:509)

AUKS : Alcidae

Guillemot

Aak, Skout

Uria aalge

Common breeding species, present throughout the year.

It appears that this species has always been the most numerous of the auk family in Orkney. In the past, the Guillemot, together with other seabirds, constituted an important element in the economy of certain areas within Orkney, providing both food and feathers. Eggs were collected and birds trapped either on the ledges or in the air by a technique known as "swappin" — catching the bird in a net on the end of a long pole.

On Copinsay, Guillemot eggs were gathered regularly until the end of the 19th century, with a short revival of interest just before 1914. In Papa Westray the last auk "swappin" took place during the 1920's (Fenton, 1978).

Today the cliffs of Orkney continue to support large breeding concentrations of Guillemots, estimated to total 160,000 birds or 22% of the British and Irish population (R.S.P.B., 1979).

The largest colonies counted are:

West Westray   60,000-70,000 individuals (Seafarer, 1968-70, Cramp et al. 1974)
Marwick Head   32,000 individuals (R.S.P.B. 1979, unpublished)
Copinsay   30,000 individuals (R.S.P.B. 1979, unpublished)

Other counts include:

Papa Westray: Fowl Craig   2,060 individuals, 28th June 1977
                           2,070 individuals, June 1981
Pentland Skerries: 22 individuals, 6th June 1982
Switha: 280 individuals, mid-June, 1977

Regular occupation of the breeding ledges occurs during March and April, although birds may be seen on the cliffs, particularly during early morning, in the late autumn and winter. Large numbers of birds attend the colonies in May and June and include many non-breeding birds. During the breeding season, the numbers of Guillemots present on the cliffs exhibit a diurnal pattern of attendance, in which numbers are usually low at each end of the day, with two peaks being recorded in the 24 hour period (Hope Jones, 1978).

Eggs are laid on narrow cliff ledges and on scree slopes, the earliest date being 20th April 1981. A study in 1982, in which the hatching date for 44 chicks was determined, showed that the median date was 13th June (range 6th-22nd June) (Wanless, Reynolds and Langslow, 1982). The same study examined chick feeding frequencies during a 24 hour period on 16th-17th June 1982. Adult Guillemots brought in fish for the chicks throughout the hours of daylight (0230-2330), the rate being sightly higher just after dawn.

The flightless young leave the cliffs in large numbers during the third and fourth weeks of June. The colonies rapidly become deserted and the ledges are empty by late July-early August. In the winter months, however, birds can always be seen in limited numbers in such areas as Scapa Flow.

The monitoring programme (Appendix III) has shown that between 1976 and 1980 Guillemot numbers increased annually at all the monitored colonies, but since 1980 the increase has apparently halted and at present numbers appear relatively stable (Wanless, Reynolds and Langslow, 1982; Wanless, French, Harris and Langslow, 1982).

Balfour (1970), at Marwick Head, 1st June 1969, found 181 bridled birds (13.4%) out of 1,350 counted. Counts of bridled birds in 1981 were:

Papa Westray: Fowl Craig   173 out of 1,787 = 9.7%
Westray: Noup Head   140 out of 1,318 = 10.6%

Young birds ringed in Orkney have been recovered during August and September from Northumberland, Norway and Outer Hebrides and during November to March from Fife, Guernsey, Holland, Norfolk, Northumberland, Sussex and Yorkshire.

A young bird ringed on the island of Canna off the west coast of Scotland, was found in Orkney in October of the same year and a full grown bird from the island of Handa, off North-west Sutherland, was recovered in Orkney four years later, in March.

Brünnich's Guillemot
Uria lomvia

Very rare.

The only authenticated record is of a bird found dead in the Bay of Ireland, Stenness on 29th December 1981 (B.B.75:511).

Baikie and Heddle (1848) stated that the first specimen in Britain was shot in Orkney several years before their book was written and the specimen was preserved in the College Museum, Edinburgh. Witherby (1939) recorded that this species had possibly occurred in Orkney. Baxter and Rintoul (1953) considered all early records to be unsatisfactory and there is no mention of any Orkney records in the 1971 B.O.U. list.

Razorbill   Coulter-neb
Alca torda

Common breeding species, recorded throughout the year.

The Razorbill has been recorded as common since the time of Wallace (1700). It is widely distributed although not as numerous as the Guillemot. The Orkney population is estimated to consist of 9,000 birds (R.S.P.B., 1979) or 6% of the British and Irish population. The most important colonies include:

West Westray   3,000-4,000 individuals (Seafarer, 1968-70, Cramp et al. 1974).

Copinsay   1,000-1,200 individuals (R.S.P.B. 1979, unpublished).

Marwick Head   718+ individuals (R.S.P.B. 1979, incomplete survey, unpublished).

An additional count is:

40 individuals, Pentland Skerries, 6th June 1982.

The monitoring programme (Appendix III) has shown that at all colonies, except Row Head (Mainland), Razorbill numbers increased between 1976 and 1980. Since then the increase has apparently halted and numbers now appear to be relatively stable. At Row Head, where the number of Razorbills sampled is low, the population seems to have changed little since 1976 (Wanless, Reynolds and Langslow, 1982).

Razorbill numbers build up at the breeding cliffs during March and April. Eggs are usually laid in May and are incubated in crevices and ledge corners, in contrast to the more exposed ledges used by Guillemots. The earliest sighting of young is 27th May, the majority usually hatching during the third week of June.

There are the following ringing recoveries of young birds:

Ringed	Recovered
Orkney, July 1976	France, February 1977
Iceland, July 1982	Orkney, February 1983

A full grown bird, ringed on St Kilda in July 1976, was found in Orkney in June 1981.

Great Auk

Pinguinus impennis

Extinct.

A full account of the Great Auk in Orkney was given by Buckley and Harvie-Brown (1891). This species, which was said to have been always rare, was restricted to a single site on one island, namely, near Fowl Craig on Papa Westray.

The last known birds in Orkney were a female, killed in the summer of 1812, while incubating an egg, and the male, killed in May 1813.

Black Guillemot   Tystie, Tyste

Cepphus grylle

Resident breeding species.

All previous writers considered the Black Guillemot to be a fairly common breeding species in Orkney. Balfour (1972) stated that it bred in smallish, widely spread colonies on rocky coasts. Lack (1943) recorded that North Ronaldsay was colonised about 1939; 45 nests were counted there in 1969 (Cramp et al., 1974).

The Black Guillemot, which is predominantly an inshore and sedentary species, nests on boulder beaches, under flat stones, in crevices on cliffs and in caves, in rabbit burrows and on piers. During the period 1974-1982, a bird in full breeding plumage has been recorded on 23rd December, but most do not reach this plumage until early February. Display has been noted on 8th February and birds have been reported at their breeding sites from 11th March to mid-August.

The Seafarer count, 1968-1970 (Cramp et al., 1974) estimated Orkney's breeding population at 2,240 pairs, approximately 27% of the total British population. This figure was based on the number of individuals counted, converted to pairs on the assumption that only one bird of each pair would be visible. It seems likely that this figure is only an extremely rough guideline. The counts were not standardised in terms of time of year, time of day or coverage of potential breeding locations.

In 1982 the following counts were made at breeding colonies:

Auskerry	262 birds
Holm of Papa Westray	481 birds, 89 nests found
Hoy: Lyness Pier	50+ pairs

In a survey of 220 km of coastline in April 1983 (Tasker and Reynolds, 1983), 4,176 Black Guillemots were counted (see table on next page). 810 birds were found associated with breeding sites around Scapa Flow (including Switha) and this number may be regarded as virtually a total for this area as only two small potential breeding sites remain to be surveyed.

From winter counts made in Scapa Flow during the period 1974-1978, Lea (1980) concluded that at certain times there could be well over 1,000 Black Guillemots in the Flow and that the area supported between 5%-10% of the British population.

A colour ringed bird, ringed as a pullus on Fair Isle in 1973, was seen on Pentland Skerries in June 1982. Two young birds ringed in Orkney have been recovered in Caithness.

Survey of Black Guillemots, April 1983 (Tasker and Reynolds)

Island	Counts of individual birds
Papa Westray	150
Holm of Papa Westray	517
Eday	261
Calf of Eday	111
Faray	164
Holm of Faray	170
Kili Holm	13
Holm of Scockness	0
Egilsay	0
Wyre	0
Eynhallow	213
Muckle Green Holm	73
Little Green Holm	41
Stronsay	456
Auskerry	206
Gairsay	9*
Sweyn Holm	2*
Grass Holm	35*
Mainland	910*
Hoy	242*
Cava	42
Rysa Little	0
Fara	0
Flotta	98
Calf of Flotta	0
Switha	180
Hunda	0
South Ronaldsay	283

*Incomplete survey of island; all suitable habitats on the other islands listed were surveyed.

Little Auk   Rotchie

Alle alle

Winter visitor, generally in small numbers; irregular.

Sightings of this species depend mainly on the weather, when the birds are driven inshore by severe gales. Baikie and Heddle (1848) said that they occasionally appeared in great numbers and that they were "very abundant" in 1803, January 1812 and the winter of 1846/47. Baxter and Rintoul (1953) reported that the severe gale of December 1894 drove thousands of birds inshore. Balfour (1972) said the Little Auk occurred in small and irregular numbers.

During the period 1974-1982, most of the sightings were of single birds, with a maximum of 3 on 30th April 1976, just south of Hoy. Extreme dates for this period were 8th October and 30th April. An unusual record was of a bird in summer plumage, which came ashore on North Ronaldsay on 19th July 1976.

Distribution of monthly sightings, 1974-1982

J	F	M	A	M	J	J	A	S	O	N	D
8	8	0	1	0	0	1	0	0	2	6	6

Puffin
Tammy-norrie, Lyer, Lyre

Fratercula arctica

Widespread but local breeding species in small numbers.

The Puffin was known in Orkney at the time of Wallace (1700). Buckley and Harvie-Brown (1891) described the species as an abundant summer visitor, breeding on many of the islands. They were not aware of any large colonies. Balfour (1972) stated that it bred in smallish numbers at several places around the coast, including St John's Head and The Berry on Hoy, Costa Head on Mainland and Swona, but that there was a very large colony on Sule Skerry.

There does not appear to have been any recent change in status and groups of 1 to 5 birds may be seen on many of the cliffs. However, there is an indication of a long term decline in at least one area. Serle (1934) noted that the Puffin nested in great numbers in the sandy soil at the summit of the cliffs near St John's Head, Hoy. Although still nesting in the cliff face, they no longer nest in any numbers on the cliff top.

There is a large colony on Sule Skerry which has been studied by Blackburn and Budworth (1975-1982). They give the following population estimates:

1975	44,289 pairs
1979	35,622 pairs
1980	34,841 pairs
1982	44,000 pairs

Counts of birds from other colonies are:

Auskerry	250, mid-June 1977
	276, 2nd July 1982
Pentland Skerries	233, 17th May 1975
	250, 3rd July 1980
	259, 6th June 1982
Swona	439, July 1974
	200, 3rd July 1980

Birds return to their breeding cliffs from the end of March onwards and the last birds are seen there in mid-August. In 1982, birds were reported close to their breeding sites on 16th February.

There are few sightings after August and only three December records for the period 1974-1982.

Puffins ringed on Sule Skerry have been recovered from Algeria, Canary Islands, Cornwall, the Faeroes, France, Iceland, Newfoundland and Spain.

Colour ringed birds seen on Pentland Skerries were ringed as pulli as follows:

Date of sighting	Ringed
3rd July 1980	Isle of May, 1974
6th June 1982	Farne Islands, 1976
6th June 1982	Farne Islands, 1977
6th June 1982	Isle of May, 1979

There are also additional recoveries in Orkney of birds ringed as pulli on the Farne Islands, Isle of May and St Kilda.

A full grown bird, ringed in Norway in July 1979, was found in Orkney in November 1980.

SANDGROUSE : Pteroclididae

Pallas's Sandgrouse

Syrrhaptes paradoxus

Very rare.

There are records from two irruptions of this species in the 19th century:

1863   Observed on 8th June (Buckley and Harvie-Brown, 1891)

1888   Large scale irruption with birds reported from many areas from 17th May until October (Buckley and Harvie-Brown, 1891)

Although Balfour (1972) gives the most recent irruption as 1908, it has been impossible to confirm that birds occurred in Orkney.

PIGEONS AND DOVES:
Columbidae

Rock Dove   Doo
Columba livia

Common resident and breeding species.

Buckley and Harvie-Brown (1891) said this species was common everywhere, breeding in all the cliffs and rocks of the sea coast. Lack (1943) recorded the Rock Dove as abundant and Balfour (1972) said it was a widespread, common resident breeding species and that there was some inter-breeding with domestic pigeons gone feral. There is no change in status.

The Rock Dove is still mainly a bird of the rocky coasts, breeding in caves, rock fissures, quarries and derelict buildings, but it also nests on beaches of the more isolated holms.

This species is under-recorded and there is very little information. For the period 1974-1982, the only breeding counts are:

Holm of Papa Westray   12-15 pairs, July 1982
Switha   16 pairs, mid-June 1977

A nest with 2 young, about a week old, has been found on 24th April, while a late nest with a 2-week-old chick was seen on 20th October.

Peak flock counts include 700 on 12th December 1982 at Bookan, Sandwick and 550 at Birsay on 1st September 1979.

Stock Dove
Columba oenas

Very rare.

Records for 1849, 1859 and 1861 have been given by Buckley and Harvie-Brown (1891), but the only satisfactory record is 1 on Auskerry on 4th October 1913 (S.N.1914:8).

Balfour (1972) described this species as a passage visitor, rather irregular and numbers small. There are no records to support this statement.

Woodpigeon
Columba palumbus

Common breeding species, present throughout the year; possible passage migrant in small numbers.

This species was very rare in Orkney up to 1845, but it then spread rapidly on Mainland and there were occasional breeding records from Hoy. In 1883 a flock of 150-200 was seen in Orphir (Buckley and Harvie-Brown, 1891). Hale (1909) noted the colonisation of Shapinsay in 1907, and Lack (1943) recorded a continuing increase and spread and found the Wood Pigeon abundant in woods on Mainland and Rousay. He also reported a number on Shapinsay and saw 20 birds on Eday. A local inhabitant said that the species had only recently spread to Eday. Balfour (1968) stated that there had been a further small increase.

The Wood Pigeon is under-recorded as a breeding species and, during the period 1974-1982, there have been definite breeding reports from Eday, Hoy, Mainland, Rousay and Westray.

This species nests in trees and bushes, but in Orkney it has also adapted to ground nesting. Lack (1943) said that it nested regularly on the ground amongst heather and quoted G. T. Arthur as saying that this was unusual twenty years before. During the period 1974-1982, there are reports of nests in heather from Hoy, Mainland, Rousay and Westray and amongst *Juncus* and *Phragmites* from Birsay. In 1982, a nest was found under a rock, on a grassy cliff in St Ola. First young were seen on 5th May and a late nest found, with full grown young, on 18th October.

There are reports of passage movements from North Ronaldsay and Papa Westray. The majority of sightings are of 1-4 birds, but 6 were noted on North Ronaldsay on 9th August 1977.

Monthly distribution of sightings on North Ronaldsay, 1976-1982

J	F	M	A	M	J	J	A	S	O	N	D
0	2	8	10	15	4	1	3	1	6	0	0

Peak flock counts are 180 at Firth on 22nd October 1978 and 101 flying from Stenness towards Hoy on 5th December 1981.

A full grown bird ringed in Orkney in October 1979 was found in Caithness in January 1981.

Collared Dove

Streptopelia decaocto

Local but fairly common breeding species, present throughout the year.

The first record of this species in Orkney was from St Margaret's Hope, South Ronaldsay on 23rd July 1962 (S.B.2:247). Details of further sightings are given by Hudson (1965) and Macmillan (1965) and are summarised below:

1963	1 Holm, 25th April
	3 Balfour Castle Woods, Shapinsay, June, when a pair partly built a nest
	Records from Kirkwall, Binscarth Wood, Finstown, Firth and Rousay in the autumn
1964	A nest with eggs found in Binscarth Wood in May or June, 7 birds present in September
1965	20 birds seen in Binscarth Wood after the breeding season (Balfour, 1968)

Balfour (1972) stated that it was established in many locations but most numerous around Finstown, Kirkwall and Stromness.

There are sightings, during the period 1974-1982, of birds from almost all the islands, but it is an under-recorded species with the only definite breeding reports from Mainland. One pair attempted to breed at Widewall, South Ronaldsay in 1982. In 1976, a pair in Kirkwall reared two broods, the one young from the second brood fledging on 29th October. In 1977, 8-10 pairs were counted breeding at Berstane, St Ola.

There are reports of cream-coloured birds from Kirkwall and Stromness.

Flocks of 10-20 birds have been recorded fairly regularly from Mainland and South Ronaldsay, with peak counts of 60 at Berstane Wood, St Ola in August 1978 and 45 in Kirkwall in December 1974.

Possible migrant birds have been reported from April to October from Auskerry, Copinsay, North Ronaldsay and Papa Westray. The extreme dates are 5th April and 23rd October. The majority of sightings is of 1 to 5 birds, but 13 were recorded on North Ronaldsay on 4th June 1981.

A full grown bird ringed in Orkney in June 1979 was recovered in Kent in September 1981.

Turtle Dove
Streptopelia turtur

Regular passage migrant in small numbers.

The Turtle Dove has been described by early writers as an occasional visitor. Balfour (1972) said it was a regular passage visitor, in small numbers, in both spring and autumn.

This species has been recorded annually during the period 1974-1982. The extreme dates are 1st May and 23rd October and most of the sightings are of 1-2 birds, with a maximum of 4 on Westray on 8th May 1977.

Monthly distribution of sightings, 1974-1982

May	June	July	Aug.	Sept.	Oct.
21	25	12	1	10	20

CUCKOOS : Cuculidae

Great Spotted Cuckoo
Clamator glandarius

Very rare.

There is one record, an immature bird in Rendall from 14th-30th August 1959, which was seen to feed on caterpillars taken from cabbages. (B.B.53:421; S.B.1:153).

Cuckoo

Cuculus canorus

Regular passage migrant; occasionally breeds.

The Cuckoo in Orkney was first mentioned by Low (1813) and it appears to have occurred in small numbers and bred from time to time. Balfour (1972) described it as "a passage visitor and occasional migrant breeder. Regular in small numbers". Lack (1943), quoting G. T. Arthur, recorded that it parasitised Meadow Pipits and Dunnocks. In June 1975, a young one was seen being fed by Skylarks near Finstown and this was the only definite breeding record for the period 1974-1982. Displaying birds, however, were reported from Harray and Orphir in May and June, 1976-1979.

There are the following sightings of juvenile birds; it is unfortunately not possible to distinguish birds bred in Orkney from migrants:

1974	1 Shapinsay, September
	1 Kirkwall, September
1975	1 dead, Kirkwall, 18th August
1976	1 Evie, 31st July-4th August
1979	1 Papa Westray, 1st-4th August
1981	1 Holm, 24th September
1982	1 Kirkwall, 3rd August
	1 Kirkwall, 4th August
	1 dead Shapinsay, 26th August
	1 Rose Ness, Holm, 29th August

Monthly distribution of sightings, April-September, 1974-1982

April	May	June	July	Aug.	Sept.
3	84	36	5	19	8

The extreme dates for the above sightings are 27th April and 25th September.

Yellow-billed Cuckoo
Coccyzus americanus

Very rare.

The only records are of single birds:

1936	Birsay, a female on 22nd October (S.N.1937:46; B.B.31:125)
1956	Sandwick, 12th October (*The Orcadian*, 25th October, 1956)

BARN OWLS : Tytonidae

Barn Owl
Tyto alba

Very rare.

There are five records, all of single birds, of which four were definitely of the dark-breasted form *T.a.guttata:*

1900	Yesnaby, Sandwick (A.S.N.H.1900:246)
1925	Near Langskaill, Stromness, February (dark breasted) (Baxter and Rintoul, 1953)
1928	Near Kirkwall (dark-breasted) (Baxter and Rintoul, 1953)
1944	Dead, North Ronaldsay, 2nd November (dark-breasted) (*Island Saga*, 1967)
1979	Sanday, 22nd May (dark-breasted)

L

OWLS : Strigidae

Scops Owl
Otus scops

Very rare.

There are four records, all of single birds:

1892	North Ronaldsay lighthouse, caught 2nd June (A.S.N.H.1893:158)
1948	Westray, 30th April (Baxter and Rintoul, 1953)
1965	Kirkwall, 11th June (B.B.59:291; S.B.3:417)
1970	Holm, dead, 27th November (B.B.64:356)

Eagle Owl
Bubo bubo

Very rare.

The only record is of a bird shot on Sanday in 1830 (Baikie and Heddle, 1848; 1971 B.O.U. list).

Snowy Owl
Nyctea scandiaca

Rare.

This species has long been known in Orkney. Balfour (1972) said it was an irregular visitor, generally occurring in winter.

The following records have been obtained from the *Annals of Scottish Natural History* and *The Scottish Naturalist:*

1892	1 North Ronaldsay, 2nd November
1893	1 female, North Ronaldsay, 27th February
1899	1 North Ronaldsay, 1st February
	1 North Ronaldsay, 9th November
1913	1 Sule Skerry, 5th February

In 1963, a pair summered in suitable breeding habitat on Eday, but they did not breed (Balfour, 1972). Since then there have been the following sightings:

1965	1 North Ronaldsay, 11th-17th April
	1 North Ronaldsay, 5th-7th May (a different bird to the one recorded in April) (B.B.59:291)
1967	1 North Ronaldsay, 11th-26th May
	1 Westray, 19th May (B.B.61:347)
1972	1 Eday, 11th May; possibly the same bird on Papa Westray a few days later (B.B.66:344)
1974	2 Loch of St Tredwell, Papa Westray, 5th November (B.B.69:364)
1977	1 Birsay, 13th-16th May (B.B.71:510)
1981	1 first year female, Papa Westray, 21st May (B.B.75:511)
	1 adult female, North Ronaldsay, 27th May (B.B.75:511)
	1 first year male, North Ronaldsay, 2nd-4th June (B.B.75:511)
1982	1 female, Evie, 27th June (B.B.76:503)

[Little Owl]

Athene noctua

Balfour (1972) was extremely doubtful if this species ever occurred in Orkney. According to *Orcadian Papers* (1905), a nest of the Little Owl was taken in Woodwick Dale, but Omond (1925) thought this was most unlikely.

This species was probably confused with Tengmalm's Owl and cannot be included in the Orkney list.

[Tawny Owl]

Strix aluco

Although Low (1813) and Baikie and Heddle (1848) said this species occurred, there is no reliable evidence for this. Buckley and Harvie-Brown (1891) gave only one record, which they considered to be unsatisfactory, that of a bird shot on Sanday about 1869.

Omond (1925) stated that a specimen in Stromness Museum was obtained in Orkney, but this cannot be verified. Balfour (1972) regarded this record as doubtful and, as such, this species cannot be included in the Orkney list.

Long-eared Owl

Asio otus

Passage migrant and winter visitor; has bred.

Pennant (1789) wrote that the Long-eared Owl bred in Orkney, but Baikie and Heddle (1848) knew of only one record, a bird that had been killed on Sanday in 1817. Buckley and Harvie-Brown (1891) stated that it had become commoner, at least on Hoy, where it bred at Melsetter in 1882. They quoted Ranken who frequently saw this species in winter.

Omond (1925) said it was scarce, but resident, and that it bred at Binscarth, near Finstown. Lack (1943) saw several pairs which nested regularly in woods and, according to G. T. Arthur, rarely in heather on Mainland; he too mentioned wintering birds. According to Balfour (1968), possibly four to six pairs had nested annually for about ten years and, in 1972, he noted that small numbers wintered and a very few pairs bred in tree plantations, as at Binscarth and Trumland, Rousay.

There are very few details of the recent breeding history of this species in Orkney and these are given below:

1954	Brood of 3 young, ready to fly, Eday, 11th July
1955	1 pair, presumed nesting, Eday, 2nd July
1956	At least 1 pair breeding, Eday, 21st June
1968	At least 3 pairs, probably more, bred in Orkney
1970	A few pairs bred
1971	A few bred. This was the last breeding record

It is possible that the Long-eared Owl has been overlooked as a breeding species during the period 1974-1982, as it has only been recorded as a passage migrant and winter visitor. There are sightings for every month except August, with the majority reported from October to May. Numbers fluctuate from year to year, especially at winter roosts, as is shown in the following table:

Peak counts, Berstane Wood, St Ola, December/January, 1975-1982

1975/76	1976/77	1977/78	1978/79	1979/80	1980/81	1981/82
20-25	15-20	1	20-22	5	0	10

Winter roosts may be found wherever there are suitable groups of trees and bushes, but occasionally buildings are used. Peak counts from other winter roosts are:

Binscarth	15-20	February, 1977
Holm	6	January, 1979
Rendall	20	January, 1979
St Margaret's Hope	7	January, 1976
St Ola	10	December, 1978
Stromness	8	November, 1892

Analysis of pellets from winter roosts of the Long-eared Owl has shown that the Orkney Vole is one of the main prey items. Balfour (1963), at a roost in Binscarth Wood, found that this vole made up 78% of all prey taken, with House Mouse 14%, Brown Rat 5% and small birds about 3%. He noted that when there was a long period of snow cover, the percentage of voles in the pellets dropped to 37% and that of the House Mouse increased to 66%.

Other analyses are given below:

Roost site	Number of skulls						Bird remains
	No. of pellets	Ork. Vole	Wood Mouse	House Mouse	Brown Rat	Pygmy Shrew	
Binscarth, 1970-72 (Booth, 1972)	86	81	9	12	1	2	
St Ola, April 1971 (Booth, 1972)	26	26	2	0	1	1	
Binscarth, April 1982 (E. R. Meek, unpublished)	100	89	4	0	1	0	present in 5 pellets

Adam (1981) examined 500 pellets from a roost at Berstane Wood, St Ola, in 1979 and found that 40% contained bird remains, and there were also 26 B.T.O. rings. He thought that this very high percentage of bird remains was not typical and was due to exploitation, by the owls, of a readily available food supply during a prolonged period of snow cover. There was a very large roost of Starlings, Redwings and other thrushes in the wood at this time.

A Long-eared Owl roosted in farm buildings on the island of

Copinsay in March, 1976 and analysis of 12 pellets showed that they contained 20 skulls of House Mice.

There are the following ringing recoveries of full grown birds:

Ringed	Recovered
Orkney, February 1971	Ireland, March 1974
Orkney, December 1978	Lapland, Sweden, May 1979

Short-eared Owl   Cattie-face
Asio flammeus

Fairly common breeding species and passage migrant.

Low, during his tour of 1774, saw several Short-eared Owls on Hoy and Baikie and Heddle (1848) stated that this species was very common, remaining throughout the year, but that it was especially abundant about harvest time. Buckley and Harvie-Brown (1891) said that it was decreasing because of egg collecting and the burning of heather for pasture land. They noted breeding on Mainland and Rousay. In 1910, Hale and Aldworth found several nests on Mainland and Shapinsay, also one on Sanday (Lack, 1943). Baxter saw "a good many" pairs on Sanday in 1927 (Baxter and Rintoul, 1953) while Lack (1943) recorded breeding on Mainland, with one or more pairs on Rousay and Sanday. He said that the numbers of Short-eared Owls had increased, thanks to protection, but had not reached former levels. Balfour (1972) commented that the species bred fairly commonly in fluctuating numbers on most of the larger islands.

The Short-eared Owl nests in heather, *Juncus* and coarse grass, from 15 metres up to 150 metres above sea-level. In 1982, a nest was found in a silage field on Sanday. Eggs have been found in the first week of April, but young from late nests may not fledge until the end of July.

In the period 1974-1982, the number of nesting pairs has fluctuated and breeding has been reported as follows:

Eday	1 pair definitely bred in 1982; birds present in other years.
Hoy	Single pairs definitely bred in 1974, 1975 and 1976. Maximum of 2-3 pairs in any one year. Birds noted at two and sometimes three different sites.

Mainland	Probably 40-60 pairs annually.
Rousay	c6 pairs bred in 1977.
	2 pairs on Central moorland in 1981 (Lea, 1982).
Sanday	4 pairs bred in 1982; this would probably be the maximum annual number for 1974-1982. Birds were seen during the breeding season from 1974-1979, but none were present in 1981.
South Ronaldsay	2 Pairs bred in 1982.
	Birds seen in summer, 1974-1981.

The number of sightings of birds increases from late February and appears to fall in August, with few reported from November to mid-January. An unusual record is of 4 birds engaged in high altitude chasing and calling on Sanday on 2nd November 1982.

The lack of sightings in autumn and winter may be due to fewer owls being present at this time, but there may also be a change in feeding behaviour, with the birds hunting at dawn, dusk and at night, when they are less obvious.

Probable migrants have been seen on North Ronaldsay from April to June and August to November, on the Pentland Skerries in April and Papa Westray in May and September.

The Orkney Vole has long been known as an important prey item of the Short-eared Owl in Orkney. Heppleston (1978) analysed 205 pellets, collected between the winter of 1973 and the summer of 1975. He found that they contained 300 prey items The percentage representation of the different prey species is shown below:

Orkney Vole	Wood Mouse	House Mouse	Pygmy Shrew	Brown Rat	Rabbit
82.7	2.0	1.0	2.0	5.0	7.0

In terms of weight, the Orkney Vole accounted for 56% of the diet, with young Rabbits and Brown Rats together providing 41%. It can be seen that, combined, young Rabbits and Brown Rats are almost as important in nutritional value as the Orkney Vole. Remains of young Rabbits are frequently found at nests where there are young owls. Bird remains found at nests include full grown Arctic Tern and Blackbird and the young of Common Gull, Lapwing and Redshank (Booth, unpublished).

There are the following recoveries of birds ringed as pulli:

Ringed	Recovered
Orkney, June 1977	Dumfriesshire, October 1977
Grampian, May 1981	Orkney, October 1981

Tengmalm's Owl

Aegolius funereus

Very rare.

There are the following records, all of single birds:

1959/60 Cruan, Firth, 26th and 27th December 1959 and
        1st January 1960 (B.B.55:565, 566)
1961   Stromness, 1st May (B.B.55:576)
1980   Binscarth (trapped) 13th-20th October (B.B.74:479)
        Binscarth (died), 18th November (B.B.74:479)

A small owl, possibly of this species, was killed at Melsetter, Hoy on 7th November 1851 and was reported by Buckley and Harvie-Brown (1891) as follows: "The bird had remained all summer in a tree near the house, within 12 feet of the dining-room window. Dr Heddle, who had only arrived the evening before, was not aware of this and killed it with such a large charge of snipe-shot at close range, that the skin was spoilt—the wings, however, were put in spirits". There is a note at the foot of the page—it reads "The wings are not now forthcoming"!

NIGHTJARS : Caprimulgidae

Nightjar
Caprimulgus europaeus

Rare pasage migrant.

Balfour (1972) described this species as a scarce and irregular passage visitor.

It has been possible to trace 20 records between 1810 and 1971, all of single birds except for the following:

1810	2 Lopness, Sanday, during summer.
1868	2 Kirkwall, April.
1888	2 Sanday, about 4th June.

Most sightings have occurred in the spring and, excluding the above records, the extreme dates for all other spring sightings are 6th May and 18th June.

Fortnightly distribution of sightings, 1810-1971

May 6th- May 19th	May 20th- June 2nd	June 3rd- June 16th	June 17th- June 30th
3	7	4	1

The only autumn records are:

1906	Pentland Skerries, 2nd October
1968	North Ronaldsay, for at least two weeks in early September

Common Nighthawk
Chordeiles minor

Very rare.

1 near Kirkwall, trapped, 12th September 1978 (B.B.72:529; S.B.11:85) is the only record.

SWIFTS : Apodidae

Swift

Apus apus

Regular passage visitor.

The Swift was recorded as an infrequent visitor by Buckley and Harvie-Brown (1891), but Balfour (1972) described it as a fairly regular passage visitor in small numbers.

This species has been reported annually from 1974-1982, with the extreme dates of 7th May and 26th October. The majority of sightings have been of 1-6 birds, with a maximum of 40 on Papa Westray in July 1980. In 1969, a count of 45 was reported from Rendall on 23rd July.

Monthly distribution of sightings, 1974-1982

May	June	July	August	September	October
38	66	84	36	31	14

Alpine Swift

Apus melba

Very rare.

The only record is of 1 trapped on North Ronaldsay, 8th June 1965 (B.B.59:292;S.B.3:418).

KINGFISHERS : Alcedinidae

Kingfisher

Alcedo atthis

Very rare.

Low (1813) mentioned seeing one in Orkney. There are four other records, all of single birds:

1936   Voy, Sandwick (now in Stromness Museum).
1952   Harray, August (*The Orcadian*, 18th September 1952).
1953   Rendall, 2nd September (Balfour, unpublished).
1975   Near Scapa Distillery, Kirkwall, 10th May.

BEE-EATERS : Meropidae

Bee-eater
Merops apiaster

Very rare.

There are the following records:

1966   3 Binscarth, Firth, 31st May-5th June (B.B.60:322)
1969   1 dead, Sanday, 25th May
        1 Westray, 29th and 30th May (B.B.63:282)
1979   1 Kirkwall, 15th-26th July (B.B.73:516)
1982   1 Rousay, 7th June (B.B.76:504)

ROLLERS : Coraciidae

Roller
Coracias garrulus

Very rare.

The first mention of the Roller in Orkney was made by Wallace (1700). Baikie and Heddle (1848) gave several reports and Buckley and Harvie-Brown (1891) noted the following records:

1843   1 South Ronaldsay, caught by a cat, mid-June.
1869   1 Sanday, shot, October.
1874   1 Eday, dead, in winter.
1889   1 Sandwick, October.
1890   2 Westray, 10th November.

Buckley and Harvie-Brown also stated that one was shot at Melsetter, Hoy, but no date was given, and that 7 were seen in 30 years on Sanday.

The only other records, all of single birds, are:

1896   Westray, June (A.S.N.H.1896:252).

1937   Stronsay, May (*The Orcadian*, 8th July 1937).

1950   Westray, July (*The Orcadian*, 10th August 1950).

1958   Rendall, 27th May, then possibly the same bird at East Mainland on 5th-7th June, 19th June and at Wideford Brae, near Kirkwall until 21st July. (S.B.1:96; F.I.B.O.B.4:65).

1966   North Ronaldsay, 11th June (B.B.60:323; S.B.4:375).

HOOPOES : Upupidae

Hoopoe

Upupa epops

Scarce and irregular visitor.

Wallace (1700) reported that the Hoopoe occurred in Orkney. During the 19th century, there are a number of records, including that of a flock of 14 on Sanday in 1842 (Buckley and Harvie-Brown, 1891).

There are several reported sightings of this species for the period 1915-1982. The extreme dates in spring are 3rd April and 19th May and, in autumn, 17th September and 17th October.

Fortnightly distribution of sightings, 1915-1982

Apr. 1st- Apr. 14th	Apr. 15th- Apr. 28th	Apr. 29th- May 12th	May 13th- May 26th	Sept. 15th- Sept. 28th	Sept. 29th- Oct. 12th	Oct. 13th- Oct. 26th
1	4	4	1	5	4	2

From 1974-1982, there have been 6 records, two each in 1975 and 1978 and single birds in 1977 and 1981.

WOODPECKERS : Picidae

Wryneck

Jynx torquilla

Uncommon but regular passage migrant.

This species, according to Balfour (1972), was a rather scarce, but more or less regular passage visitor.

During the period 1974-1982, it has been recorded annually, being more numerous in autumn. The extreme dates, in spring, are 3rd and 29th May and, in autumn, 14th August and 6th October. Most sightings are of single birds, but a maximum of 3 was seen on North Ronaldsay on 14th September 1981.

Monthly distribution of autumn sightings, 1974-1982

August	September	October
9	26	5

Green Woodpecker
Picus viridis

Very rare.

The only authenticated record is that of one seen in a Kirkwall garden in July, 1885 (Buckley and Harvie-Brown, 1891).

Great Spotted Woodpecker
Dendrocopos major

Irregular passage migrant and occasional winter visitor.

From the time of Baikie and Heddle (1848), this species has been noted as an occasional visitor. In September 1861, there was an irruption, mainly of immature birds, and an even greater influx in 1868, again involving young birds (Buckley and Harvie-Brown, 1891). Balfour (1972) recorded it as a passage and occasional winter visitor, tending to be irruptive.

During the period 1974-1982, the Great Spotted Woodpecker has been reported annually, except for 1977, 1978 and 1981. All the sightings have been of single birds and occurred between 30th March and 20th November.

In 1976 a bird was seen and heard drumming in June and July in Trumland Woods, Rousay.

Monthly distribution of sightings, 1974-1982

Mar.	Apr.	May	June	July	Aug.	Sept.	Oct.	Nov.
1	1	2	2	1	1	3	8	4

In 1968, there was a moderate influx from about 7th September continuing into October, with sightings of 2-6 birds from several islands. A few birds wintered and there were reports from Binscarth, Firth (1), Woodwick, Evie (2), Rousay (1) and Stromness (1) until late April 1969.

[Lesser Spotted Woodpecker]
Dendrocopos minor

This species was listed by Baikie and Heddle (1848), Buckley and Harvie-Brown (1891) and Omond (1925) as having occurred in

Orkney. Baxter and Rintoul (1953), however, concluded that all records were unsatisfactory. This species therefore cannot be included in the Orkney list.

LARKS : Alaudidae

Short-toed Lark
Calandrella brachydactyla

Very rare visitor.

There is just one record, that of a single bird on Auskerry on 1st October 1913 (S.N.1914:6).

Woodlark
Lullula arborea

Very rare visitor

Only four birds have been recorded:

1911	1 Pentland Skerries, 21st October (S.N.E.P. No.1 1912:33)
1912	1 Auskerry, 26th October (S.N.E.P. No.2 1913:41)
1913	Single birds, Auskerry 11th and 21st October (S.N.E.P. No.3 1914:41)

Skylark   Laverock, Lavero, Lady's Hen
Alauda arvensis

Common breeding species; some birds winter; passage migrant.

Recorded by Buckley and Harvie-Brown (1891) as very abundant and resident in all the islands. Lack (1943) found it common in all cultivated and grass land, very scarce in pure heather moorland but common on grass moorland, including bogs and the bare hilltops of Hoy above 1,000 feet. Balfour (1968) noted no change in status, but subsequently (1972) indicated that the species was less numerous than formerly. There does not appear to be any recent change.

During the period 1974-1982, the earliest recorded date for song was 20th January. The only breeding counts available are:

Cava	3 pairs, 1980
Gairsay	17 pairs, 1981
Rousay:	
Central Moorland	41 pairs, 1981 (Lea, 1982)
North Fara	c10 pairs, 1982

The main passage movements occur in March and early April and during the last two weeks of September and throughout October. Wintering birds have been recorded in many areas, although they are usually absent from hilltops at this time of the year. Maximum counts include 150 on South Ronaldsay, 8th December 1981 and 73 on Sanday, 8th February 1982. During periods of snow cover, birds may be found feeding on the shore.

A bird ringed on North Ronaldsay in September was recovered in January over 4 years later in Lincolnshire, and a pullus ringed in Shetland was controlled in September two years later on North Ronaldsay.

Shore Lark
Eremophila alpestris

Rare passage migrant.

There are the following records:

1913	1 Pentland Skerries, 13th October
	2 Auskerry, 30th October, 1 on 2nd November, 2 on 3rd November (S.N.E.P. No. 3 1914:42)
1915	1 Graemsay, 25th March
	2 Swona, 16th October (S.N.1916:177)
1972	2 Papa Westray, 18th May
1976	3 Copinsay, 24th April
	1 Hundland, 9th October
	2 Sandwick, 31st October
	North Ronaldsay—3 on 5th October, 60 on 6th October, 40 on 7th October, 20 on 21st October

1977	2 North Ronaldsay, 3rd March
	3 Birsay, 1st April
	1 Westray, 28th September
1981	1 Papa Westray, 22nd May
	North Ronaldsay—2 on 9th October, 1 on 10th and 11th October, 4 from 15th to 24th October, 2 Westray, 15th November

MARTINS AND SWALLOWS:
Hirundinidae

Sand Martin   Witchuck
Riparia riparia

Passage migrant; has bred.

Recorded by Low (1813) as "the most common bird of the Swallow tribe in the Orkney Isles". He found it breeding on Mainland at the Loch of Stenness and at Skaill, Sandwick. Baikie and Heddle (1848) also recorded breeding at these places and on Sanday. There must then have been a decrease, as Buckley and Harvie-Brown (1891) stated that it no longer bred at Skaill and mentioned a letter from Moodie-Heddle in which he said that "the Sand Martin is much scarcer than formerly, perhaps owing to an increase in Brown Rats; it used to breed near Melsetter, Hoy". Lack (1943) noted that G. T. Arthur had only twice found a nest since 1918, both times on Mainland. There are no further breeding records.

It is a regular passage migrant but only in small numbers, the maximum recorded at one time being 10 on Sanday on 22nd May 1979. During the period 1975-1982, the extreme dates were 14th April and 13th October.

Monthly distribution of sightings, 1975-1982

April	May	June	July	Aug.	Sept.	Oct.
3	50	6	1	4	11	2

M

Swallow
Hirundo rustica

Uncommon breeding species and passage migrant.

The number of Swallows breeding in Orkney seems to have fluctuated. Low (1813) found them breeding, although not in great numbers, in Kirkwall, while Buckley and Harvie-Brown (1891) suggested that, having at one time been fairly common, they had become scarce but were apparently increasing. Lack (1943) found no nests in 1941, but stated that in normal years they were liable to breed on any island. Balfour (1972) noted that the Swallow bred regularly in very small numbers.

There has probably been an increase during the period 1974-1982, although perhaps no more than 50 pairs bred in any one year. Nesting has been recorded on the following islands: Flotta, Hoy (Lyness and Melsetter), Mainland (Birsay, Deerness, Dounby, Evie, Firth, Orphir, Sandwick, Stenness, Stromness and Tankerness), Rousay, Sanday and South Ronaldsay.

In 1982 a total of 25 pairs were located on Mainland, of which 13 definitely raised two broods. The majority of pairs were in the West Mainland and most of the sites were in buildings away from farms, mainly old air-raid shelters.

The main passage occurs in May and September, the extreme dates being 4th April and 7th November.

Red-rumped Swallow
Hirundo daurica

Very rare.

There is only one record, a single bird seen on North Ronaldsay on 7th October 1976 (B.B.71:511).

House Martin
Delichon urbica

Passage migrant, occasionally breeds.

The House Martin was found by Low (1813) nesting in the corners of the windows of St Magnus Cathedral, Kirkwall. Buckley and Harvie-Brown (1891) also recorded that nesting had occurred on the Cathedral and mentioned breeding having taken place at Birsay, Evie, Hoy, Skaill (Sandwick) and St Margaret's Hope, South Ronaldsay. They also thought that the House Martin fluctuated both as a breeding species and a migrant. Lack (1943) did not find a nest in 1941, but stated that in normal years G. T. Arthur had found nests both on buildings and cliffs. Balfour (1968) commented that it had not bred regularly since 1941.

The only recent breeding records available, all of single pairs are:

1956	Skaill, Sandwick
1969	Finstown
1977	Pierowall, Westray

The main passage movements occur in May and June, and again in late September and early October. The extreme dates for the period 1974-1982 are 21st April and 31st October. There is a late record of a bird seen on 2nd November 1963.

PIPITS AND WAGTAILS:
Motacillidae

Richard's Pipit
Anthus novaeseelandiae

Very rare.

There are eight records, all of single birds:

1967	North Ronaldsay, 13th April (B.B.61:353)
1968	North Ronaldsay, 2nd October and 26th October (B.B.62:482)
1969	North Ronaldsay, 1st-3rd November (B.B.63:287)
1970	North Ronaldsay, 28th September (B.B.64:362)
1975	Deerness, 2nd November (S.B.9:228)
1981	Deerness, 12th September (B.B.75:514)
1983	North Ronaldsay, 21st September (in litt.)

Tree Pipit
Anthus trivialis

Passage migrant.

A regular passage migrant in May, September and October, usually in small numbers. All sightings between 1974 and 1982 have been of 1-5 birds. The extreme dates in spring are 3rd May and 28th May. There is a single record on 28th June and in autumn all reports have been from 25th August to 19th October.

Monthly distribution of sightings, 1974-1982

May	June	July	August	Sept.	Oct.
14	1	0	2	19	4

In May 1969 there was an exceptional fall of Tree Pipits with over 300 counted in a small part of South Ronaldsay on the 5th.

Meadow Pipit   Teeting, Titlark
Anthus pratensis

Common breeding species and passage migrant; a few birds winter.

The Meadow Pipit was recorded as a common species by earlier writers, although Buckley and Harvie-Brown (1891) thought that it was less common than in other parts of Scotland. Balfour (1972) stated that it was common on all islands with moorland and there does not appear to have been any change in status.

Breeding counts include:

Cava	4 pairs, 1980
Gairsay	26 pairs, 1981
Rousay: Central moorland	77 Pairs, 1981 (Lea, 1982)
Pentland Skerries	at least 1 pair, 1982

An increase in numbers takes place during August, with the main passage occurring in September and early October. The majority of birds have departed by the end of October. There are records of probable wintering birds in December and January with 1-5 individuals being involved; reports have come from Burray, Evie, Firth, Holm, Gairsay, North Ronaldsay, Orphir, Rousay, St

Ola, Stenness, Stromness and Tankerness. The return to the breeding territories occurs in March and early April.

A pullus ringed in Orkney was recovered in Spain in December of the same year and a full grown bird from Orkney, ringed in September, was found in Spain a month later.

Red-throated Pipit
Anthus cervinus

Very rare.

There are two records, both of single birds:

1913	Auskerry, 1st October, a first year male. (S.N.1914:6).
1978	Mull Head, Papa Westray, 4th June (B.B.72:531).

Rock Pipit   Tang Sparrow
Anthus spinoletta

Common resident, passage migrant and winter visitor.

This species is widely distributed around the coasts of all the islands and, in autumn, flocks of up to 20 birds are not unusual. In winter it is not confined to the coast and there are a number of records from inland localities. Song has been heard as early as 27th February. Breeding counts include:

Cava	3 pairs, 1980
Gairsay	min. 11 pairs, 1981
Papa Westray: North Hill	14 pairs, 1981
Pentland Skerries	min. 3 pairs, 1982

A bird of the Scandinavian race *A.s.littoralis* was recorded on Pentland Skerries on 9th May 1912 (S.N.E.P. No. 2, 1913:9).

Five birds, two of them pulli, ringed on Fair Isle between June and August have been recovered in Orkney from November to March, indicating that there is some movement of birds between the islands.

Yellow Wagtail
Motacilla flava

Passage migrant; has bred.

The record of breeding at Melsetter, Hoy in 1880 and 1881, given by Buckley and Harvie-Brown (1891), has not been generally accepted by later writers, due to possible confusion with the Grey Wagtail and the fact that Orkney is well beyond the normal breeding range in Britain. However, in 1979 a pair bred successfully on Papa Westray, rearing three young, and in 1980 a pair was seen on Westray carrying food on 11th June; they were very agitated but no nest or young were found.

This species is a passage migrant in very small numbers, the majority of sightings being in May and September. The extreme dates in spring are 3rd May and 12th June, in autumn 12th September and 30th September.

Monthly distribution of sightings (excluding those breeding on Papa Westray and Westray), 1968-1982

May	June	July	August	September
12	2	0	0	8

The only record in which the race was specified was that of a male *M.f.flavissima* on Copinsay, 3rd and 4th May 1975.

Grey Wagtail
Motacilla cinerea

Passage migrant; irregular breeding species.

The first mention of nesting was by Buckley and Harvie-Brown (1891); quoting Moodie-Heddle, they stated that the species bred occasionally on Hoy. Lack (1943) noted that G. T. Arthur had twice found a nest by streams on Mainland since 1918. Balfour (1968) stated that it had not bred in the last 25 years.

A bird was seen on Hoy, near suitable breeding habitat, in July 1973 and during the period 1974-1982 breeding has been proved annually, except in 1975. Details of breeding are given below:

    1974   A pair bred in Firth, rearing 4 young.

1975	Birds seen in April near site where they bred in 1974, also seen in July when there was a juvenile in the area.
1976	Pairs bred successfully in Evie, Firth and St Ola.
1977	A pair reared two broods in St Ola.
1978	A pair reared two broods in St Ola.
1979	A pair failed, St Ola; there was probably a second pair.
1980	A pair bred in St Ola, rearing 6 young.
1981	A pair bred in St Ola, with possibly a second brood. A pair was seen feeding a fledged young, Hoy, on 22nd July.
1982	A pair seen on Hoy, with at least 1 fledged young.

Breeding birds have been noted on territory from 2nd February and the earliest date for fledged young is 8th May.

Balfour (1972) stated that this species was a rather scarce passage visitor. From 1974-1982, it has been recorded regularly on passage in September and October, with a number of sightings in November and December.

Pied Wagtail   Willie Wagtail
Motacilla alba yarrellii

Widespread breeding species, passage migrant; a few birds winter.

The status of the Pied Wagtail in Orkney has fluctuated during the last two hundred years. Low (1813) considered it migratory, while Baikie and Heddle (1848) said that it was very abundant, but Buckley and Harvie-Brown (1891) stated that it was resident, breeding on some of the larger islands, although less numerous in winter. Lack (1943) found it very local in 1941, with a few pairs breeding on several islands. Balfour (1968) noted that it was formerly a common breeding species which had decreased rapidly from 1935 and was still scarce; however in 1972 he commented that it had begun to increase. During the period 1974-1982, this increase continued and the Pied Wagtail is now widespread, as a breeding species, throughout the islands. Counts made in 1981 include 4 pairs on Gairsay, 3 pairs on North Ronaldsay and several pairs on Papa Westray.

The influx of breeding birds starts in early March and they are well distributed by the end of the month. In autumn there is a build-up of numbers in August, with an obvious decrease during October.

The majority of records of wintering birds are from Kirkwall and St Ola, but there are also some from Evie, Sandwick and Stromness. Most sightings are of single birds, but two have been recorded on a number of occasions. A favoured area for these birds is the Papdale School complex in Kirkwall.

Pulli ringed in Orkney have been recovered in Aberdeen (January), Cornwall (April), Merseyside (November) and Avon (December). An adult bird, ringed in Orkney in April, was recovered in Spain in October.

White Wagtail *M.a.alba.* This species is a regular passage migrant and has also bred on rare occasions (Balfour, 1972). During the period 1974-1982, it has been recorded in spring between 28th March and 10th June, with a maximum of 10 in South Ronaldsay on 14th April 1980, and in autumn between 23rd August and 22nd September, with a maximum of 10 in Deerness on 22nd September 1975.

WAXWINGS : Bombycillidae

Waxwing
Bombycilla garrulus

Irregular passage migrant and winter visitor.

This is an irruptive species, in some years occurring in moderate numbers, but in others none are seen. It is most often reported from gardens in Kirkwall and Stromness, where it is found feeding on Cotoneaster and other berries. During the period 1974-1982, it was recorded from October to April, the majority of sightings being in the last two weeks of October and throughout November, with the extreme dates of 2nd October and 22nd April. There were no sightings in 1978 or 1980 and only two each in 1979 and 1982.

The last large influx was in 1975, when a maximum of 30 was seen in Kirkwall on 1st November. Other recent irruptions have occurred in 1957, 1960, 1965 and 1970 (Balfour, unpublished). A flock of c200 was recorded in Tankerness on 1st March 1957 (Clouston).

The Waxwing probably occurs more regularly now than it did in the 19th century, as Buckley and Harvie-Brown (1891) gave only four records, all of birds killed, two in 1851 and singles in 1852 and 1864.

A bird ringed in Norway in late October was recovered ten days later in Kirkwall.

DIPPERS : Cinclidae

Dipper

Cinclus cinclus gularis

Rare visitor; has bred.

There was only one record given by Buckley and Harvie-Brown (1891), a single bird seen at Rackwick Burn, Hoy at the end of August 1883. The next report of this species in Orkney was again from Hoy in 1919 (Baxter and Rintoul, 1953) and breeding probably occurred there fairly regularly during the next twenty years.

Omond (1925) stated that, although formerly a rare visitor, the Dipper had been seen in summer on Hoy and could be considered a resident breeding species. There is a record in *The Orcadian* of 15th December 1927 of a bird found dead on Hoy, probably on 10th December; in addition there is a specimen in Stromness Museum, dated 1928. Serle (1934) saw Dippers on Rackwick Burn in 1933 and noted that they were said to breed there every year. Lack (1943) found one on Segal Burn, Hoy in 1941 but none on Rackwick or Pegal Burns; he did not visit Mill or Lyrawa Burns where it had been reported in previous years. The Dipper ceased to nest on Hoy in 1940-41 (Balfour, 1968).

In 1969 a bird was seen on 23rd and 24th June on Hoy in suitable breeding habitat and in 1970 there were several sightings and an empty nest was found. Since then there have been the following records:

1972   1 Hoy, 9th September.
1973   1 Hoy, 5th May.
1974   A pair was present on Rackwick Burn throughout the summer, but breeding was not proved.

Black-bellied Dipper *C.c.cinclus.* A bird of this race was seen on North Ronaldsay on 4th April 1965 (S.B.3:374).

WRENS : Troglodytidae

Wren   Jenny Wren

Troglodytes troglodytes

Common resident, passage migrant.

The status of the Wren does not appear to have changed significantly in the last two hundred years. Balfour (1968) said that it was common and widespread but declined in hard winters. During the period 1974-1982, the effect of cold weather on numbers was noticeable in both 1979 and 1982.

This species is most commonly found in areas of thick heather, along burns and ditches, on low cliffs, dry stone walls, in woods and amongst bushes. In 1975 and 1976 it bred on North

Ronaldsay, the first definite proof of nesting in this island, and on Papa Westray the first breeding for many years was noted in 1980. Song has been heard as early as 15th February; the only breeding counts available are:

Cava   2 pairs, 1980
Rousay: Central moorland 5 pairs, 1981 (Lea, 1982)

There is some evidence of passage during the autumn; on 12th October 1913, forty were counted on the Pentland Skerries. Nine were ringed on North Ronaldsay between 18th September and 9th October 1974, compared to one or two in other years. Influxes have also been noted in late October 1976 on North Ronaldsay and Papa Westray, on 6th October 1979 in Holm and on 27th October 1980 on Papa Westray.

ACCENTORS : Prunellidae

Dunnock
Prunella modularis

Resident and passage migrant, possible winter visitor.

The Dunnock was recorded by Baikie and Heddle (1848) as a winter visitor and it was still rare in 1862, but by 1887 it was more common, breeding at Melsetter, Hoy and around Kirkwall (Buckley and Harvie-Brown, 1891). This increase continued and Lack (1943) found it to be common on Mainland and gave the following information for additional islands:

Eday   2 or more pairs in Carrick Wood
Hoy   4 or more pairs around Melsetter and
              another four or five pairs at the north end
Rousay   3 or more pairs at Trumland and one at
              Westness
Shapinsay   2 pairs in Balfour Castle Woods

He found most birds in woods, gorse patches and bushy gardens. One pair was seen in very thick heather.

Balfour (1972) noted that it bred regularly in small numbers in woods and gardens. During the period 1974-1982, the status does not appear to have changed. Breeding has definitely been recorded on Mainland at Berstane Woods (St Ola), Crantit (St Ola), Evie, Kirkwall and Stromness. During summer, birds have been seen in suitable habitat on Eday, Hoy and Mainland (Binscarth, Finstown, Orphir and Stenness). Song has been heard as early as 5th February.

In winter there are records from Hoy, Mainland (Berstane, Binscarth, Finstown, Kirkwall, Orphir, Rendall, Stenness, St Ola and Stromness) and South Ronaldsay.

In spring, obvious passage migrants have been noted from 27th March to 24th May, with a maximum of 55 on North Ronaldsay on 30th March 1980; and in autumn from 15th September to 10th November, with a maximum of 12 on North Ronaldsay on 25th September 1980.

Birds of the Continental race *P.m.modularis* have been identified on a number of occasions.

ROBINS, CHATS and THRUSHES:
Turdidae

Robin   Robin Redbreast
Erithacus rubecula

Recorded throughout the year, breeds in very small numbers, passage migrant, winter visitor.

This species was considered resident by Low (1813) and Baikie and Heddle (1848) noted that although it was not very numerous, it remained throughout the year. Buckley and Harvie-Brown (1891) recorded breeding on Mainland, Hoy and Rousay but said numbers had been much reduced by a cold winter in 1878. Lack (1943) found it much scarcer than usual in 1941, with a number of pairs in Mainland woods and gardens, 1 pair on Shapinsay and two or three pairs on Hoy. Balfour (1972) stated that it bred in small numbers in woods and gardens and ascribed these birds to the British race *E.r.melophilus.*

It remains a very uncommon breeding species. During the period 1974-1982, there are definite breeding records from Hoy and Mainland (Evie, Firth, Orphir and Stenness) and birds have been seen in suitable habitat in summer on Flotta and Rousay. Apart from 3 pairs at Binscarth and 3 pairs on Hoy in 1976, all other records are of single pairs.

In winter it is much more widespread with records from Burray, Egilsay, Gairsay, North Ronaldsay, Papa Westray, Sanday, South Ronaldsay and various sites on Mainland.

It is a regular passage migrant, sometimes occurring in quite large numbers. In spring, migrants have been noted from 26th March to 31st May, with a maximum of 15 on North Ronaldsay on 27th March 1980 and 15 on Pentland Skerries on 19th April 1975. In autumn, they have been seen from 1st September to 31st October, with a maximum of 400 on North Ronaldsay on 23rd October 1976. These migrant birds, and many of those wintering, are considered to be of Continental race *E.r.rubecula.*

There was a remarkable influx on 31st March and the first days of April 1958, when there were reported to be hundreds of birds, mainly pale-breasted, throughout Orkney. Almost every farm was said to shelter between 2-30 birds (F.I.B.O.B.4:65).

There are the following ringing recoveries:

Ringed in Orkney	Locality recovered
September 1969	Norfolk, November 1969
October 1970	Holland, January 1971
March 1980	France, November 1981

Ringed outwith Orkney	Recovered in Orkney
Yorkshire, April 1958	April 1959
Sweden, October 1960	March 1961
Finland, September 1976	October 1976
Heligoland, October 1976	January 1977

Nightingale

Luscinia megarhynchos

Very rare.

The only definite record is of a single bird trapped on North Ronaldsay on 11th May 1967 (S.B.4:517).

Bluethroat

Luscinia svecica

Regular but scarce passage migrant.

The Bluethroat occurs fairly regularly in small numbers, but there was an exceptional influx in 1981, with records from many parts of Orkney and two singing males were heard in Birsay, Mainland.

Annual number of daily individual sightings, 1974-1982

1974	1975	1976	1977	1978	1979	1980	1981	1982
1	2	12	2	1	0	3	47	1

Most records are in May with a smaller peak at the end of September and early October. Extreme dates for the period 1974-1982 are:

Spring, 9th May and 14th June and autumn, 22nd September and 7th October.

Daily individual sightings in fortnightly periods, 1974-1982

May 1st- May 14th	May 15th- May 28th	May 29th- June 11th	June 12th- June 25th	Sept. 15th- Sept. 28th	Sept. 29th- Oct. 12th
24	35	1	2	3	4

The majority of sightings refer to the red-spotted form *L.s.svecica* but there are two definite records of the white-spotted form *L.s.ceyanecula,* both of single birds:

> 1958   St Ola, Mainland, 31st March (F.I.B.O.B. 4:65; S.B.1:257).
>
> 1967   North Ronaldsay, 6th May (S.B.4:517).

Black Redstart
Phoenicurus ochruros

Regular passage migrant in small numbers.

Between 1975 and 1982 the majority of records of this species were of single birds, but 3 were noted on Sule Skerry on 8th May 1975 and 5 on North Ronaldsay on 20th October 1982.

In spring, the main passage occurs in May, but there are records from 25th March to 7th June, while in autumn the peak is recorded during October, especially the last 2 weeks; extreme dates are 20th September and 13th November.

There is a winter record given by Buckley and Harvie-Brown (1891) of a bird shot in Kirkwall on 20th December 1859.

On 30th June 1973, a nest with 4 eggs was found in a farm building on Copinsay. The eggs proved to be infertile and only a female bird was seen. (Lea, S.B.8:80).

Redstart
Phoenicurus phoenicurus

Regular passage migrant.

The Redstart, a common migrant, is usually more numerous in autumn than in spring. During the period 1974-1982, the peak passage in spring occurred during the first three weeks of May, with extreme dates of 19th April and 15th June. There was a maximum of 23 on Copinsay on 9th May 1975. In autumn the main passage took place during the last three weeks of September and first two weeks of October, with extreme dates of 26th August and 7th November. A maximum of 20 was recorded on North Ronaldsay on 24th September 1980.

Whinchat
Saxicola rubetra

Regular passage migrant; has bred.

In spring, the majority of records has been in May and, apart from 1 in North Ronaldsay on the exceptionally early date of 23rd March 1977, all other records during the period 1974-1982 have occurred between 14th April and 25th June. Most sightings are of single birds, but 8 were noted on Sanday on 14th May 1981.

Larger numbers occur in autumn with the peak passage in September, extreme dates being 15th August and 9th November. There was a big influx from 11th September 1981, with maximum counts of 40 in Deerness and at Grimness, South Ronaldsay on 12th September.

This species was noted by Baikie and Heddle (1848) as an occasional summer visitor, while Buckley and Harvie-Brown (1891) stated that, prior to 1888, breeding apparently occurred for some years on Hoy, near Melsetter and a valley near Berriedale. Lack (1943) saw none in 1941, but mentioned that two or three pairs had bred each year since 1918, in areas of gorse with grass, on Mainland. Balfour (1968) reported that there was no recent proof of breeding.

A bird was seen carrying food on 24th June 1969 on Hoy (S.B.5:101) and in 1975 a pair was suspected of breeding near the Glen of the Berry, Hoy. A pair was found holding territory on Hoy during May 1976 and singing males have been reported from Hoy in 1980 and 1981 and Cottascarth, Mainland in 1982, but there has been no further evidence of nesting.

Stonechat
Saxicola torquata

Local breeding species in small numbers, passage migrant.

The population of Stonechats in Orkney has fluctuated over

N

the years, being particularly affected by severe winters. Baikie and Heddle (1848) stated that it "makes its appearance very rarely", but Buckley and Harvie-Brown (1891) recorded breeding pairs on Hoy and at Orphir and Quanterness, Mainland. Lack (1943) indicated that, from 1918, it was confined to Hoy, but had since spread to Mainland within the preceding decade. Serle (1934) found 4 pairs on Hoy in 1933 and in 1938 there were 10 pairs (Lack, 1943); however, in 1941, following a severe winter, only 2 birds were seen. The Venables (1955) were told by G. T. Arthur that a few pairs did eventually come back but that they were exterminated by the 1946/47 winter. There had obviously been no recovery by 1950 as G. T. Arthur stated that "Stonechats are completely out to date". An increase took place during the next twenty years, as Balfour (1972) noted that Hoy had a thriving population and a few pairs bred regularly on Mainland and Rousay.

This increase continued through the 1970's, but a cold winter in 1981/82 again saw a reduction in numbers. The main concentrations of breeding birds are on North Hoy and the Hobbister Reserve, Mainland.

During the period 1974-1982, breeding pairs were recorded from:

Flotta
Hoy (including 12 pairs along the Rackwick road in 1978)
Rousay (2 pairs in 1977)
Mainland: Orphir (9 pairs Hobbister Reserve in 1980)
           Rendall
           Stenness
           St Ola

In 1982 breeding pairs were confined to Hoy (4 pairs counted along the Rackwick road) and the Hobbister Reserve (5 pairs).

At least two pairs produced three broods on the Hobbister Reserve in 1980, with the first brood fledging on 7th May, the second brood on 27th June and the third brood on 10th September.

During the autumn and winter, birds have been recorded away from their breeding areas in several parts of Mainland and South Ronaldsay. Possible migrants were noted on Eday on 22nd and 24th September 1976 and North Ronaldsay on 5th and 7th October 1976, 23rd and 24th September 1977, 4th April and 16th October 1978.

A bird showing the characteristics of one of the eastern races *S.t.maura* or *S.t.stejnegeri* was seen at Birsay on 21st October 1981 (B.B.75:517).

Wheatear

Stonechat, Chuckie

Oenanthe oenanthe

Widespread breeding species in small numbers, passage migrant.

The Wheatear was a common visitor to all the islands, according to Buckley and Harvie-Brown (1891). Lack (1943) found it to be widely distributed, with scattered pairs on most islands. He quoted G. T. Arthur, who was of the opinion that the species had much decreased during the previous twenty years. Balfour (1972) recorded that it bred in smallish numbers, widely scattered.

Although found breeding on many islands, nowhere is it common. Recent counts include:

Swona	3 pairs, 1974
Cava	2 pairs, 1980
Gairsay	3 pairs, 1981
Rousay: Central moorland	10 pairs, 1981 (Lea, 1982)

On North Hill, Papa Westray, there has been an increase from 8 pairs in 1980 to 15 pairs in 1982. Nesting on Copinsay was noted for the first time in 1976. Singing males on territory have been heard as early as 4th April.

On migration, it sometimes occurs in quite large numbers, when it is common throughout the islands. In spring, the first birds usually arrive at the end of March, the extreme dates for first arrival in the period 1974-1982 being the 13th March and 10th April. The main passage occurs during the last two weeks of April and the whole of May, with the last migrants noted on Copinsay on 9th June 1975. In autumn, movement has been recorded from 3rd August and the main influxes take place at the end of August and during September, with a noticeable decrease in numbers in October. Some years a few birds are reported in November, the latest date being the 16th. Birds of the Greenland race *O.o.leucorrhoa* have been recorded on both spring and autumn passage.

Birds ringed in Orkney have been recovered in Spain in

autumn, Morocco in October and January and in Algeria in March.

Pied Wheatear
Oenanthe pleschanka

Very rare.

There is one record of a single bird, a female, on Swona on 1st November 1916 (S.N.1916:293).

Desert Wheatear
Oenanthe deserti

Very rare.

A male of the eastern form *O.d.atrogularis* on Pentland Skerries on 2nd June 1906, is the only record (S.N.1906:138).

Rock Thrush
Monticola saxatilis

Very rare.

A male was obtained and another seen on Pentland Skerries on 17th May 1910 (A.S.N.H.1910:148)

Ring Ouzel
Turdus torquatus

Passage migrant and irregular breeding species.

This species was first recorded breeding on Hoy in 1847, and subsequently one or two pairs were said to have nested in most seasons at Berriedale or Segal (Buckley and Harvie-Brown, 1891). Traill (1888) recorded finding a nest near Harray, Mainland. Lack (1943) doubted the regularity of the nesting on Hoy and stated that the only recent record was of a pair, obviously breeding, found by G. T. Arthur, at the Kame valley on Hoy. Balfour (1968) mentioned a nest on Hoy in 1963 and indicated that breeding had been strongly suspected at three other localities in recent years.

Since 1968 there have been the following records of nesting or suspected nesting:

1969	Probably at least 2 pairs, Hoy.
1970	1-2 pairs bred, Hoy.
1971	Apparently bred, Hoy.
1972	At least 1 pair bred, Hoy.
1974	A male singing at one site on Rousay, and at another a pair was holding territory, but breeding was not proved. A singing bird on Hoy on 2nd July.
1975	Birds singing at two sites on Hoy and a juvenile seen on 2nd August.
1976	Nest with 4 young, Hoy on 22nd May. Singing birds at two other sites.
1977	Nest with 4 eggs, Hoy 21st May. Male singing, Rousay, in suitable habitat, 6th July.
1978	Singing birds noted at several sites on Hoy.
1981	Singing bird, Hoy on 23rd April.

The Ring Ouzel is a regular passage migrant, most sightings in spring consisting of 1-3 birds. The main passage takes place between 18th April and 20th May, with the extreme dates of 30th March and 28th May (1974-1982). In autumn, the extreme dates are 17th September and 7th November, with the main passage during the last week of September and throughout October. The majority of records are of 1-5 birds, but an exceptional influx took place on 26th October 1976 and birds were widespread throughout the islands. Peak counts were 200 in Orphir on 26th and 100 in Kirkwall on 27th.

A bird ringed in Orkney in October 1969 was recovered in France in November 1973.

Blackbird   Blackie

Turdus merula

A common breeding species and passage migrant.

The Blackbird has increased as a breeding species since the

early part of the 19th century. Baikie and Heddle (1848) described it as breeding, but not in good numbers. The increase was noted by Buckley and Harvie-Brown (1891), who thought that it was due to the planting of trees and bushes, which provided more cover. Lack (1943) recorded a continuing increase and noted that, apart from breeding in woods, bushy places and gardens, it was present throughout all cultivated land, locally on moorland and on some small treeless islands. Balfour (1972) listed it as a common breeding species.

There has been no change in status. Recent breeding counts include:

Cava	1 pair, 1980
Gairsay	8 pairs, 1981
Rousay: Central moorland	1 pair, 1981 (Lea, 1982)

First song has been heard on 22nd January. In 1982, a pair reared four broods in St Ola, the first egg being laid on 29th March with the fourth brood hatching on 4th August.

The spring passage is not always well marked, but, during the period 1974-1982, influxes have been noted between 7th March and 19th April.

In 1975, there were peak counts of 100+ on Copinsay on 16th April and 115 on Pentland Skerries on 19th April. In autumn, numbers are much larger, with influxes noted as early as 31st August. However, the main passage begins at the end of September and continues throughout October and the first two weeks of November. Peak counts are 300 on 24th October 1969 and 300 at Widewall, South Ronaldsay on 30th October 1982. A roost at Berstane Wood, St Ola reached 1,200 to 1,500 between 12th and 25th November 1978.

Birds ringed in Orkney from October to March have been recovered as follows:

April to August	Norway, Scotland and Sweden
September to March	Heligoland, Ireland, Norway and Scotland

Birds ringed in West Germany, Norway and Sweden in October have been found in Orkney from November to February and birds ringed in spring and summer in Denmark and Norway have been found in Orkney in December.

Fieldfare

Turdus pilaris

Passage migrant, some birds winter; has bred.

This species sometimes occurs in very large numbers, especially in autumn. During the period 1974-1982, spring passage has been noted as early as 12th March, although the main movements take place in April and early May, the latest date being 25th May; occasionally single birds are reported in June and July. A very large passage occurred in April 1975, when between 18th and 22nd there were 1,000 in Harray and Tankerness and c3,000 in North Ronaldsay.

Autumn migrants have been reported from 8th August, but numbers do not build up until the end of September, with the largest influxes in October and occasional ones during the first two weeks of November. By the end of this month, the majority of birds have left the islands and only the wintering flocks remain. There was a fall of about 20,000 on North Ronaldsay on 22nd October 1969. On 26th October 1976 an estimated 5,000 passed over Kirkwall; on the same day, between 0830 hrs and 1000 hrs, 9,000 were counted passing WSW over Orphir, with another 2,000-3,000 beween 1000 hrs and 1300 hrs.

Wintering flocks of 100-300 birds are not uncommon, although in some years very few birds are present in December and January.

In 1967 a pair was found breeding in the West Mainland (Balfour, 1968; S.B.5:31) and successful nesting occurred at Evie in 1969, when 3 young fledged about 1st August. The only other breeding record is of a pair feeding 2 young on Westray in mid-June 1974.

There are the following ringing recoveries, all of full-grown birds:

Ringed	Recovered
Orkney, February 1971	Norway, March 1971
Orkney, October 1978	Norway, June 1979
Orkney, October 1979	Sweden, August 1980
Orkney, October 1979	Norway, December 1980

Song Thrush   Mavis
Turdus philomelos

Locally common breeding species and passage migrant.

Recorded as a common species on most of the larger islands by Buckley and Harvie-Brown (1891); Lack (1943) found it to be abundant in all woods and gardens with trees. It was fairly common in and around shrubs and hedges and on Westray throughout the cultivated land, breeding in ditches and walls. According to Balfour (1972) it bred fairly commonly. There has been no change in status.

In 1975 there was a minimum of 12 territories in Balfour Castle Woods, Shapinsay and 18 nests were found in Berstane Woods in 1976. In 1980, Papa Westray and North Ronaldsay each had at least two pairs breeding. It is interesting to note that Briggs, in 1892, found 1-2 pairs breeding on North Ronaldsay (Briggs, 1893).

During the period 1974-1982, song has been heard on 21st January and the first fledged young seen at the end of April.

In spring, passage has been recorded from the first week of March until 14th May. Numbers are usually quite small, with the peak count being 12 on North Ronaldsay on 27th March 1980. The autumn passage is more marked, with movements reported from 13th September to 5th November. The largest influxes occur during October and the maximum recorded was 450 on North Ronaldsay on 19th October 1976.

The following ringing recoveries of full grown birds have been reported:

Ringed	Recovered
Orkney, October 1972	Norway, October 1973
Orkney, September 1980	Highland Region, Oct. 1980
Orkney, November 1980	Denmark, April 1981

Redwing
Turdus iliacus

Passage migrant and winter visitor; has bred.

This is a common migrant. Spring passage during the period 1974-1982 has been noted between 14th March and 5th June; only small numbers of birds are usually involved, with flocks of over ten being uncommon. The autumn movements, however, can be very spectacular with thousands of birds passing through the islands. Migrants have been reported from 16th August, but numbers are low until the last week of September, with the main passage occurring in October. On 23rd October 1969, there were estimated to be 20,000 birds on North Ronaldsay and there were approximately 15,000 there on 14th October 1970. The largest movement recorded in recent years was in October 1976, when on the 26th between 40,000 and 70,000 were estimated to have passed over Kirkwall and there were many thousands throughout Orkney on that day, including 25,000 in one field on Shapinsay.

Following the autumns when there have been large influxes, many birds stay on to winter and in December 1977 there was a roost of 10,000 at Berstane Woods, St Ola. These birds remained into January, but had declined to 150 by 25th February. In other years only small numbers are present, with flocks of 30 being the largest recorded.

Although singing birds have been noted in suitable habitat during May on several occasions, there is only one authenticated breeding record, that of a pair which successfully reared young in Orphir in 1975.

Recoveries of passage and possible wintering Redwings ringed in Orkney indicate that birds of both Continental (including Finland, Norway and Russia) and Icelandic origins are involved. Birds ringed in Orkney have also been recovered from October to March in the following countries: Denmark, France, Germany, Ireland, Italy, Portugal, Spain, Sweden.

Mistle Thrush

Turdus viscivorus

Passage migrant in small numbers; has bred.

This species was regarded by Buckley and Harvie-Brown (1891) as a rare visitor and they mentioned breeding in the garden at Westness, Rousay in 2 years between 1845 and 1856 and in Kirkwall in 1874 and 1875. In 1910 at least 3 pairs bred near Finstown and on 20th May two of the nests had 4 eggs each (Hale and Aldworth, 1910).

According to Robertson (1934) it had become much more common in Orkney and a good many pairs bred in the county every year. Lack (1943) suggested that it had bred regularly since 1908 and recorded that G. T. Arthur had found nests each year on Mainland since 1919. In 1941 two pairs were feeding young in Balfour Castle Woods, Shapinsay and there were a number of pairs at Berstane (St Ola), Binscarth (Firth) and Kirkwall. There must then have been a decrease, as Balfour (1968) indicated that it was very scarce, with not more than two or three pairs. He later considered the breeding status to be "uncertain" (Balfour, 1972).

The only recent records of breeding are in 1971, when pairs apparently bred at Binscarth and Kirkwall. In 1972, a pair was present in Kirkwall, but probably failed to breed.

As a passage migrant, the Mistle Thrush has been recorded annually between 1975 and 1982; the majority of sightings are of one to three birds, with a maximum of 10 on North Ronaldsay on 29th March 1981. In spring, it has been reported from 9th March to 18th May, with most records in the period 26th March to 25th April. In autumn, the main passage occurs during the last two weeks of October, with extreme dates of 12th September and 1st November. There is one winter record of two birds in Kirkwall on 24th January 1977.

American Robin

Turdus migratorius

Very rare.

The only record is of a single bird at Grimsetter Aerodrome on 27th May 1961 (B.B.55:577; S.B.2:343).

WARBLERS : Sylviidae

Lanceolated Warbler
Locustella lanceolata

Very rare.

There is just one record, a single bird on Pentland Skerries on 26th October 1910 (A.S.N.H.1911:71).

Grasshopper Warbler
Locustella naevia

Rare passage migrant.

The following records are available, all of single birds:

1913	Pentland Skerries, 9th May (S.N.E.P. No.3 1914:51).
1968	North Ronaldsay, 20th April (trapped).
1969	Deerness, first week of May.
1970	Graemsay, 18th May.
1971	Singing, Hoy in June.
	1 singing, St Ola, 23rd June.
1975	Near Stromness, 7th May.

1980	Singing, Orphir, 7th August.
1981	North Ronaldsay, 22nd September.
	Carness, St Ola, 23rd September.
1982	Kirkwall, 7th June.

Sedge Warbler

Acrocephalus schoenobaenus

Local breeding species and passage migrant.

The Sedge Warbler was first recorded on 29th July 1857, since when it had increased, according to Buckley and Harvie-Brown (1891). They mentioned three pairs nesting at Westness, Rousay in 1883, and on Mainland documented nesting at Swanbister, Orphir in 1884 and at St Ola in 1886. In 1888 there were three pairs at Melsetter, Hoy, where breeding had been noted for the previous twenty years. There must have been a decrease, as Lack (1943) stated that very few pairs usually bred on Mainland and in 1941 he found none. However, Balfour (1968) noted that it had increased and regularly bred at several places on Hoy, Mainland, Sanday, Westray and Stronsay, the latter two islands having only recently been colonised.

During the period 1974-1982, there are definite breeding records from:

> Mainland: Dee of Durkadale, Birsay
> Kirbister, Orphir
> Longhouse, St Ola
> Stenness
> Wideford Burn, St Ola.
> Rousay: Wasbister.

Singing birds have been noted in suitable habitats as follows:

Hoy: Melsetter   Sanday: Bea Loch
North Hoy   North end.
Ore Burn.   South Ronaldsay: Burwick
Mainland: Deerness   East Dam
Dounby   Graemston
Evie   Hoxa
Loch of Banks   Widewall.
Loch of Harray

Loch of Isbister
The Loons, Birsay
Sandwick
Waulkmill.

There is no recent data on the status of this species in Stronsay and Westray.

The extreme dates (1974-1982) for the Sedge Warbler in Orkney are 19th April and 25th September.

A bird ringed near Kirkwall in autumn was recovered two years later in France in August and two birds ringed in Orkney were controlled a year later at their ringing site.

Marsh Warbler

Acrocephalus palustris

Very rare.

There are only 5 records:

1968	1 North end, Sanday, 21st September.
1979	1 found dead, Copinsay, 1st June. This bird had been ringed in Denmark as a pullus on 3rd August 1978.
	1 singing, Orphir, 20th June and trapped there, 21st June.
1983	1 Windwick, South Ronaldsay, 1st June (trapped)
	1 North Ronaldsay, 8th June (trapped)

Reed Warbler

Acrocephalus scirpaceus

Uncommon passage migrant, the majority of sightings being in autumn.

Since the first record of this species in Orkney, which was on Auskerry on 28th September 1912 (S.N.1912:278), there have been 47 individual sightings. Most reports are of single birds, but there were 6 at Holm on 26th September 1982 and 3 on North Ronaldsay on 13th September 1981.

The only spring record is of a single bird at St Ola on 23rd

May 1977. In the period 1974-1982, the extreme dates for autumn are 17th August and 10th October, with the last two weeks of September being the peak period.

Daily individual sightings in autumn, in fortnightly periods, all available records, 1912-1982

Aug. 15th- Aug. 28th	Aug. 29th- Sept. 11th	Sept. 12th- Sept. 25th	Sept. 26th- Oct. 9th	Oct. 10th- Oct. 23rd
3	4	21	17	1

This species has been recorded annually from 1976-1982.

Icterine Warbler
Hippolais icterina

Rare passage migrant.

There have been 17 records, all of single birds, the first being on Pentland Skerries on 10th and 11th June 1914. (S.N.1914:237).

Years and numbers of records of Icterine Warblers, 1914-1982

1914	1966	1971	1972	1977	1978	1979	1980	1981	1982
2	1	2	1	1	1	2	1	2	4

The 10 spring records of the above period fall between 6th May and 19th June and the 7 autumn records from 10th August to 3rd October.

Melodious Warbler
Hippolais polyglotta

Very rare.

There are four records, all of single birds:

1971	North Ronaldsay, 23rd-24th August (trapped).
1979	Papa Westray, 11th June.
1983	St Ola, 10th September (trapped),
	Holm, 2nd October (trapped).

Subalpine Warbler

Sylvia cantillans

Very rare.

There are 3 records, all of single birds:

1967	Male, North Ronaldsay, 14th-17th September (trapped) (B.B.61:351; S.B.5:223).
1968	Auskerry, 29th May (B.B.62:479, S.B.5:394).
1971	Male, Binscarth, 26th April (trapped). (B.B.65:343).

Barred Warbler

Sylvia nisoria

Regular passage migrant in autumn.

All records between 1968 and 1982 have been in autumn and are of immature birds. The extreme dates are 7th August and 16th October, the maximum recorded being 6 on North Ronaldsay on 16th October 1970. The peak period of passage occurs at the end of August and beginning of September.

Daily individual sightings in fortnightly periods, 1968-1982

Aug. 1st- Aug. 14th	Aug. 15th- Aug. 28th	Aug. 29th- Sept. 11th	Sept. 12th- Sept. 25th	Sept. 26th- Oct. 9th	Oct. 10th- Oct. 23rd
5	20	35	25	17	11

Lesser Whitethroat

Sylvia curruca

Regular passage migrant in small numbers.

Although recorded annually between 1974 and 1982, numbers have fluctuated, with over 40 records in 1981 and only one in 1982; this species is slightly more numerous in autumn.

During the period 1974-1982, the spring passage has been noted between 8th May and 26th June, with the peak numbers occurring from 8th to 26th May. A maximum of 5 was noted on North Ronaldsay on 12th May 1981. Autumn migration has been recorded from 1st September to 5th November, with peak passage from 14th September to 10th October; a maximum of 8 was seen on North Ronaldsay on 30th September 1978.

Singing birds have been reported from a number of areas in May and June, but there has been no evidence of breeding.

A bird trapped in St Ola on 5th November 1981 was probably of the Siberian race *S.c.blythi.*

Whitethroat
Sylvia communis

Regular passage migrant in small numbers; has attempted to breed.

The Whitethroat has occurred in about equal numbers in spring and autumn during the period 1974-1982, although the distribution of records has fluctuated from year to year. The earliest spring record is 17th April, but the majority have been reported from 3rd-28th May and the last have been seen at the end of June. The maximum noted was c20 on Copinsay on 26th May 1976, but all other records have been of 1-3 birds. In autumn the extreme dates are 15th August and 22nd October, with peak passage from 11th-30th September.

A pair was seen at Balfour Castle, Shapinsay from 30th May to 3rd June 1910 (Hale and Aldworth, 1910) which from their behaviour, had a nest close by. Lack (1943) saw a nest which was fully lined at Smoogro, Orphir in 1941, but no eggs were laid. More recently singing birds have been noted in May and June, but there has been no further indication of nesting.

Garden Warbler
Sylvia borin

Regular passage migrant; has bred.

The only record given by Buckley and Harvie-Brown (1891) was considered by them to require further confirmation. It is now a regular passage migrant, being much more numerous in autumn. Only small numbers have been recorded in spring, with a maximum of 4 on Copinsay on 26th May 1976 and 4 on North Ronaldsay on 20th May 1981. During the period 1974-1982, the earliest recorded date is 19th April, but most sightings occur between 9th May and 9th June.

In autumn the extreme dates are 10th August and 7th November, with the main passage from 10th September to 12th October. The largest number noted is 40 on North Ronaldsay on 21st September 1981.

A pair was seen carrying food in Binscarth Wood, Firth on 15th and 16th July 1964 (S.B.3:268) and nesting may have also occurred in 1965 (Balfour, 1968). In June and early July 1976, singing birds were noted at Binscarth, Finstown and Trumland, Rousay. The Rousay bird was heard giving alarm calls, but no definite proof of breeding was obtained.

Blackcap

Sylvia atricapilla

Regular passage migrant; has bred, occasionally attempts to winter.

This species occurs regularly in spring in small numbers and most sightings are of single birds. During the period 1974-1982, the earliest record is 14th April with the main passage occurring between 7th and 31st May. A maximum of 5 was seen on North Ronaldsay on 12th May 1981. A few birds have been noted in June and there are two July records of single birds.

It is much more numerous in autumn and, during the period 1974-1982, has been recorded from 26th August, with peak passage between 14th September and 16th October. A maximum of 70 was present on North Ronaldsay on 27th September 1981. The majority of birds have departed by the end of October, but in most years sightings continue into November and occasionally December.

Single birds in Kirkwall on 20th January 1975 and in Holm on 14th January 1982 may have been attempting to winter, while one seen in a Kirkwall garden from 9th-26th March 1971 may have successfully wintered.

Buckley and Harvie-Brown (1891) gave two breeding records from near Kirkwall, which they considered to be doubtful, suggesting that the birds were probably wrongly identified. Hale and Aldworth (1910) saw and heard a male singing on Mainland on 26th May 1910 and stated that a pair on Shapinsay in early June undoubtedly had a nest, but this was not found. The only definite breeding record is of a male singing and a female carrying food in the grounds of Balfour Castle, Shapinsay on 29th June 1949 (B.B.43:222). In 1976 two singing males were found in Binscarth Wood, Firth on 18th June and one was heard there on 1st July. Single singing birds were heard on Hoy on 7th June 1979 and 1st June 1981.

Ringing recoveries are as follows:

Ringed	Recovered
Orkney, September 1969	Italy, October 1969
Belgium, August 1976	Orkney, September 1976
Belgium, September 1979	Orkney, May 1980
Holland, October 1980	Orkney, October 1980
Norway, July 1981	Orkney, September 1981
Belgium, July 1981	Orkney, September 1981
Holland, September 1982	Orkney, October 1982

Greenish Warbler
Phylloscopus trochiloides

Very rare.

There are three records of single birds, all of them occurring in 1981 (B.B.75:522).

North Ronaldsay, 17th September (trapped).

Holm, 26th-27th September (trapped).
North Ronaldsay, 10th October.

The 1967 record given by Balfour (1972) has not been accepted by the B.B.R.C.

Arctic Warbler
Phylloscopus borealis

Very rare.

There are just three records, all of single birds. The 1969 record given by Balfour (1972) has not been accepted by the B.B.R.C.

1902	Sule Skerry, 5th September (A.S.N.H.1909:114).
1972	Stenness, 3rd September (trapped). (B.B.66:349).
1981	Holm, 15th September (trapped). (B.B.75:523).

Pallas's Warbler
Phylloscopus proregulus

Very rare.

The only records occurred in 1982, following a large influx of this species on the east coast of Britain. All records were of single birds (B.B.76:516):

Windwick, South Ronaldsay, 14th October (trapped).
Berstane Wood, St Ola, 15th October.
Rackwick, Hoy, 15th October.
Windwick, South Ronaldsay (trapped), 15th October.
Berstane Wood, St Ola (trapped), 31st October.

Yellow-browed Warbler
Phylloscopus inornatus

Scarce passage migrant in autumn.

This species was first recorded on 29th September 1913 on Auskerry (S.N.E.P.No.3 1914) and during the period 1974-1982 there have been sightings annually, except in 1976 and 1977.

Daily individual sightings, 1974-1982

1974	1975	1976	1977	1978	1979	1980	1981	1982
1	4	0	0	7	3	1	5	1

All records have been in autumn, with the extreme dates of 18th September and 22nd October.

Individual sightings in weekly periods, all available records from 1913-1982

Sept. 14th-Sept. 20th	Sept. 21st-Sept. 27th	Sept. 28th-Oct. 4th	Oct. 5th-Oct. 11th	Oct. 12th-Oct. 18th	Oct. 19th-Oct. 25th
1	7	13	9	4	2

Radde's Warbler
Phylloscopus schwarzi

Very rare.

There are two records of single birds, both in 1982 (B.B.76:518):

Near Kirkwall, 10th October (trapped).
Holm, 17th October (trapped).

Dusky Warbler

Phylloscopus fuscatus

Very rare.

There is only one record, that of a bird on Auskerry on 1st October 1913 (S.N.1913:271; S.N.1914:7).

Wood Warbler

Phylloscopus sibilatrix

Scarce but regular passage migrant; has bred.

The Wood Warbler has been a regular passage migrant in small numbers during the period 1974-1982.

Daily individual sightings, 1974-1982

1974	1975	1976	1977	1978	1979	1980	1981	1982
0	1	1	25	4	2	9	4	3

Spring sightings, all of single birds, have been recorded between 3rd May and 14th June. There was a bird on Sule Skerry on 17th July 1977. In autumn the records fall within the period 4th August to 3rd October, the maximum noted in one day being 3 on North Ronaldsay on 11th September 1980.

Daily individual sightings in fortnightly periods, 1969-1982

May 1st- May 14th	May 15th- May 28th	May 29th- June 11th		
8	3	1		

Aug. 1st- Aug. 14th	Aug. 15th- Aug. 28th	Aug. 29th- Sept. 11th	Sept. 12th- Sept. 25th	Sept. 26th- Oct. 9th
1	16	10	9	1

A pair bred in Binscarth Wood, Firth in 1914 and 1915 rearing three and five young respectively (Wood, 1916), the only breeding records for Orkney. Balfour (1968) regarded these breeding records as doubtful, but included them in his 1972 list without any comment.

Chiffchaff

Phylloscopus collybita

Regular passage migrant; occasionally birds are present in summer and in some years one or two may winter.

Although mentioned by Baikie and Heddle (1848) as an occasional summer visitor, Buckley and Harvie-Brown (1891) preferred not to include this species until they had further and more accurate information of its occurrence. It is difficult to know whether there has been any real change in status since the late 19th century, but it is now a regular passage migrant. In spring, obvious migrants have been noted from 28th March and small numbers are recorded through until June, with a maximum of 6 at Holm on 29th March 1980. There is no definite peak period of movement.

In autumn, there are records from 5th September with the main passage in the last week of September and throughout October. A maximum of 40 was counted on South Ronaldsay on 27th October 1980. In several years an obvious influx has occurred in the first week of November and some birds are still present in December. Many of these have been reported as showing the characters of the Siberian race *P.c.tristis*. There are records of successful wintering from Orphir in 1974/75, Binscarth wood and Kirkwall in 1975/76 and Kirkwall in 1979/80 (it is likely that these birds were of the race *P.c.tristis.)*

During the period 1974-1982, singing birds have been reported regularly in summer, but there has been no definite proof of breeding, although it was suspected at Trumland, Rousay in 1977. Other places where possible breeding birds have been noted are:

> North Hoy plantations,
> Binscarth Wood, Firth,
> Woodwick, Evie.

Small numbers of the Scandinavian race *P.c.abienitis* were identified on Auskerry from 14th September to 6th October 1913 (S.N.1914:8). A single bird of the race *P.c.tristis* was recorded on Sule Skerry on 23rd September 1902 (Baxter and Rintoul, 1953) and two from Kirkwall on 5th February 1908 (A.S.N.H.1908:80).

A bird ringed in Yorkshire in October was controlled in Orkney the following May and one ringed in Estonia in September was controlled 23 days later in Orkney.

Willow Warbler

Phylloscopus trochilus

Common passage migrant; breeds in small numbers in woods and areas with shrub cover.

The status of the Willow Warbler as a breeding species in Orkney in the 19th century was not made clear by Buckley and Harvie-Brown (1891). From reports they had received, they assumed it to be quite rare, but suggested that it could have been overlooked. They gave a possible breeding record from Melsetter, Hoy and mentioned that when visiting Binscarth in 1888 they saw and heard several birds. According to Lack (1943) it bred in most of the woods on Mainland (Berstane, Binscarth, Woodwick); six were heard singing in Balfour Castle Woods, Shapinsay and one at Trumland, Rousay. He stated that it was gradually increasing and spreading. Balfour (1968) listed it as regular and widespread, although not numerous.

During the period 1974-1982, there are definite breeding records from Hoy (White Glen plantation), Mainland (Firth and Orphir) and Rousay (Trumland), but it is almost certainly under-recorded. Singing birds in suitable breeding habitat have been noted on Hoy (Berriedale, Hoy Lodge plantation, Rackwick, Segal Burn) and Mainland (Holm and St Ola). In 1975 there were 3-5 territories in Binscarth Wood, Firth and 4 territories in Balfour Castle Wood, Shapinsay, and in 1976, 3 singing birds in Binscarth and 4 singing at Trumland, Rousay.

In spring, migrants have been noted from 8th April to 8th June, with the main passage in the first two weeks of May. Most records are of 1-6 birds, but there were 400 in South Ronaldsay on 5th May 1969. Autumn passage has been recorded from 4th August to 31st October, with peak numbers occurring from the last week of August to the beginning of October, with a maximum count of 40 noted on North Ronaldsay on 31st August 1980.

A bird ringed in Orkney in May was recovered 2 years later in Algeria in April.

Goldcrest

Regulus regulus

Common passage migrant, a few birds may winter. An irregular
breeding species in small numbers during recent years.

There were two records of nesting given by Buckley and
Harvie-Brown (1891), one at Woodwick, Evie about 1830 and the
other of an empty nest in a Kirkwall garden, which Lack (1943)
considered to be highly unsatisfactory for a breeding record. A pair
bred at Binscarth, Firth in 1945 and a pair at Carrick Wood, Eday
in 1962 (Balfour, 1968). In 1972 two pairs bred at Binscarth and 1
pair in a plantation on Hoy. Since then there have been the
following breeding records and reports of birds seen in suitable
breeding habitat in summer:

1973	Bred Binscarth and Hoy.
1974	Bred Binscarth.
	Singing birds in Berriedale and Lyrawa plantations, Hoy.
1975	1 pair bred Binscarth.
	A nest at Whitehall, Stronsay failed.
	Singing birds at Hoy Lodge plantation and Rackwick, Hoy.
1976	Singing birds Binscarth and Hoy.
1978	2 singing birds, Lyrawa plantation, Hoy.
1980	1 bird seen Lyrawa plantation, Hoy.
1981	Fledged young seen Lyrawa and White Glen plantations, Hoy.
	2 birds seen Carrick Wood, Eday.
1982	Singing birds Hoy Lodge and White Glen plantations, 1 seen Lyrawa plantation, Hoy.

In spring, migrants have been noted from 18th March to 18th
May, with the main passage from 26th March to the end of April.
In autumn, there are reports from 13th August, with most records
in the period 16th September to the end of October. Up to 60
birds were present on North Ronaldsay between 15th and 25th
October 1976. There are many records in November, while some
birds are still present in December. Wintering birds have been
noted at Berstane, St Ola in 1976/77, 1979/80, 1981/82 and in
Binscarth in 1976/77 and 1980/81.

A bird ringed in Orkney in October was recovered in Norway a month later, and a bird ringed in Finland in September was controlled 9 days later in Orkney.

Firecrest
Regulus ignicapillus

Very rare.

There is only one fully authenticated record, that of a single bird seen on Auskerry on 13th September 1967 (S.B.5:224).

The 1971 record given by Balfour (1972) was not accepted by *Scottish Birds.*

FLYCATCHERS : Muscicapidae

Spotted Flycatcher
Muscicapa striata

A regular passage migrant in small numbers. One or two pairs have bred fairly regularly in recent years.

This was a very rare species in Orkney, according to Buckley and Harvie-Brown (1891). They mentioned that a pair bred at Melsetter, Hoy in 1867 and for several years after that date. Lack (1943) noted that a pair bred in Binscarth Wood, Firth in 1915 and 1916 and two pairs in 1917; he saw a nest with young at Melsetter in 1941. Balfour (1968) stated that it had bred regularly in small numbers during the preceding decade. There has possibly been a slight decline since then, as definite proof of breeding has been obtained in only seven years during the period 1972-1982, but not all suitable breeding habitat has been visited each year.

All records of breeding and possible breeding since 1972 are given below:

1972   2 pairs bred Binscarth.
1973   A few pairs bred.
1975   2 pairs bred Binscarth.

1976	2 pairs present Binscarth, 1 pair feeding young in early July.
	1, possibly 2 pairs bred at Trumland, Rousay.
1977	Present Binscarth and Trumland during breeding season.
1980	1 pair bred Balfour Castle Wood, Shapinsay.
1982	1 pair bred Kirkwall,
	1 bird calling repeatedly Binscarth, 16th July.

In spring, it has been recorded from 5th May, with a maximum of 10 on Auskerry on 29th May 1969. The main passage was from 15th May to 7th June. In autumn there were records from 7th August to 24th October, with most sightings falling within the period 11th September to 6th October. A peak count of 8 was reported on South Ronaldsay on 19th September 1981.

A bird ringed on Heligoland in May 1964 was recovered in Orkney in May 1965.

J.F.H.

Red-breasted Flycatcher
Ficedula parva

A scarce, but regular, passage migrant in autumn, rare in spring.

There were only four spring records during the period 1974-1982 and these were all between 21st May and 9th June.

Numbers of Red-breasted Flycatchers recorded annually,
1974-1982

1974	1975	1976	1977	1978	1979	1980	1981	1982
3	0	6	3	5	4	2	7	2

In autumn the majority of sightings have occurred during the last two weeks of September and the first two weeks of October, the extreme dates being 6th September and 31st October. All records in the above period were of single birds, but two were seen on Sanday on 21st September 1968.

Collared Flycatcher
Ficedula albicollis

Very rare.

There are just two records, both of single birds:

1963   Male, Hunscarth, Harray, 30th May (B.B.57:275; S.B.2:478).

1980   Male, Stronsay, 31st May (B.B.74:487).

Pied Flycatcher
Ficedula hypoleuca

Regular passage migrant in spring and autumn.

During the period 1974-1982, this species has probably been slightly more numerous on autumn passage. In spring the main movement takes place in May, with extreme dates of 30th April and 18th June and a maximum of 9 on Copinsay on 26th May 1976. There was a record of a single bird on North Ronaldsay on 9th July. The autumn sightings fell between 11th August and 14th November, but the majority of these were from the end of August to 7th October. Peak counts included 20 on Hoy on 13th September 1981 and 20 on North Ronaldsay on 14th September 1981.

A breeding record from Melsetter, Hoy in 1864, given by Buckley and Harvie-Brown (1891), was considered doubtful by both Lack (1943) and Balfour (1968).

LONG-TAILED TITS:
Aegithalidae

Long-tailed Tit
Aegithalos caudatus

Very rare.

There are only 7 records of this species:

1966	2 North Ronaldsay, 20th October (British race), (S.B.4:387).
1969	5 Binscarth, Firth, 28th and 29th October (British race).
1973	1 Kirkwall, 19th November-3rd December (British race).
1974	1 Westray, 27th June.
1975	4 Eday, 28th October.
1980	3 Stromness, 29th October.
1983	1 Berstane Wood, St Ola was trapped on 20th November (British race) and had been ringed in July 1983 at Conon Bridge, Highland Region. It was retrapped on 3rd December at Crantit, St Ola.

TITS : Paridae

Coal Tit
Parus ater

Very rare.

The only records of this species were given by Balfour (1972). In an unpublished note he stated that both referred to birds of the Continental race.

1946	2 Binscarth, 20th October.
1949	1 Binscarth, 20th November.

Blue Tit

Parus caeruleus

Very rare.

All available records are given:

1845	1 Kirkwall, 23rd Ocotber (Baikie and Heddle, 1848).
1887	1 Stromness, April (Buckley and Harvie-Brown, 1891).
1888	1 Kirkwall, 20th May (Buckley and Harvie-Brown, 1891).
1912	1 North Ronaldsay, 10th May (S.N.E.P.No.2, 1913:45).
1969	3 Binscarth, Firth, 14th May.
1971	1 North Ronaldsay, 2nd October.
1973	2 Kirkwall, 13th October. One was seen frequently in Kirkwall from 26th October until 27th January 1974.
1977	1 Stronsay, 9th October.
1982	1 North Ronaldsay, 9th October.

Great Tit

Parus major

Rare.

All available records are given:

1884	1 Kirkwall, 2nd July (Buckley and Harvie-Brown 1891).
1915	1 Stromness (Stromness Museum).
1957	1 Binscarth, Firth, 1st December (F.I.B.O.B.4:226).
1966	1 North Ronaldsay, 9th September (Balfour, 1972).
1973	1 Birsay, late November.
1974	1 Stromness, 17th January.
1975	5 Balfour Mains, Shapinsay, 14th April.
	1 Copinsay, 14th April.
1977	1 North Ronaldsay, 21st March,
	1 South Ronaldsay, 30th November.
1981	1 Binscarth, 19th and 20th April.

1982   Single birds, Hoy 25th October,
            Eday 27th October,
            Binscarth 5th December,
            Pierowall, Westray 22nd December
            until the end of the year.

TREECREEPERS : Certhiidae

Treecreeper
Certhia familiaris

Rare passage migrant and winter visitor.

Baikie and Heddle (1848) stated that this species had been occasionally shot in Orkney. Buckley and Harvie-Brown (1891) mentioned one shot near Stromness in 1841 and 2 birds reported from Kirkwall, one of which was last seen in June 1884. Balfour (1972) referred all occurrences to the Northern race *C.f.familiaris*. All other known records are listed:

1941   1 Kirkwall, 10th October (Baxter and Rintoul, 1953).

1960   1 Binscarth, 5th September, 2 on 2nd October, 1 on 3rd November (Balfour, unpublished).

1961   1 Stromness, 10th October (Groundwater, 1974),
            1 St Margaret's Hope, South Ronaldsay, 20th October,
            1 Binscarth, 6th November, 2 on 14th November (Balfour, unpublished).

1964   1 wintered in a Kirkwall garden (S.B.3:322).

1970   1 Binscarth, 11th January to 13th February.

1971   1 Binscarth, 9th and 30th October.

1980   1 Balfour Woods, Shapinsay, 5th December.

1981   1 Binscarth, 7th December.

ORIOLES : Oriolidae

Golden Oriole
Oriolus oriolus

Scarce passage migrant, more numerous in spring.

The only early records for Orkney are of a male and female in the collection of Stromness Museum and one from Sanday on 20th May 1893, which is now in the Royal Scottish Museum (Omond, 1925). It has been reported more frequently since the early 1960's and in 1964 a maximum of 6 birds was seen.

The majority of records were in spring with the extreme dates 16th May and 5th June. There were two autumn records, both of single birds, from Sule Skerry on 9th September 1964 and Toab, East Mainland on 18th September 1971.

Number of Golden Orioles recorded annually, 1974-1982

1974	1975	1976	1977	1978	1979	1980	1981	1982
1	2	3	0	1	0	0	2	1

SHRIKES : Laniidae

Red-backed Shrike
Lanius collurio

Regular passage migrant in small numbers.

This species is usually more numerous in spring than in autumn. In the period 1974-1982, it has been recorded on spring passage from 27th April to 14th June, with most sightings from 20th May to 10th June. In autumn, there were records from 22nd August to 23rd Ocotber, but the main passage occurred during the last two weeks of September. The majority of sightings were of single birds, but up to three have been present in a day on Copinsay and North Ronaldsay.

A pair was seen displaying on Hoy in early June 1970. At the end of May 1977, a pair was reported from Firth, Mainland, but there was no proof of breeding.

Lesser Grey Shrike

Lanius minor

Very rare.

There are 3 records, all of single birds:

1962	A first winter bird, Finstown, 11th November (B.B.59:300; S.B.4:232).
1965	North Ronaldsay, found dead 30th May (B.B.59:296; S.B.3:420).
1967	North Ronaldsay, 27th September (B.B.61:354; S.B.5:224).

Great Grey Shrike

Lanius excubitor

Regular passage migrant.

The Great Grey Shrike has been recorded as a passage migrant since at least the 19th century, as Buckley and Harvie-Brown (1891) stated they had known many instances of its capture in Orkney. The number of records fluctuates from 1-20 annually; it is more numerous in autumn.

During the period 1974-1982, the extreme dates in spring were 28th March and 17th May, with most sightings occurring in April. In autumn it has been noted from 26th September to 14th November, with peak numbers from 12th October to the end of the month. Usually records are of single birds, but there were 4 on North Ronaldsay on 24th October 1976.

Woodchat Shrike

Lanius senator

Very rare.

There are five records, all of single birds in either May or June:

1913	Auskerry, 6th June (S.N.1914:45).
1953	Rendall, Mainland, 23rd June (Balfour, 1972).
1964	Male, North Ronaldsay, 8th May (B.B.60:333; S.B.4:508).
1971	North Ronaldsay, 26th May (B.B.65:346).
1974	Orphir, 9th-16th June (B.B.69:365).

CROWS : Corvidae

Jay

Garrulus glandarius

Very rare.

There is just one record, that of a single bird seen on North Ronaldsay on 11th May 1967 (S.B.4:516).

Magpie

Pica pica

Very rare.

All the records available involve single birds:

1845	Hoy (Buckley and Harvie-Brown, 1891).
1849	Hoy (Buckley and Harvie-Brown, 1891).
1892	Loch of Kirbister, Orphir, end of August (A.S.N.H.1893:114).
1900	Noup Head, Westray, 14th April (Baxter and Rintoul, 1953).

1960	Sanday, 2nd November (*The Orkney Herald*, 20th Dec. 1960).
1963	Sanday, 15th January (*The Orcadian*, 14th Feb. 1963).
1970	Kirkwall Airport, 13th-26th February.
1976	North Ronaldsay, 12th October.

Nutcracker

Nucifraga caryocatactes

Very rare.

The only record is of a single bird shot on Sanday on 1st October 1868 (Buckley and Harvie-Brown, 1891).

Chough

Pyrrhocorax pyrrhocorax

Very rare.

There are four records, all of single birds:

1935	Westray, 19th October (Baxter and Rintoul, 1953).
1942	Westray, 14th May (*The Orcadian* 11th June 1942).
1951	Herston, South Ronaldsay, 10th December (Balfour, 1972).
	This record is attributed to G. T. Arthur; the Venables (1955) referred to probably the same bird when they noted that G. T. Arthur saw one around Kirkwall from 10th-24th December.
1965	Windwick, South Ronaldsay, 6th January (S.B.3:377).

Jackdaw

Jackie, Kae

Corvus monedula

Resident; widespread, but local, breeding species; passage migrant.

This species has apparently increased during the last two hundred years. Low (1813) recorded only a few breeding pairs, from Stews Head (South Ronaldsay) and Walls (Hoy). Buckley and Harvie-Brown (1891) mentioned that several were seen about Kirkwall during the springs of 1855 to 1858 and appeared to have bred there. However, one of their correspondents noted that, although there were birds present in Kirkwall in 1866, they were not breeding. Quoting Ranken, they stated that the Jackdaw was only an occasional visitor thirty or forty years ago, but had since become numerous. In 1888 they found pairs breeding in the chimneys of the Earl's Palace, Kirkwall and large colonies were seen at Hersta and Stews Head, South Ronaldsay in 1889.

Lack (1942) found it to be common on Mainland with several cliff colonies, some nesting in Kirkwall and probably others among the Rooks at Berstane, St Ola. Birds were seen on both the east and west cliffs of South Ronaldsay. On Hoy there was a cliff colony at Melsetter and some birds were with Rooks at Orgil. Cliff colonies (20-50 pairs) were noted at Faraclett (Rousay), Calf of Eday, Noup Head (Westray) and near Housebay (Stronsay). He stated that, although there had been a decrease in South Ronaldsay, it had increased elsewhere. Baxter and Rintoul (1953), during visits to Orkney from 1927-1948, thought that it was more numerous in Kirkwall than elsewhere, but saw small numbers in a good many places.

The Jackdaw has a very local distribution as a breeding species with extensive, unoccupied stretches of cliffs and coastline between colonies. There has been a decrease in Kirkwall, probably because fewer nesting sites are now available.

During the period 1974-1982, colonies of over 50 birds have been reported from:

> Mainland: Black Craig, Stromness
> Costa Head, Birsay
> Gaitnip, Holm
> Gultack, Holm
> South Ronaldsay: Stews Head

Smaller colonies have been noted on:

> Copinsay: 3-4 pairs, 1974; 1 pair, 1981
> Calf of Eday: 15 birds, 1973; 19 birds, 1982
> Hoy: The Kame and South Walls
> Mainland: Berstane, min. 1 pair amongst Rooks
>   Kirkwall, less than 10 pairs
>   Marwick Head, Birsay
>   Mull Head, Deerness
>   Point of Ayre, Deerness
>   Row Head, Sandwick
>   Stromness, less than 10 pairs
>   Woodwick, Evie, max. 3 pairs amongst Rooks
> Rousay
> Sanday: Breeding took place at Scuthi Head between 1972
>   and 1982 with a max. of 14 birds. There was one
>   nest at Lamba Ness in 1982
> South Ronaldsay: Halcro Head
> Stronsay
> Westray: Noup Head

This species is under-recorded and the above counts are not comprehensive.

The earliest date for fledged young is 23rd May. In winter the maximum flock noted was 500 at Stenness on 5th December 1982. Probable migrant birds have been reported from North Ronaldsay in March, April, May and October and from Papa Westray in October. Numbers are generally small, with a peak count of 9 on North Ronaldsay on 15th March 1977 and 27th March 1981. In May 1966 up to 50 were recorded on North Ronaldsay (*Island Saga*, 1967).

Rook

Corvus frugilegus

Resident breeding species and passage migrant.

There were few occurrences of the Rook in Orkney in the early part of the 19th century, according to Baikie and Heddle (1848). The first record of nesting was from Muddiesdale, near Kirkwall in 1876 and by 1878 this rookery had 30 nests. In 1883 there was a colony at Tankerness and, in about 1889, the Rook was plentiful in Kirkwall in the trees around the Bishop's Palace. They were also noted breeding at Melsetter, Hoy (Buckley and Harvie-Brown, 1891). Lack (1942) stated that it had continued to increase on Mainland, with the largest colony being at Berstane Wood, St Ola and a few nesting in trees in Kirkwall. There were also other small colonies. On Hoy, they no longer bred at Melsetter but nested at Orgil, where they were noted by Serle in 1934. There was a single pair at St Margaret's Hope, South Ronaldsay. Baxter and Rintoul (1953) recorded a total of 583 nests in 1945, while the Venables (1955) gave a count of about 720 pairs in 1950. Unfortunately it has not been possible to obtain further details of these counts, as they show a definite increase. Balfour (1968), commenting on Lack's observations, stated that there had been no further increase.

Complete censuses were undertaken in 1975 and 1982 and the results are given in the table. It would appear that the Rook is still increasing but there are changes in distribution, probably due to persecution. Another change noted is in the size of the rookeries.

Nesting first took place at Grindelay, Orphir in 1973, Binscarth, Firth in 1975 and Nisthouse, Harray in 1978. There were nests at Graemeshall, Holm in 1976 and in the same year 9 nests were counted at Tankerness, but these were later destroyed. The colony at St Margaret's Hope, South Ronaldsay consisted of over 30 nests during the 1960's (H. Mackenzie, pers. comm.) but is no longer in existence, with breeding last recorded in 1974. Some of the nesting trees have now been felled.

All the nests counted during the surveys were in trees, but in 1970 a pair attempted to nest on the chimney of a house near Queen Street, Kirkwall. This type of nesting site is also mentioned by Ranken (Buckley and Harvie-Brown, 1891).

Nest building has been recorded as early as 19th February, but few birds are incubating before 20th March. First fledged young have been reported on 11th May.

In winter, flocks of 1,000 birds have been noted at Berstane in October 1970 and at Binscarth on 21st November 1982.

Probable migrants have been recorded on several islands from March to June and October to November. Numbers have been small, with a maximum of 12 on Sanday on 17th April 1981.

Site	1975*		1982**	
	No. of nests	Date	No. of nests	Date
Rousay				
Westness House	52	28 Mar.	1	10 Apr.
Evie				
Woodwick House	244	15 Apr.	140	Apr.
Harray				
Nisthouse	0	—	50	5 May
Firth				
Binscarth	8	29 Apr.	218	29 Apr.
Kirkwall/St Ola				
Police Station to King St. and Queen St.	151	2 May	117	30 Apr.
Willowburn and Papdale				
Infant School	104	3 May	162	30 Apr.
Papdale House and Farm	50	5 Apr.	108	30 Apr.
New Scapa Road	2	14 Apr.	2	30 Apr.
Berstane Woods	225	26 Apr.	337	29 Apr.
Holm				
Graemeshall	0	—	17	3 May
Orphir				
Grindelay House	29	29 Apr.	80	30 Apr.
Stromness				
Hillside Road	18	11 Apr.	54	22 Apr.
John Street	9	11 Apr.	0	22 Apr.
Primary School	7	11 Apr.	39	22 Apr.
Bea, Back Road	5	11 Apr.	21	22 Apr.
Church Road	0	—	1	22 Apr.
Hoy				
Bu	43	1 May	0	7 May
Longhope				
Melsetter House	10	1 May	0	7 May
Totals	957		1,347	

* Lea, 1975
** Adam and Corse, 1983

Carrion Crow

Corvus corone corone

Regular visitor in small numbers, occasionally pairs with Hooded Crow.

Only one record of the Carrion Crow was given by Buckley and Harvie-Brown (1891), that of a bird shot in 1856. It has become much commoner in recent years and the first recorded nesting of a bird paired with a Hooded Crow occurred on the West Mainland cliffs in 1974. Since then definite breeding has been noted in 1976, 1981 and 1982, a mixed pair being involved on each occasion. Apart from these breeding birds, individuals have been recorded regularly during the period 1974-1982, with sightings from many of the islands. There have also been a number of reports of hybrid birds.

Hooded Crow   Craa, Hoodie

Corvus corone cornix

Common resident breeding species.

This species was persecuted during the 19th century in the interests of game preservation and Buckley and Harvie-Brown (1891) recorded that, although not so numerous as formerly, all the islands had a pair or two. Lack (1942) stated that there were a few pairs on all the larger islands; however, Balfour (1972) noted that it had increased considerably over the past decade or more.

It is now a common breeding species, being well distributed throughout the islands. Recent counts include:

Cava	2 pairs, 1980
Rousay: Central moorland	7 pairs, 1981 (Lea, 1982)
Papa Westray	1 pair, 1982
Pentland Skerries	1 pair, 1982

In 1976, 3 pairs were breeding on a 1½-mile stretch of cliff and 5 pairs on a 3-mile stretch in the West Mainland.

A variety of breeding sites are used including buildings, cliffs, quarries, steep banks, amongst thick heather, trees, bushes, telephone poles and pylons. One pair has recently attempted to nest on the mast of a wreck in Burra Sound. First eggs have been noted on 22nd April and fledged young on 9th June.

Flocks of non-breeding birds can be seen throughout the year and there were between 200 and 300 roosting in Binscarth Wood, Firth in December 1982.

Raven   Corbie

Corvus corax

Resident breeding species, well distributed throughout the islands.

The Raven was noted by Baikie and Heddle (1848) as a constant inhabitant, although most common in winter and spring, while Buckley and Harvie-Brown (1891) thought that, from all accounts, it was much scarcer than formerly. Lack (1942) stated that there were under 10 pairs at the end of the 19th century, while Wood (1916) indicated that it was restricted to perhaps four or five pairs. No mention was made as to whether complete surveys of all the islands had been undertaken. By 1941 it was well distributed and Lack found one pair, and in some cases two, on South Ronaldsay, South Walls, Copinsay, Shapinsay, Rousay, Eday, Sanday and Westray, with more on Hoy and Mainland (Lack, 1942).

Numbers probably increased after Lack's time and now, despite the continuing destruction of some nests, the shooting of adult birds, possible competition with Fulmars for nest sites and Fulmar oiling of juveniles, the Raven population appears to be maintained.

During the period 1974-1982, breeding has taken place on the following islands:

Eday	at least 4 pairs
Flotta	2 pairs
Hoy	c12 pairs
Mainland	22-26 pairs
Rousay	3 pairs on central moorland 1981 (Lea, 1982) and several pairs on the coast
Sanday	4-5 pairs
Shapinsay	min. 2 pairs
South Ronaldsay	min. 6 pairs

| Stronsay | several pairs |
| Westray | several pairs |

Single pairs have nested on:

Calf of Eday	Glims Holm
Cava	Holm of Papa Westray
Copinsay	North Ronaldsay
Gairsay	

The favoured nesting sites are high sea cliffs, but some pairs nest on inland cliffs and quarries, buildings (Mainland, North Ronaldsay and Sanday) and trees (one pair only, Mainland). Nesting pairs are regularly spaced along the West Mainland coast with a mean distance of 3.5kms between nests (Booth, 1979); 2 pairs nested only 800m apart in Rousay in 1977 and 3 pairs were found on a 1.3km stretch of cliff on Mainland in 1980.

Some sections of cliff are traditional nesting sites and have probably been used over hundreds of years, as they have been given the name of Ramnageo, which is the Orkney form of the old Norse Hrafna-gja—Raven's Gap.

Ravens are early nesters and eggs have been found on 26th February, although most clutches are laid in the first two weeks of March. A few broods fledge at the end of April, but the majority leave the nest during the first two weeks of May.

Flocks of 20-25 birds have been reported gathering where there is a plentiful food supply and, between 1974 and 1977, there was a regular roost of 100-150 birds on a Mainland cliff. More recently, in 1981 and 1982, the largest roosts recorded have been of about 60 birds.

Single birds ringed as pulli in Orkney have been recovered in Caithness and Sutherland, while one from Stenness, Mainland was found injured eleven years later on Eday.

STARLINGS : Sturnidae

Starling

Stare, Stroling, Strill

Sturnus vulgaris

Common breeding species, winter visitor and passage migrant.

This species has been regarded as abundant by all writers since the 18th century and there does not seem to have been any change in status. It is present throughout the islands and is only absent from the high hills of Hoy.

Nests can be found in a variety of habitats including buildings, cliffs, stone walls, holes in the ground in heather moorland, including rabbit burrows, and among boulders.

Movements of birds, probably on passage, have been recorded from Pentland Skerries (Groundwater, 1974) and North Ronaldsay. Briggs (1894) noted that several thousand visited North Ronaldsay on the evening of 10th October 1893, but was not sure whether they were migrants or a collection of birds from neighbouring islands.

During the autumn and winter large roosts form, with up to 5,000 being regularly recorded at Berstane Wood, St Ola in November and December, 1976-1982. A peak count of 17,500 occurred there on 17th December 1977.

There is evidence of some movement into Orkney during the winter, as birds ringed here in December and January have been found in North-east Scotland, Arran, Northumberland, Shropshire and Norway from March to May. One bird ringed in Orkney in December 1981 was recovered in Iceland in October 1982. A bird ringed as a nestling in Norway in 1979 was found in Orkney in February 1980, while an adult ringed in Norway in September was controlled in Orkney the following October.

Rose-coloured Starling
Sturnus roseus

Rare visitor.

Several records of the Rose-coloured Starling were mentioned by Baikie and Heddle (1848), while Buckley and Harvie-Brown (1891) stated that it had occurred on several occasions. They quoted Moodie-Heddle, who had known five or six instances of its occurrence on Hoy during the period 1882 to 1886.

It was noted by Balfour (1972) as a rather scarce, irregular visitor with less than ten occurrences during the preceding fifteen years, but there is only one authenticated record for this period. Unfortunately no details of any of the other sightings are available.

The following 20th century occurrences are known, all of single birds:

1932 Holm 25th August, now in Stromness Museum (Groundwater, 1974).

1962 Rousay, dead, 1st August (B.B.56:407).

1975 Finstown, adult, 17th-26th July (B.B.69:353).

1980 Sandwick, Mainland, first summer, 14th-23rd June (B.B.75:527).

1982 Wyre, adult female, 31st August-7th September (B.B.76:521).

As this species is kept in captivity, it is possible that any of the above records could refer to an escaped bird.

SPARROWS : Passeridae

House Sparrow
Passer domesticus

Common resident breeding species.

In the 18th century this species must have been very common, as Low (1813) stated that "sparrows are here in myriads, they make a vast destruction among early corn". It was described as abundant by both Baikie and Heddle (1848) and Buckley and Harvie-Brown (1891). Lack (1943) found it extremely common, but restricted to houses and cultivated land, absent from moorland and from those holms with only moorland and grazing land. Balfour (1972) noted that it was fairly numerous on most inhabited islands.

Although remaining common, this species may have declined since the 18th century as the acreage of cereal crops has decreased. Locally this has almost certainly occurred as it is now a scarce bird in Rackwick, Hoy, where formerly it was common (J. Rendall, pers. comm.). Unfortunately there is remarkably little information available for such a relatively common species.

Flocks of between 50 and 100 birds have been reported from Deerness, Holm, St Ola and Weyland Bay from August to October, with smaller numbers during winter. A maximum count from North Ronaldsay, during the period 1974-1982, was 400 on 14th December 1981. Leucistic birds are occasionally reported.

Tree Sparrow

Passer montanus

Scarce migrant, has bred.

As a passage migrant, the Tree Sparrow has been recorded in small numbers and, during the period 1968-1982, most of the sightings have been in spring, with extreme dates of 13th May and 21st June. The majority of records occur during the last two weeks of May. The peak count was 25 on North Ronaldsay from 17th-20th May 1971; all other sightings have been of 1-6 birds. There were only four autumn records, all from North Ronaldsay:

    1968   3 on 20th September.
    1976   1 on 22nd October.
    1977   1 on 14th and 15th October.

A small breeding colony was found in Carrick Wood, Eday in 1961 (Balfour, 1968) although the year is given as 1962 both in S.B.2:350 and *Bird Notes*, 30:154. This colony continued until at least 1974, with the maximum number of pairs being 10-12 in 1971. A single pair nested on Papa Westray in 1972. An earlier record of possible nesting was given by Wood (1916) who stated that "in

Binscarth Wood high up in the spruce trees the Tree Sparrows are chattering and the huge nest can be seen almost at the top of the tree". This was not referred to by either Lack or Balfour in their lists of breeding birds.

FINCHES : Fringillidae

Chaffinch
Fringilla coelebs

Local breeding species in small numbers; regular passage migrant, winter visitor.

The Chaffinch was very common in spring and winter, large flocks appearing in October after easterly gales, according to Baikie and Heddle (1848). They stated that it might breed as several remained throughout the summer.

The first definite breeding record was from Hoy in 1859 and mentioned by Buckley and Harvie-Brown (1891). They noted that the species was by no means common, even in winter, and rare in summer. They saw birds at Muddiesdale, Kirkwall in 1889, which were evidently breeding.

There was probably an increase during the early part of the 20th century as Lack (1943) found it fairly common in Mainland woods and gardens. There were 2 pairs at Melsetter, Hoy, five or more in Balfour Castle Woods, Shapinsay and two pairs at Trumland, Rousay. Balfour (1972) stated that it bred in limited numbers and was regular on passage.

During the period 1974-1982, breeding pairs have been reported from Hoy, Mainland, Rousay and Shapinsay. Singing males have been noted on Hoy at Berriedale, Lyrawa, White Glen and Hoy Lodge plantations and Rackwick.

In 1976 the following counts of singing birds were obtained:

Mainland: Berstane, St Ola 1
                    Binscarth, Firth 6
                    Gyre, Orphir 1
                    near St Magnus Cathedral, Kirkwall 2

Rousay: Trumland   2
Shapinsay: Balfour Castle Woods   7

A pair was seen at Carrick Wood, Eday in June 1982.

Spring passage has been noted from 20th March to 1st June, with a maximum of 120 on North Ronaldsay on 30th March 1980. The main movement occurred during the last week of March and throughout April. In autumn, migrants have been recorded during the period 11th September to 30th October, with a peak count of 80 on South Ronaldsay on 3rd October 1982. Small flocks of 10-20 birds are often reported during November and may remain to winter. The maximum wintering numbers recorded were 30-40 from both Kirkwall and Rousay in January 1976 and 35 in Finstown on 13th January 1980.

Briggs (1893) noted that large numbers, mainly females, occurred on North Ronaldsay on 3rd October 1892.

A bird ringed in Orkney in March 1980 was controlled in March 1982 at a roost in Belgium.

Brambling

Fringilla montifringilla

Regular passage migrant, some may winter and birds are occasionally present in summer.

Buckley and Harvie-Brown (1891) gave very little information on this species and it would appear to have been uncommon in the 19th century. Briggs (1893) recorded some on North Ronaldsay from 5th-10th October 1892 and a few on 4th October 1893 (Briggs, 1894).

It is a regular passage migrant, being more numerous during autumn. During the period 1974-1982, spring passage has been noted from 26th March to 2nd June, with the main movements in April and the first two weeks of May. The peak count was 200 at Finstown on 9th May 1969. In autumn, there were records of migrants from 11th September to mid-November, with the majority of sightings in October. A maximum of 360 was seen in Orphir on 26th October 1976. Small numbers are present through November to December and a few birds may winter. The largest winter flocks recorded were 10 in Kirkwall on 25th January 1976 and 20 in Firth on 20th February 1975.

A bird was reported singing in Binscarth Wood during early June 1974, but there was no evidence of breeding.

Birds ringed in Orkney in autumn have been recovered in Germany (October), Lanarkshire (November) and Highland Region (January). A bird ringed in Norway in October was controlled three days later in Orkney and a bird ringed in Germany in December was controlled the following October in Orkney.

Greenfinch
Carduelis chloris

Scarce breeding species, passage migrant and winter visitor.

According to Baikie and Heddle (1848) this species was a winter visitor. Breeding was first recorded at Swanbister, Orphir in either 1879 or 1880 and in 1883 there were 3 or 4 pairs at Westness, Rousay. By 1889 it had increased on Mainland and was considered common (Buckley and Harvie-Brown, 1891).

Lack (1942) said that the Greenfinch had increased further and spread to Hoy and Shapinsay, where a nest was found in 1910. In 1941 he found it fairly common on Mainland, with 2 pairs at Melsetter, Hoy, over 6 pairs in Balfour Castle Woods, Shapinsay and about a dozen pairs at Trumland, Rousay. Breeding occurred mainly in woods, but one pair on Hoy and one on Rousay were nesting in gorse and, on Mainland, gorse and thorn hedges were regular habitats.

Balfour (1972) considered that a further change in status had occurred; he recorded that, although fairly common up to the late 1940's, breeding numbers had become very low. The decrease continued and there were no breeding records for the period 1972-1976, in fact there was only one sighting in both 1974 and 1975. In December 1976 there was an influx and in the summer of 1977 birds were reported in suitable breeding habitat. Breeding was confirmed at Binscarth, Firth in 1978.

For the period 1979-1982 there are the following confirmed and possible breeding records:

> 1979   A bird seen carrying nesting material, St Ola, 20th April
> 2 singing, Orphir, 13th April

1980   2 fledged broods, Orphir, 31st May
        A pair probably nesting Balfour Castle Woods,
        Shapinsay, 4th June
1981   Singing birds Binscarth, Finstown and Orphir,
        March-June
1982   A pair nested Trumland, Rousay with fledged
        young on 18th July
        Nest building noted Finstown, 21st May
        Display noted Orphir, Waulkmill and one other
        site, 29th and 30th May

When Buckley visited Rousay in 1883, he found that there was an influx of birds in the autumn and that they became even more numerous in the winter. A rather similar pattern occurred in December 1976 and, from January to April 1977, up to 60 were present in Berstane Wood, St Ola. Since then the maximum number reported has been 12 at Binscarth on 16th February 1982.

During the period 1976-1982, migrant birds have been recorded on North Ronaldsay in March and May and on Sanday in April. Away from the breeding areas, there have been reports of 1-7 birds at Deerness, Holm, Hoy, St Ola and Stromness from October to April.

Goldfinch

Carduelis carduelis

Rare.

The Goldfinch was described by Balfour (1972) as a scarce and irregular visitor with only a few recent occurrences. There are the following authenticated records:

1858   1 shot near Kirkwall (Buckley and Harvie-Brown,
        1891)
1968   2 Mainland, 30th April
        12 North Ronaldsay, late April (S.B.5:352)
1972   1 South Ronaldsay, 10th May
1976   1 Birsay, 2nd December
1977   1 Westray, 20th May
1981   Single birds, St Ola, 18th May
        Binscarth, Firth, 21st May
        Wideford Burn, St Ola, 29th May

Siskin
Carduelis spinus

Passage migrant, regular in autumn, but numbers fluctuate.

Buckley and Harvie-Brown (1891) considered this species to be "extremely rare if not of doubtful occurrence in the Orkneys." It must have become a more frequent visitor in the next twenty years as Omond (1925) noted it as being present annually in both spring and autumn. Balfour (1972) recorded it as a passage visitor in rather irregular numbers.

During the period 1974-1982, it has been recorded each year, although numbers have fluctuated from one in 1974, two in 1975 and four in 1976, to many in 1980 and 1981. Spring migrants have been noted in 1975, 1980, 1981 and 1982 from 17th April to 26th May. The numbers have been small, with all sightings being of from 1-5 birds; there were two July records of single birds on Hoy. The Siskin is much more numerous during the autumn passage with extreme dates of 10th September and 29th November. The majority of records occurred in the last two weeks of September and first two weeks of October, with a maximum of 75 in Holm on 24th September 1980.

An unusual record was of a single bird in Rendall on 4th January 1982.

There was a large influx in the autumn of 1961, when peak counts were c200 in St Ola on 29th September and at least 200 at Scapa on 8th October (Balfour, unpublished).

Birds ringed in Orkney in October have been controlled in Highland Region (February) and Suffolk (April) and a bird ringed in Norway in September was controlled in Orkney 12 days later.

Linnet   Lintie, Rose Lintie, Lintick
Carduelis cannabina

Resident breeding species and passage migrant.

This species was considered to be a very common resident by Low (1813). Similar views were expressed by Buckley and Harvie-Brown (1891), who added that numbers increased in winter and that breeding occurred in many localities on Mainland and on Rousay and Hoy.

In 1927 Linnets were found on Sanday, Stronsay and Westray and in 1928 on Papa Westray (Baxter and Rintoul, 1953). Lack (1942) described it as common on Eday, Rousay and Hoy, in woods with bushes and also in gorse, but scarce away from such sites. Only single pairs were seen on Shapinsay and Fara, while it was not uncommon on South Ronaldsay where gorse bushes occurred. He found that the Linnet was common throughout the cultivated land of Sanday, Stronsay and Westray and that it bred occasionally in reedy marshes. On North Ronaldsay and Papa Westray, it was found primarily around the main house with its bushes; on Mainland it was widespread and common in cultivated land. Lack concluded that, in addition to the colonisation of North Ronaldsay since 1893, there had been a general increase in Orkney.

Balfour (1968, 1972) thought that the status was much as formerly but that it no longer nested on North Ronaldsay. In addition to the nest sites already noted, he mentioned grass-covered quarry faces and dry stone walls and stated that it bred in fair numbers.

As a breeding species the Linnet appears to have declined in recent years and this may, to some extent, be due to the ploughing out of gorse bushes in some areas. During the period 1974-1982, breeding birds have been recorded from:

> Eday (4 pairs in 1982)
> Gairsay
> Hoy
> Mainland: Evie   Orphir
>   Firth   Rendall
>   Harray   St Ola
>   Kirkwall Stromness
> Rousay
> Sanday (2 pairs in 1982)
> South Ronaldsay (7 pairs in 1982)
> Stronsay (7 or 8 pairs in 1979)

There were several pairs on Papa Westray in 1981, but no proof of breeding.

Passage movements are difficult to identify because of the presence of local birds, but there were records of 1-2 birds on North Ronaldsay in April, May, June, September, October and

November and 2 on Copinsay in May. Numbers appear to increase in spring and again in autumn, with the maximum recorded being 120 in Finstown on 29th September 1982. During the winter, flocks of between 20 and 50 birds have been reported regularly and the peak count was 60 in Evie on 17th December 1974.

A bird ringed in Norfolk in October was controlled the following April in Orkney.

Twite   Heather Lintie

Carduelis flavirostris

Resident breeding species and passage migrant.

The Twite was mentioned as breeding in Orkney by Pennant (1789) and Low (1813) recorded it as an abundant species. Buckley and Harvie-Brown (1891) also considered it to be abundant everywhere throughout the year and breeding predominantly amongst heather, but also in trees, bushes and even ivy.

There must have been a decrease during the next fifty years as Lack (1942) found it widely distributed although nowhere abundant. It was found to be present in all islands visited, but absent from high and exposed moorland. No change of status was given by Balfour (1968, 1972); he noted that it was more common than the Linnet and that it bred in tall Fuchsia bushes in North Ronaldsay.

Although no longer abundant, the Twite remains widely distributed in small numbers. It has probably been under-recorded as a breeding species during the period 1974-1982. There are reports of nesting from:

    Copinsay
    Flotta
    Gairsay (6 pairs in 1981)
    Hoy
    Mainland: Deerness
                Evie
                Holm
                Orphir
                Sandwick
    North Ronaldsay (where it was noted as becoming scarcer
        in 1981)

Shapinsay (nesting in fair numbers in Balfour Castle Woods, 1975)
South Ronaldsay
Stronsay (8 or 9 pairs in 1979)

In 1981 and 1982, flocks of over 100 birds were reported from several areas from September to December, with a peak count of 400 in Holm on 28th November 1982. The only records that may refer to passage movements are a flock of 40 on Pentland Skerries on 18th September 1976 and 100 on North Ronaldsay on 24th and 25th October 1981.

Redpoll

Carduelis flammea

Regular passage migrant, a few may winter; has bred.

The status of the Redpoll in the 18th and 19th centuries is not clear and all the records of breeding were considered unsatisfactory by both Lack (1943) and Balfour (1968), because of possible confusion with the Linnet and Twite.

During the period 1974-1982, the Redpoll has been a regular passage migrant, but numbers have fluctuated from year to year. Very small numbers of spring migrants have been noted from 27th March to 25th May, with a maximum of 3 on North Ronaldsay from 23rd-25th May 1981. There were a few records of 1-2 birds away from the possible breeding areas in June and July. It was much more numerous in the autumn and passage has been reported from 10th September, with the main movements in the last week of September and throughout October. Flocks of over 50 birds were unusual and the peak count was of 100 in Kirkwall from late September to the end of October 1975. Smaller numbers may remain throughout November and into December, the maximum recorded being 50 in Rendall on 1st December 1976. There were reports of sightings of 1-3 birds in January and February.

Many of the birds have been identified as Mealy Redpolls *C.f.flammea* but there were several records of the Greenland Redpoll *C.f.rostrata*, including 6 at Harray on 10th December 1972, 14 at St Ola on 8th October and 3 on 20th October, 1976 and 1 on 15th October 1978. There are no recent definite sightings of the Lesser Redpoll *C.f.cabaret* although Briggs (1893) noted 4 on North

Ronaldsay on 15th September 1892, a few on 18th October 1892 and a single bird on 13th January 1893.

A pair was seen in suitable breeding habitat on Hoy in June 1971 and breeding was proved in 1975 for the first time. Details of breeding and possible breeding are as follows:

1975	2 pairs holding territory and displaying, Balfour Castle Woods, Shapinsay on 17th May.
	Pair feeding young, Hoy Lodge plantation, Hoy, 6th June. This was the first confirmed breeding.
1976	A pair Balfour Castle Woods, Shapinsay, 9th July.
	A pair feeding newly fledged young, Hoy, late July.

No mention of the race concerned was given in the breeding records.

A bird ringed in Orkney in October was found in West Lothian, Scotland in November of the same year.

Arctic Redpoll
Carduelis hornemanni

Very rare.

There are three records, all of single birds:

1970	North Ronaldsay, 11th October (trapped) (B.B.64:365).
1972	Adult male, North Ronaldsay, 12th October (trapped) (B.B.66:351).
1975	Immature bird North Ronaldsay, 15th October (trapped) (B.B.69:355).

Two-barred Crossbill
Loxia leucoptera

Very rare.

There is only one record, that of a male shot on North Ronaldsay on 13th June 1894 (A.S.N.H.1895:54).

Crossbill

Loxia curvirostra

Irregular visitor in summer and autumn.

The Crossbill has been an irregular visitor to Orkney since at least the beginning of the 19th century and a number of years were given by Buckley and Harvie-Brown (1891) when irruptions of this species occurred.

There were many recorded in late June and during July 1909, with a maximum of 42 on Sule Skerry in July (S.N.1909:216). Unfortunately there is very little data for the next forty years, but irruptions took place in June and July 1953 and 1956 (Balfour, unpublished), September and October 1962 and June 1966 (Groundwater, 1974). The last large influx was in 1972, when over 20 birds were noted on Sule Skerry on 17th June and there were reports from several parts of Orkney through into July, with a maximum of 30 in Kirkwall on 6th.

In seven years, during the period 1974-1982, there have been records involving from 1-27 birds, with extreme dates of 25th May and 27th October. A male was heard singing in Hoy on 1st June 1973.

Parrot Crossbill

Loxia pytyopsittacus

Very rare.

There is only one authenticated record, that of a bird found dead in Lyrawa Plantation, Hoy on 29th October 1982, (B.B.76:522).

Trumpeter Finch

Bucanetes githagineus

Very rare.

A single bird, which was present on Sanday from 25th May to 29th May 1981, is the only record. (B.B.76:523; O.B.R.1982:51).

Scarlet Rosefinch

Carpodacus erythrinus

Scarce but regular passage migrant, more numerous in autumn.

There are no 19th century records of this species, but recent observations have shown it to be a regular passage migrant in small numbers.

Numbers of Scarlet Rosefinches recorded annually, 1970-1982

1970	1971	1972	1973	1974	1975	1976	1977	1978	1979	1980	1981	1982
1	3	1	0	2	1	1	5	0	12	3	11	2

In the period 1970-1982, there have been 16 birds recorded in spring with extreme dates of 21st May and 19th June. It was more numerous in autumn, with a total of 26 birds reported between 4th August and 5th October.

Three birds were present on North Ronaldsay on 21st May 1981, but otherwise only single birds have been seen in any area in one day.

Numbers of Scarlet Rosefinches in fortnightly periods, 1970-1982

May 20th- June 2nd	June 3rd- June 16th	June 17th- June 30th	Aug. 1st- Aug. 14th
14	1	1	1

Aug. 15th- Aug. 28th	Aug. 29th- Sept. 11th	Sept. 12th- Sept. 25th	Sept. 26th- Oct. 9th
4	5	9	7

Only three adult males in full breeding plumage have been recorded during this period; all other sightings have been of either immature or female birds.

Bullfinch

Pyrrhula pyrrhula

Passage migrant and winter visitor in very small numbers.

This species was rare in Orkney in the 19th century with only two records, one in 1809 (Baikie and Heddle, 1848) and the other in 1865 (Buckley and Harvie-Brown, 1891). It is now a regular passage migrant and winter visitor, although numbers are small, with the majority of sightings consisting of 1-2 birds. During the period 1974-1982, it has been recorded annually except for 1981. The earliest autumn date was 10th October. Some birds may remain throughout the winter, particularly in the gardens of Kirkwall and Stromness. It is difficult to distinguish the arrival of spring migrants due to the presence of wintering birds. The last recorded spring date was 16th April. The maximum number of birds seen together is 4 on 29th March 1980, in Kirkwall. There is an unusual record from Hoy of a single bird on 6th July 1976.

All the birds that have been critically examined have been ascribed to the Northern form *P.p.pyrrhula*.

Hawfinch

Coccothraustes coccothraustes

Scarce passage migrant.

The first satisfactory record of this species in Orkney was from Harray on 5th April 1923 (Omond, 1925) and since then it has been possible to trace details of a further 22 birds. The majority of records have occurred in spring. There are two autumn sightings, one in October and the other in November, while a bird was present in Binscarth Wood, Firth from the second half of December 1969 until January 1970.

The extreme dates in spring are 27th March and 9th June, but most sightings are in the period 27th March to 15th April. Apart from two birds seen at Finstown on 31st March 1980, all other records are of single birds.

Numbers of Hawfinches recorded annually, 1974-1982

1974	1975	1976	1977	1978	1979	1980	1981	1982
0	0	1	0	2	2	7	1	0

NEW WORLD WARBLERS: Parulidae

Tennessee Warbler

Vermivora peregrina

Very rare.

There is only one record, that of a single bird trapped at Holm, which was there from 5th-7th September 1982 (B.B.76:524).

BUNTINGS : Emberizidae

Lapland Bunting
Calcarius lapponicus

Scarce and irregular passage migrant, usually occurring in autumn.

Balfour (1972) stated that, as a passage migrant, the Lapland Bunting was more or less regular in small numbers. There is only one spring record, that of a bird seen at Evie on 4th May 1977. In autumn, the extreme dates of all known records are 11th September and 1st November, with the majority of birds reported from 19th September to 5th October. Most sightings are of 1-2 birds, but three have been recorded on the following occasions: Birsay on 11th September 1962, Auskerry on 20th September 1964, North Ronaldsay on 11th October 1968 and Finstown on 1st November 1975.

Numbers of Lapland Buntings recorded annually, 1974-1982

1974	1975	1976	1977	1978	1979	1980	1981	1982
0	3	3	3	0	0	0	2	2

Snow Bunting   Snowflake
Plectrophenax nivalis

Regular passage migrant and winter visitor.

The Snow Bunting was recorded as a winter visitor, in large numbers, by both Low (1813) and Baikie and Heddle (1848). Buckley and Harvie-Brown (1891) described it as a very abundant winter visitor to all the islands, numbers varying according to the severity of the winter. Balfour (1972) stated that it was common in both small numbers and large flocks, occasionally up to about 5,000 birds.

From 1974-1982, the earliest date for the first autumn arrival was 5th September, while the main movements occurred at the end of September and throughout October and November. Numbers have not been as large as those recorded by earlier writers and the peak count was 800 on North Ronaldsay on 27th November 1977.

Wintering flocks of about 100 birds have been noted in many areas, with a maximum of 400 in Harray during early February 1980. The spring passage is less obvious and the majority of birds have left by the end of April. There are occasional records in May and June, while a single bird was seen at Sandwick on 7th August 1977.

An indication of the large numbers that have occurred is given by Briggs (1893) in his notes on North Ronaldsay—"On 19th October 1892 and for some time after this date, they were simply in thousands—required to be seen to be believed." Large flocks recorded in recent years include 3,000 in Orphir on 23rd February 1957 (Clouston), 2,000 at Loch of Skaill, Mainland on 10th March 1968 and 2,000 in Sandwick on 10th December 1970.

Baxter and Rintoul (1953) noted that in 1874 there were seen, near Stromness about 2nd August, quite young birds which could have been bred in the islands.

A bird ringed at Spurn Point, Yorkshire in February was found two years later in Orkney in May and another ringed at Spurn in December was recovered in Orkney in March of the following year.

Pine Bunting

Emberiza leucocephalos

Very rare.

There are two records, both of single birds:

1943   Male, Papa Westray, 15th October (B.B.37:196)
1967   Male, North Ronaldsay, 7th-11th August (B.B.61:359 S.B.5:225)

Yellowhammer   Yellow Yarling

Emberiza citrinella

Rare passage migrant; formerly bred regularly.

In the first part of the 19th century, this species was by no means plentiful and, according to Baikie and Heddle (1848), it was chiefly a winter visitor, but they noted that, in 1846, two pairs bred near Kirkwall. Buckley and Harvie-Brown (1891) stated that it had become abundant and resident in most of the South Isles, especially since the 1860's; they suggested that the sowing of whin hedges and the making of small plantations had encouraged it to breed. The Yellowhammer was resident in Rousay in 1883 but was not common; in 1888 it was seen on Hoy and considered to be common around Kirkwall.

A male was seen in 1910 on Shapinsay (Hale and Aldworth) where it may have been breeding. Omond (1925) thought it more common than the Corn Bunting around Finstown and Kirkwall. Baxter and Rintoul (1953) recorded that Serle saw at Melsetter, Hoy in May 1929 a pair that was believed to be breeding. Lack (1943) found it only on Mainland, where it was not uncommon in hedgerows and gorse, in several places. He quoted G. T. Arthur who said that it was more restricted than formerly and decreasing. Balfour (1972) stated that it had become an increasingly scarce breeding species within the preceding 30-40 years.

By 1970 there were very few breeding birds and a pair that had nested regularly in an area of gorse near Finstown was not seen after 1974, when the gorse was destroyed. The last known breeding record is of a pair feeding young near the Bay of Houton, Orphir in July 1975.

As a passage migrant, during the period 1974-1982, except for 1978 and 1979, there have been from 1-4 records annually. In spring, it has occurred between 18th March and 6th May and, in autumn, from 13th September to 7th November. The maximum number seen was 4 on North Ronaldsay on 27th October 1980, all other sightings having been of 1-2 birds.

Ortolan Bunting

Emberiza hortulana

Rare passage migrant.

All known occurrences are listed:

1913	2 Pentland Skerries, 7th May,
	1 Auskerry 11th, 12th and 15th May
	2 Pentland Skerries, 19th September
	(all in S.N.E.P.E, 1914:39)
1914	1 Pentland Skerries, 8th and 9th May (S.N.1915:184)

1965	2 North Ronaldsay, 1st October
1970	1 Westray, 7th May
1971	1 North Ronaldsay, 6th June (trapped)
1973	1 Copinsay, 8th May
1976	1 male, Stronsay, 4th and 5th October
1977	1 Tankerness, 9th October
1981	1 Sanday, 28th May

Rustic Bunting

Emberiza rustica

Very rare.

There are four records, all of single birds:

1927	Male, Finstown, killed by a cat on 13th October (S.N.1928:107)
1976	Copinsay, 9th-12th June (B.B.71:527)
	North Ronaldsay, immature male, 1st-7th October (trapped) (B.B.70:442)
1979	North Ronaldsay, juvenile, 29th September (trapped) (B.B.73:529)

Little Bunting

Emberiza pusilla

Very rare.

There are five records, all of single birds:

| 1903 | Pentland Skerries, 15th October (A.S.N.H.1904:14) |

1908   Sule Skerry, 22nd September (A.S.N.H.1909:48)
1913   Auskerry, 21st September (S.N.1914:6)
1915   Pentland Skerries, 12th October (S.N.1916:150)
1980   North Ronaldsay, 13th Oct. (trapped) (B.B.75:530)

Yellow-breasted Bunting

Emberiza aureola

Very rare.

A single bird was seen on Auskerry on 22nd September 1964 (B.B.58:370, S.B.3:317 corrected p.381).

Reed Bunting

Emberiza schoeniclus

Fairly common breeding species in suitable habitat; passage migrant.

The Reed Bunting was probably uncommon at the beginning of the 19th century and Baikie and Heddle (1848) recorded that several specimens had been shot within the previous few years. In the summer of 1845, a pair was observed breeding in the plantations at Muddiesdale, near Kirkwall. It is possible that breeding had occurred before this, as Buckley and Harvie-Brown (1891) mentioned a pair at Papdale in July 1839 and at Scapa in April 1840. They stated that it had become more numerous, but was by no means common. Buckley in 1883 saw this species only on two or three occasions on Rousay and a nest was found at Melsetter, Hoy in 1865.

Omond (1925) thought that it was scarcer than either the Corn Bunting or the Yellowhammer, while Lack (1943) recorded a "rapid increase and spread in recent years". He found it common on Mainland, Sanday and Stronsay and to a lesser extent on South Ronaldsay and Westray, but local and scarce on Hoy, South Walls, Rousay and Eday. Balfour (1968) confirmed that it had increased and thought that it had benefited from the spread of willow bushes by burnsides and other wet places.

There is very little information on the breeding status of this widespread species for the period 1974-1982 and it has obviously been under-recorded.

The only counts available are:

North Ronaldsay	2 pairs, 1977
Papa Westray	several pairs, 1981
South Ronaldsay	7 pairs, 1982
Wideford Burn	6 pairs, 1982

Passage movements have been recorded on North Ronaldsay during September and October and Mainland in October. Small wintering flocks can be found throughout the islands and there was a peak count of 60 in Deerness on 28th November 1982.

A bird ringed in Orkney in October 1976 was controlled in Belgium in April, 1982.

Black-headed Bunting

Emberiza melanocephala

Very rare.

There are two records of single birds, both seen in 1967:

Papa Westray, male, 25th June to mid-July
North Ronaldsay, male, 4th-7th Aug. (B.B.61:359; S.B.5:225)

Corn Bunting
Miliaria calandra

Skitter Broltie,
Common Bunting, Thistlecock

Rare breeding species and possible passage migrant.

This species was common in the 18th century and Low (1813) stated that "it continues with us the whole year and is shot in farm yards in winter in great numbers, it is good eating being full and fat". Buckley and Harvie-Brown (1891) found it common and resident in all the cultivated islands, though less abundant in North Ronaldsay and the Westray group. Briggs (1893) recorded 15-16 pairs on North Ronaldsay in 1892.

In 1927 Baxter noted that it was fairly common on Sanday, Stronsay and Westray, with some on Hoy, but was less numerous on Mainland. In 1928 it was common on Papa Westray (Baxter and

Rintoul, 1953). Serle (1934) found it breeding abundantly on Hoy in 1933, wherever there was ploughed land and Lack (1943) found it common on all islands where there was sufficient cultivated ground.

A decrease occurred during the next twenty-five years as Balfour (1968) recorded that it had become very scarce, with the largest numbers in the North Isles, although it had ceased to breed on North Ronaldsay in 1967.

A rough census was undertaken in 1969 and 1970 (Balfour, 1971) with the following results:

Burray	East Mainland	Eday	Sanday	Shapinsay	Stronsay
1 pair	2 pairs	4 or 5 pairs	21 pairs	1 pair	1 or 2 pairs

The decline continues, with the islands of Sanday and Stronsay remaining the stronghold of this species, although singing males have been reported from Eday, Mainland and Shapinsay between 1979 and 1982. A further survey was carried out in 1979 (Lea, 1979), when only 21 singing males were found.

Counts of singing male Corn Buntings reported in 1979, 1981 and 1982

	Eday	East Mainland	West Mainland	Sanday	Shapinsay	Stronsay
1979	3	-	-	8	-	10
1981	-	-	1	4	2	7
1982	-	1	-	8	-	1

No comprehensive surveys were undertaken in either 1981 or 1982 so the actual totals of possible breeding pairs could have been higher in these years.

There has been no definite evidence of passage movements during the period 1974-1982, but in spring single birds have been reported from Mainland (Evie, St Ola, Stromness), North Ronaldsay and Papa Westray. The extreme dates were 29th March and 24th May. The only flocks recorded were from Sanday, where there was a winter roost of 35 birds in 1974, two separate groups of 12 each in 1980 and 16 near Lady Village, in September 1982.

ESCAPES AND CATEGORY "D" SPECIES

The following species have also been recorded in Orkney, but are either escaped birds or are listed as Category "D" by the British Ornithologists' Union, as there is reasonable doubt that they have ever occurred in a wild state:

Flamingoes : Phoenicopteridae

1974   A bird of the Chilean race at Carness, St Ola from 14th January until it was found dead on 30th January.

1979   1 Loch of Saintear, Westray, 19th June.

Bar-headed Goose

Anser indicus

1969   A pair on Swona, 11th May (Balfour, 1972).

1975   1 Copinsay, 23rd-29th May.

Demoiselle Crane

Anthropoides virgo

1863   2 Deerness, 14th May, one of which was shot (Buckley and Harvie-Brown, 1891).

Blue Rock Thrush

Monticola solitarius

One was seen on North Ronaldsay from 29th August to 6th September 1966. Because numbers of this species are imported as cage birds, this record is placed in Category "D". (B.B.60:324).

Red-headed Bunting
Emberiza bruniceps

This species is often kept as a cage bird and is placed in Category "D". The following sightings, all of adult males, have been reported:

1931	1 North Ronaldsay, 19th June.
1962	1 Birsay, 17th May.
1968	1 Holm, 10th May.
1974	1 Copinsay, 8th and 11th August.
1975	1 Kirkwall, 21st June.
	1 reported present for some while on North Ronaldsay in July.
1976	Singles Deerness, 30th May-1st June and South Ronaldsay 7th June.
1977	1 Shapinsay, 16th May.
1979	1 Papa Westray, 11th-19th June.

Lazuli Bunting
Passerina amoena

1964	A male was present in Holm from 31st May for about 1 week, then it was shot (B.B.57:340).

ADDITIONAL RECORDS

Since the writing of the main text, the following records ha²
been confirmed:

1979
BLYTH'S REED WARBLER *Acrocephalus dumetorum*
1 Holm 5th-13th October (trapped)

1983
WHITE STORK *Ciconia ciconia*
1 seen South Ronaldsay, 18th April, Holm, 19th April aɪ
near Grimsetter aerodrome, 20th April.

CRANE *Grus grus*
1 Birsay, 30th April to 18th May.
1 Tankerness/Holm, 13nd June to at least 9th October.

LONG-BILLED DOWITCHER *Limnodromus scolopaceus*
1 Carness, St Ola, 24th-26th September.

NEEDLE-TAILED SWIFT *Hirundapus caudacutus*
1 South Ronaldsay, 11th-12th June.

THRUSH NIGHTINGALE   *Luscinia luscinia*
1 Holm, 12th-16th May (trapped).

SUBALPINE WARBLER *Sylvia cantillans*
1 South Ronalday, 7th-9th May (trapped).

ARCTIC WARBLER *Phylloscopus borealis*
1 Holm, 9th September (trapped).

UNCONFIRMED RECORDS

The records listed below are awaiting confirmation from the B.B.R.C.:

1980
ARCTIC REDPOLL *Carduelis hornemanni*
1 North Ronaldsay, 13th-27th October.

1982
BLUE-WINGED TEAL *Anas discors*
1 North Ronaldsay, 21st September
BRÜNNICH'S GUILLEMOT *Uria lomvia*
1 Stromness, dead, 3rd April
PALLAS'S WARBLER *Phylloscopus proregulus*
2 North Ronaldsay, 11th October (1 trapped)
ARCTIC REDPOLL *Carduelis hornemanni*
1 Deerness, 5th March.

1983
BLUE-WINGED TEAL *Anas discors*
1 North Ronaldsay, 6th-14th October.
RED-FOOTED FALCON *Falco vespertinus*
1 Harray, 13th June.
WHITE-RUMPED SANDPIPER *Calidris fuscicollis*
1 Evie, 11th October.
RING-BILLED GULL *Larus delawarensis*
1 Stromness, 27th March.
SHORT-TOED LARK *Calandra brachydactyla*
1 North Ronaldsay, 28th-29th September.
CITRINE WAGTAIL *Motacilla citreola*
1 North Ronaldsay, 19th-21st September

APPENDIX I

Count areas: Loch of Stenness, Bay of Ireland, Bay of Houton, Swanbister Bay, Waulkmill Bay, Scapa Bay, Barriers 1 and 2 west, Barriers 1, 2 and 3 east, Echnaloch Bay, Barrier 4 east, Inner Water Sound, south and east Graemsay, Weddel Sound, Switha Sound, Pan Hope, Kirk Hope, Longhope, North Bay, Gutter Sound, Rysa Sound.

APPENDIX II
Partial Wader Survey, January 1983

In order to estimate the populations of open shore waders and thus complement the B.T.O. Birds of Estuaries Enquiry (Prater, 1981), the Tay Ringing Group (with the help of the Orkney Ringing Group) undertook, as part of a more extensive programme, to survey the open sandy and rocky shores of Orkney. This two-year survey was begun in 1983. Gulls present in these areas were also counted.

Of a total of 650 km of low-lying rocky shores and sandy beaches, approximately 450 km (70%) were surveyed in 1983, between 22nd and 31st January. The coastline was walked when the tide was "low", i.e. between half ebb and half flood. Several species, e.g. Curlew, Lapwing and Redshank, also occurred in the coastal fields and these birds were included as part of the coastal population.

The remaining 30% of the coastline suitable for waders is to be surveyed in winter 1983/84. No attempt was made to count waders that were further inland, so that the island counts must not be taken as complete totals.

For further details see "Waders of Rocky Shores in Northern Scotland", preliminary report to the Nature Conservancy Council and Scottish Ornithologists' Club by the Tay Ringing Group, February 1983, written by M. W. A. Martin and R. W. Summers.

APPENDIX III

In 1976, a regular monitoring programme was initiated in order to establish the average number of cliff-nesting seabirds each year at selected colonies on Mainland Orkney, so that subsequent changes in numbers could be measured (Wanless, French, Harris and Langslow, 1982).

Scientific names of mammals mentioned in the text

Pygmy Shrew	Sorex minutus
Rabbit	Oryctolagus cuniculus
Mountain Hare	Lepus timidus
Orkney Vole	Microtus arvalis orcadensis
Wood Mouse	Apodemus sylvaticus
House Mouse	Mus musculus
Brown Rat	Rattus norvegicus

BIRDS IN ORCADIAN PREHISTORY

Beverley Smith

Bird bones have been recognised from Orcadian monuments since the late 19th century, when archaeological sites began to be opened up and investigated. The method of recovery and identification of the bones in Orkney remained unaltered until the 1970's, when new scientific methods were applied to the excavation of sites and the recovery of remains. Improvements in the knowledge of Orcadian birds of prehistory have substantially increased since what must have been a rather piecemeal and haphazard collection of interesting bones, in the Victorian era, to the recording and sampling technology and the detailed post-excavation analysis of today. The preservation of bone on Orcadian sites is normally quite good and excavation can provide an enormous amount of data on species, habitat exploitation, domestication etc.

Environmental findings from early excavations can now be viewed as disappointing and uninformative. The present-day location of bones from sites such as Burrian Broch on North Ronaldsay, Holm of Papa Westray South and Onston, Stenness chambered tomb, is unknown, although we know that bird bones were recovered. This situation is expressed in Macgregor's re-examination of the Burrian Broch finds:

"and of the birds identified (by Dr Traill in Archaeologia Scotica Vol. V) only the utilised radius (47) and a single Gannet's skull found their way to the National Museum." (Macgregor, 1972-74).

Results from the 1930's excavations at Midhowe Broch, Rousay, showed that bird bones were found, but the published report indicated only six bird species, as well as a bird bone pin or point, and a worked tube of bird bone from a "wild goose or fish eagle" (Callander and Grant, 1933; Platt, 1933). The contemporary excavation at the Broch of Gurness, Evie, across Eynhallow Sound, also produced indentifiable bird bones (see table), but the number of species is incomplete and unrepresentative of the whole site; the findings were more or less unstratified.

Not only were wild bird bones found, but bones of domestic

259

fowl have been located at Buckquoy (Birsay), Midhowe Broch (Rousay) and Quanterness (St Ola). Even more surprising, in spite of the unsophisticated excavation techniques, was the recovery of eggshell fragments from the Neolithic excavations at Skara Brae, Sandwick and at Midhowe chambered tomb. The fragments from Midhowe were identified as being eggshell fragments from Rock Dove or Owl (Henshall, 1963).

To summarise, it is possible that all pre-1950's excavations which yielded bone finds, contained some bird bones. The published excavation results and findings are meaningless, even where the bones have been identified. The unstratified bone collections, and in some cases their present day locations, preclude further detailed identification and analysis. It is impossible, for these reasons, to assess clearly the importance of bird bones from the early excavations in the prehistoric economy and the purpose they served in ritual procedures.

Since the 1950's there have been a number of excavations of Neolithic, Iron Age, Pictish and Norse structures, including the sites of Quanterness, Bu, Buckquoy and Isbister. From the table it is clear that these sites have produced more information about bird remains than the earlier excavations. The methodical and detailed collection and analyses have changed the results of bone number and bird diversity, so that a more comprehensive picture is produced. From the recent publication of the excavations at Isbister, South Ronaldsay, it is possible to reconstruct accurately where the bones were located within the tomb. From this, bird bones can be sorted from later and earlier deposits and reviewed with bones from other contemporary depositions. Not all birds were deposited within the monument at the same time, but had accumulated over a long period of use. This can produce a different emphasis on bird species at different times during the life of a site, or seasonal variations in capture, etc.

Sites, such as Isbister, were excavated stratigraphically (layer by layer) and from this it is possible to isolate intrusive bones—bones from Owl pellets, those that accumulated after the site had ceased to function, e.g. those such as the Wryneck at Quanterness in a disturbed context. The data can be refined to indicate what was present and exploited during the life of a site. From improved collections and data, it is possible to make conclusions even though these may be a little tentative. From Bramwell's work on the bird bones from Buckquoy (Bramwell,

1977), it is possible to deduce that more birds were caught, more domestic geese and fowl were kept and a greater range of species was exploited in the Norse phase compared to the earlier Pictish phase. Although such conclusions go beyond the boundary of this study, it does show what is possible from a substantial increase in recovered bird bones.

Analysing bird remains can be productive, but it can also be problematic. Individual bones are identified, but it can be difficult to differentiate clearly between species such as Blackbird and Ring Ouzel, especially when the whole skeleton is not present.

Small bird bones which have to be analysed microscopically can prove extremely difficult. The overlap of bone and skull sizes may lead to tenuous conclusions, so too does the identification of bones of bird species rare to Orkney. These limitations should be borne in mind when making generalisations. In specialist reports, numbers of bones per species are recorded, but it is not general to calculate the exact number of individuals recovered from sites. However, from the number of White-tailed Eagle talons present in the tomb at Isbister, it was possible to suggest that a minimum of six birds were represented (Bramwell, 1983).

From the table it is clear that Gannet, Cormorant and Shag are well represented at most of the sites listed, with Gulls, Curlew and Raven being the next most frequent, but the Gannet is clearly the commonest species recorded. The table also shows species that are no longer present in Orkney—the White-tailed Eagle and the now extinct Great Auk, as well as the uncommon visitors—Brent Goose, Common Scoter, Bittern and Phalarope.

From the more recent excavations at Quanterness and Buckquoy, it is shown that birds were exploited from a variety of local habitats, such as the open sea, coastal cliffs, shore lines and mud flats, marshes and fresh water areas, meadows, scrubland and moorland. Coastal exploitation of birds has been noted at Birsay by Durham University in their Birsay Bay project, but excavation data is still being processed (Donaldson, Morris, Rackham, 1981). The results of these excavations will no doubt expand this survey and provide much more information about specific habitat exploitation, especially of sea cliffs during the breeding season. Clearly there is much work to be done in this field.

The table indicates that, throughout prehistory, man has exploited many species. Apart from the obvious necessity of food, not all the species found are particularly good to eat, so we must ask why specific bird remains are found at all and found in monuments such as chambered tombs. Few bird remains, apart from Gannets at Quanterness, have provided evidence of butchering marks to indicate that they were "food for the dead". The Quanterness Gannets, however, were clearly chopped in half (Bramwell, 1979). Why should White-tailed Eagles be part of the funerary remains at Isbister? Birds, such as the Eagle, which were obviously difficult to catch, must have been of special significance. This might also be true of other species of which we are, as yet, in ignorance. Birds may also have been introduced into the tombs for their feathers, of which no evidence survives, or, in the case of falcons, the birds may have been used for hawking.

As the techniques of recovery and analysis become increasingly more sophisticated, it may be possible to assess seasonality of bird catches, to determine when domesticated birds were introduced or managed and to determine why birds were caught, if they were not considered good eating, and what part they played in the economy.

This is by no means an up-to-date or comprehensive survey of bird bone findings from Orcadian monuments, but it may give some idea of past inadequacies, the problems involved and future possibilities. The recent excavations of Pictish and Norse sites at Birsay have already been mentioned, but other sites such as Howe, Stromness; Pool, Sanday (Iron Age and Pictish); Tuquoy, Westray (late Norse and early Medieval); Noltland, Westray (Neolithic), have much still to offer. Once the results of the bird remains from these sites have been published, there should be a clearer, more interesting and more conclusive report of what bird remains have been found in the past.

Bird remains found at Archaeological sites in Orkney

BROCH OF AYRE (excavated 1901 and 1909) Holm

Great Northern Diver	Shag
Manx Shearwater	Swans
Gannet	Herring Gull?
Cormorant	Great Auk

MIDHOWE BROCH (excavated 1930-1933)

Great Northern Diver?	Goose
Gannet	Ducks
Shag	Oystercatcher?
Heron	

MIDHOWE CHAMBERED TOMB (excavated 1932-1934)

Gannet	Falcon
Cormorant	Skua
Shag	Guillemot
Buzzard	Carrion Crow
Eagle?	

KNOWE OF RAMSAY (excavated 1935) Rousay

Gannet	Pink-footed Goose
Cormorant	Ducks
Bittern	White-tailed Eagle
Swans	Great Auk

BLACKHAMMER CHAMBERED TOMB (excavated 1936)

Gannet	Cormorant
Pink-footed Goose	

GURNESS (excavated 1929-1939)

Gannet	Long-eared Owl
Cormorant	Blackbird
Gulls	

BUCKQUOY (excavated 1970-1971)

Great Northern Diver	Goldeneye	Turnstone
Fulmar	Osprey	Phalarope
Manx Shearwater	Kestrel	Skua
Gannet	Merlin	Gulls
Cormorant	Red Grouse	Guillemot
Shag	Crane	Razorbill
Swans	Water Rail	Little Auk
Shelduck	Corncrake	Great Auk
Wigeon	Oystercatcher	Puffin
Teal	Golden Plover	Rock Dove
Mallard	Knot	Ring Ouzel/Blackbird
Ducks	Dunlin	Song Thrush
Shoveler	Jack snipe	Rook/Crow
Eider	Whimbrel	Raven
Common Scoter	Curlew	Starling

QUANTERNESS CHAMBERED TOMB
(excavated 1805 and 1972-1973)

Leache's Petrel	Black-headed Gull	Fieldfare
Gannet	Great Black-backed Gull	Song Thrush
Greylag Goose	Guillemot	Redwing/Thrush
Goshawk	Wryneck	Mistle Thrush
Buzzard	Skylark	Warblers
Red Grouse	Pipit?	Goldcrest
Quail	Wagtail?	Tit?
Oystercatcher	Wren	Raven
Lapwing	Wren/Chat	Starling
Snipe	Wheatear	Brambling
Black-tailed Godwit	Ring Ouzel	Linnet?
Greenshank	Blackbird	Twite?

ISBISTER CHAMBERED TOMB
(excavated 1958 and 1976-1978)

Shag	Red Grouse	Common Gull
Goose	Oystercatcher	Great Black-backed Gull
Mallard	Snipe	Little Auk
Eider	Woodcock	Puffin
Goshawk	Curlew	Short-eared Owl
White-tailed Eagle	Gulls	Raven
Kestrel		

BU (excavated 1978) Stromness

Gannet	Dunlin	Puffin
Shag	Snipe	Skylark
Pink-footed Goose	Curlew	Tree Pipit
Brent Goose	Great Skua	Lesser Whitethroat
Merlin	Gulls	Raven
Red Grouse	Terns	Chough
Oystercatcher	Black Guillemot	Starling
Golden Plover	Little Auk	

Acknowledgements

The Scottish Development Department (Ancient Monuments) and individual site supervisors are to be thanked for allowing the use of unpublished material. Grateful thanks are also expressed to Andrewina Ross for typing the manuscript.

Bibliography

BRAMWELL, D. 1977 Appendix 2. Bird and Vole bones from Buckquoy, Orkney, pp 208-211. Ritchie, A. Excavations of Pictish and Viking Age Farmsteads at Buckquoy, Orkney. P.S.A.S.108:174-227.

BRAMWELL, D. 1979 Appendix F. pp 138-143. Bird bones. Renfrew, C. Investigations in Orkney. Soc. of Antiquaries of London.

BRAMWELL, D. 1983 Bird bones. pp 159-170. Hedges, J. W. Isbister "A Chambered Tomb in Orkney". B.A.R.115.

BRAMWELL, D. Forthcoming. The Bird remains from Bu. Hedges, J. W. (ed). Bu, Gurness—Brochs of Orkney.

CALLANDER, J. W. and GRANT, W. G. 1933 The Broch of Midhowe, Rousay, Orkney. P.S.A.S.48:444-516.

DONALDSON, A., MORRIS, C., RACKHAM, J. 1981 The Birsay Bay Project. Preliminary investigations into the past exploitation of the coastal environment at Birsay, Mainland, Orkney. Brothwell and Dimbleby, G. Environmental Aspects of Coasts and Islands. B.A.R. S.94.

GRAEME, A. S. 1914 An Account of the Excavation of the Broch of Ayre, St Mary's Holm. P.S.A.S. 48:31-51.

GROUNDWATER, W. 1974 Birds and Mammals of Orkney. Kirkwall.

HENSHALL, A. H. 1963 The Chambered Tombs of Orkney Vol. 1 Ed. U.P.

MACGREGOR 1972-4 The Broch of Burrian, North Ronaldsay, Orkney. P.S.A.S.105:63-118.

PLATT, M. 1933 Report on Animal and other Bones, pp 514-516. Callander, J. W. and Grant, W. G. 1933 The Broch of Midhowe, Rousay, Orkney. P.S.A.S.48.

SMITH, B. Forthcoming. The Environmental Remains. Hedges, J. W. (ed) Bu, Gurness—Brochs of Orkney.

NOTE: P.S.A.S. Proceedings of the Society of Antiquaries of Scotland.

B.A.R. British Archaeological Reports.

Beverley Smith,
Excavation Supervisor, for Howe Excavation,

Don,
Outertown,
Stromness.
13.1.84.

BIBLIOGRAPHY

ADAM, R. G. 1981 High incidence of ringing recoveries from Long-eared Owl pellets. S.B.11:166-167.

ADAM, R. G. and CORSE, C. J. 1983 Rookery Survey. Orkney Bird Report, 1982:58-59.

ANNALS OF SCOTTISH NATURAL HISTORY 1892-1911.

APLIN, O. V. 1915 Gannet nesting in Orkney. Zool.1915:433.

APLIN, O. V. 1916 Reported nesting of Gannet in Orkney. Zool.1916:312-313.

ARTHUR, G. T. 1950 Orkney's Birds. Bird Notes, 24:130-135.

BAIKIE AND HEDDLE. 1848 Historia Naturalis Orcadensis. Part 1. Edinburgh.

BALFOUR, E. 1955 Kestrels nesting on the ground in Orkney, Bird Notes, 26:245-253.

BALFOUR, E. 1959 Letter (Skuas). S.B.1:74-76.

BALFOUR, E. 1963 Food study of Long-eared Owls wintering in Orkney. Orkney Field Club Bulletin, 1963 No.2.

BALFOUR, E. 1967 Buzzards breeding in Orkney. S.B.4:447.

BALFOUR, E. 1968 Breeding birds of Orkney. S.B.5:89-104.

BALFOUR, E. 1970 Bridled Guillemots. Orkney Field Club Bulletin, 1970 No.1:10.

BALFOUR, E. 1971 Diminished Status of the Corn Bunting in Orkney. Orkney Field Club Bulletin, 1971 No.1:6.

BALFOUR, E. 1972 Orkney Birds: Status and Guide. Senior, Stromness.

BALFOUR, E., ANDERSON, A. and DUNNET, G. M. 1967 Orkney Cormorants—Their breeding distribution and dispersal. S.B.4:481-493.

BALFOUR, E. and CADBURY, C. J. 1975 A population study of the Hen Harrier *Circus cyaneus* in Orkney. The Natural Environment of Orkney. Nature Conservancy Council, Edinburgh 1975.

BANNERMAN, D. A. 1963 The Birds of the British Isles. Vol. 12. Oliver and Boyd, Edinburgh and London.

BARRY, Rev. George. 1805 History of the Orkney Islands.

BAUGH, I. 1981 Land use change in Orkney. Unpublished report to Nature Conservancy Council, 1981.

BAXTER, E. V. 1928 Common and Velvet Scoter in Orkney. S.N.1928:28.

BAXTER, E. V. and RINTOUL, L. J. 1953 The Birds of Scotland, 2 vols. Edinburgh.

BIRD NOTES R.S.P.B. Magazine.

BLACKBURN and BUDWORTH 1975-1982 Reports on expeditions to Sule Skerry. Seabird Group Reports.

BÖKER, VON U. 1964 Bemerkungen zur Vogelwelt der Orkneyinsel Hoy. Ornithologische Mitteilungen, 16:3-12.

BOOTH, C. J. 1972 Food of wintering Long-eared Owls. Orkney Field Club Bulletin, 1972 No.1:5.

BOOTH, C. J. 1974 Skua Survey, 1974. Orkney Bird Report, 1974-75.

BOOTH, C. J. 1976 Orkney Swan Survey, 1976. Orkney Bird Report, 1976-77.

BOOTH, C. J. 1978 Golden Plover Survey, 1977/78. Orkney Bird Report, 1978-79.

BOOTH, C. J. 1979 A study of Ravens in Orkney. S.B.10:261-267.

BOOTH, C. J. 1982 Fledging success of some Red-throated Divers in Orkney, S.B.12:33-38.

BRAZIL, M. A. and KIRK, J. 1981 The Current Status of Whooper Swans in Great Britain and Ireland. Unpublished report to the University of Stirling.

BREE, C. R. 1850 Nests of *Colymbus arcticus* and *Charadrius morinellus*. Zoologist VIII:2954.

BRIGGS, A. 1893 Bird Notes from North Ronaldsay. A.S.N.H.1893:67-79.

BRIGGS, A. 1894 Some further Bird Notes from North Ronaldsay. A.S.N.H.1894:82-87.

BRITISH BIRDS 1907-1983 Monthly publication.

BRITISH ORNITHOLOGISTS' UNION. 1971 The Status of Birds in Britain and Ireland. Edinburgh : Blackwell Scientific Publication.

BUCHANAN, Rev. J. L. 1793 Travels in the Western Hebrides.

BUCKLEY, T. E. 1896 Pochard and Tufted Duck breeding in Orkney. A.S.N.H. 5:191-192.

BUCKLEY, T. E. and HARVIE-BROWN, J. A. 1891 A Vertebrate Fauna of the Orkney Islands. Edinburgh.

BULLOCK, I. D. and GOMERSALL, C. H. 1981 The Breeding Population of Terns in Orkney and Shetland in 1980. Bird Study, 28:187-200.

CADBURY, C. J. 1980 The Status and Habitats of the Corncrake in Britain, 1978-1979. Bird Study, 27:203-281.

CLOUSTON, Mrs M. TRAILL. Unpublished Diary.

CRAMP. S., BOURNE, W. R. P. and SAUNDERS, D. 1974 The Seabirds of Britain and Ireland. Collins.

CRAMP, S. and SIMMONS, K. E. L. (eds.) The Birds of the Western Palearctic. Vol I, 1977; Vol. II, 1980; Vol. III, 1983. Oxford University Press.

CRICHTON, A. W. 1866 A Naturalist's Ramble to the Orcades.

DUNN, R. 1837 The Ornithologist's Guide to the Islands of Orkney and Shetland.

DUNNET, G. M. 1975 Seabird Studies on Eynhallow. The Natural Environment of Orkney. Nature Conservancy Council, 1975.

DUNNET, G. M. 1983 Eiders at Eynhallow. Orkney Bird Report, 1982:60.

DUNNET, G. M. and OLLASON, J. C. 1982 The Feeding Dispersal of Fulmars *Fulmarus glacialis* in the Breeding Season. Ibis 124:359-361.

DUNNET, G. M., OLLASON, J. C. and ANDERSON, A. 1983 Orkney Fulmars. Orkney Bird Report, 1982:44-50.

FEA, JAMES, 1775 The Present State of the Orkney Islands considered. Brown, Edinburgh, 1884.

FENTON, ALEXANDER. 1978 The Northern Isles : Orkney and Shetland. John Donald.

FISHER, J. 1952 The Fulmar. Collins, London. New Naturalist.

FORTESCUE, WILLIAM I. 1886 Wild Swans. The Field, April 10th 1886.

GARDEN, E. A. 1958 The National Census of Heronries in Scotland, 1954. Bird Study, 5:90-109.

GRAY, ROBERT. 1871 Birds of the West of Scotland. Collected Papers.

GROUNDWATER, W. 1974 Birds and Mammals of Orkney. The Kirkwall Press.

HALE, J. R. 1909 Increase of Wood Pigeons in Orkney. B.B.2:345.

HALE, J. R. and ALDWORTH, T. P. 1910 Notes on Birds in Orkney in 1910. B.B.4:220-221.

HARVEY, W. 1892 The Shoveler nesting in Sanday, Orkney. A.S.N.H.1892, 1:138.

HEPPLESTON, P. B. 1978 The food of Short-eared Owls in Orkney. The Western Naturalist, 1978, 7:55-62.

HEPPLESTON, P. B. 1981 The Curlew in Orkney. Orkney Bird Report, 1980:35-38.

HOPE JONES, P. 1978 Surveillance of cliff-nesting seabirds at their breeding sites in Orkney, 1976-1977. Unpublished Nature Conservancy Council Report.

HOPE JONES, P. 1979 Roosting behaviour of Long-tailed Duck in relation to possible oil pollution. Wildfowl, 30:155-158.

HOPE JONES, P. and KINNEAR, P. K. 1979 Moulting Eiders in Orkney and Shetland. Wildfowl, 30:109.113.

HUDSON, R. 1965 The spread of the Collared Dove in Britain and Ireland. B.B.58:104-139.

ISLAND SAGA 1967 Mary A. Scott. The Story of North Ronaldsay.

JOURDAIN, F. C. R. 1918 First nesting record of the Great Skua in the Orkneys. B.B.12:50-52.

JOURDAIN, F. C. R. 1919 Further notes on the breeding of the Great Skua in the Orkneys. B.B.12:170-171.

KEATINGE, T. H. and DICKSON, J. H. 1979 Mid Flandrian changes in vegetation on Mainland, Orkney. New Phytologist, 1979, 82:585-612.

LACK, D. 1942 The Breeding Birds of Orkney. Ibis, 1942:461-484.

LACK, D. 1943 The Breeding Birds of Orkney. Ibis, 1943:1-27.

LEA, D. 1975 Rookery Survey, Orkney Bird Report, 1974-75.

LEA, D. 1979 Corn Buntings in Orkney, 1979. Orkney Bird Report, 1978-79.

LEA, D. 1980 Seafowl in Scapa Flow, Orkney, 1974-1978. Royal Society for the Protection of Birds report to Nature Conservancy Council. 1980.

LEA, D. 1982 The Heathland Birds of Rousay. Orkney Bird Report, 1981: 56-58.

LEA, D. and BOURNE, W. R. P. 1975 The Birds of Orkney. The Natural Environment of Orkney. Nature Conservancy Council. 1975.

LOVE, J. A. 1983. The Return of the Sea Eagle. Cambridge University Press.

LOW, G. 1774 George Low's tour through Orkney and Schetland in 1774. Published 1879.

LOW, Rev. G. 1813 Fauna Orcadensis. Published and edited by W. Leach, Edinburgh.

MACMILLAN, A. T. 1965 The Collared Dove in Scotland. S.B.3:292-301.

MARTIN, M. W. A. and SUMMERS, R. W. 1983 Waders of Rocky Shores in Northern Scotland. Preliminary report to the Nature Conservancy Council and Scottish Ornithologists' Club by the Tay Ringing Group. February 1983.

MATHER, A. S., RITCHIE. W. and SMITH, J. S. 1975 An introduction to the morphology of the Orkney coastline. The Natural Environment of Orkney. Nature Conservancy Council, 1975.

MEINERTZHAGEN, R. 1939 A note on the birds of Hoy, Orkney. Ibis, 1939:258-264.

MOAR, N. T. 1969 Two pollen diagrams from the Mainland, Orkney Islands. New Phytologist, 1969, 68:201.

NEILL, Dr P. 1806 Tour through some of the Islands of Orkney. 1806.

NETHERSOLE-THOMPSON, D. 1971 Highland Birds. Highlands and Islands Development Board.

NOBLE, H. 1908 On the identification of ducks' eggs. B.B.2:21.

OGILVIE, M A. 1981 The Mute Swan in Britain. Bird Study, 28:87-106.

OMOND, J. 1925 How to know the Orkney Birds. Kirkwall.

ORCADIAN PAPERS. 1905 Edited by M. M. Charleson. Selection of the Proceedings of the Orkney Natural History Society from 1887-1904. Wm. Rendall, Stromness.

ORKNEY BIRD REPORT 1974-75. 1976-77, 1978-79, D. Lea (Ed.).

ORKNEY BIRD REPORT 1980, 1981, 1982. Chris Booth, Mildred Cuthbert, Peter Reynolds (Eds.).

PENNANT, T. 1789 (2nd Edition) A Tour of Scotland in 1769.

PICOZZI, N. 1983 Two hens but a single nest. An unusual case of polygyny by Hen Harriers in Orkney. B.B.76:123-128.

PICOZZI, N. and CUTHBERT, M. F. 1982 Observations and Food of Hen Harriers at a winter roost in Orkney. S.B.12:73-80.

PRATER, A. J. 1981 Estuary Birds of Britain and Ireland. Poyser.

RAWCLIFFE, C. P. 1958 The Scottish Mute Swan Census, 1955/56. Bird Study 5:45-55.

REYNOLDS, P. 1982 Wintering Whooper Swans. Orkney Bird Report, 1981:49-54.

ROBERTSON, D. J. 1934 Notes from a Bird Sanctuary. Reprinted from "The Orcadian".

ROBINSON, H. W. 1905 In "Orcadian Papers", edited by Charleson, 1905.

ROBINSON, H. W. 1934 First nesting of Leach's Fork-tailed Petrel in Orkney. S.N.1934:93.

R.S.P.B. 1979 Marine Oil Pollution and Birds. 1979.

SALMON, J. D. 1832 On Eggs and Birds met with in three weeks sojourn in the Orkney Islands. London's Mag. Nat. Hist. V.

SERLE, W. 1934 Notes on the Breeding Birds on the island of Hoy. S.N.1934:129-136.

SCOTTISH BIRDS. 1958-1982 Quarterly Publication of the Scottish Ornithologists' Club.

SCOTTISH NATURALIST, THE. 1871-91, 1912-39 and 1948-57.

SHIRREFF, J. 1814 General view of the agriculture of the Orkney Islands.

TASKER, M. and REYNOLDS, P. 1983 A survey of Tystie (Black Guillemot) *Cepphus grylle* distribution in Orkney, 1983. Report to Nature Conservancy Council.

TRAILL, J. W. H. 1888 Ring Ousel breeding in Orkney. S.N.9:344.

TUDOR, J. R. 1883 The Orkneys and Shetlands. Stanford, London.

VENABLES, L. S. V. and VENABLES, U. M. 1955 Birds and Mammals of Shetland. Edinburgh.

WALKER, K. G. 1967 Scaup breeding in Orkney. S.B.4:503.

WALLACE, Rev. JAMES 1700 (2nd Edition) A Description of the Isles of Orkney. 1693. Edinburgh.

WANLESS, S., FRENCH, D. D., HARRIS, M. P. 'and LANGSLOW, D. R. 1982 Detection of annual changes in the number of cliff nesting seabirds in Orkney, 1976-1980. Journal of Animal Ecology, 1982 51:785-795.

WANLESS, S., REYNOLDS, P. and LANGSLOW, D. R. 1982 Surveillance of cliff nesting seabirds in Orkney, 1982. Unpublished Nature Conservancy Council Report.

WITHERBY, H. F. et al 1938-41. 5 volumes. The Handbook of British Birds. London.

WOOD, A. 1916 Bird Life in Orkney. Published lecture.

YARRELL, W. 1843 History of British Birds.

INDEX